Naija Marxisms

'A splendid book – erudite, accessible, and entirely original. Mayer writes with authority on the incredible work of Nigerian Marxists, their scholarship and activism, largely ignored by Western scholarship and in contemporary histories of Nigeria, while their books are often difficult, or, for most of us, impossible to access. We hear African Marxists speaking for themselves, resolving questions of the greatest social and political significance with remarkable sophistication. But the book also does much more: it is an elegant history of modern Nigeria, which is simultaneously thorough and accessible, with a necessary focus on labour and socialist politics. A contribution of the highest order – it shows a vibrant and relevant Nigerian Marxism still engaged in a struggle to understand the present and craft possible alternatives for the future.'
—Leo Zeilig, author of *Lumumba* (2008) and *Frantz Fanon* (2014)

'In Adam Mayer's capable hands, *Naija Marxisms* offers its readers a detailed map with which to navigate the fascinating and complex landscape of Marxism in Nigeria – past, present, and even futures still to come. A wonderful, insightful introduction to a topic that everyone interested in political change and social justice should know more about.'
—Imre Szeman, Canada Research Chair in Cultural Studies, University of Alberta and co-editor of *Contemporary Marxist Theory: An Anthology*

'African Marxism has been neglected not only in Westernized Universities but also by the Marxist Left. Here is a corrective to this trend. Adam Mayer takes seriously Nigerian Marxism and shows its unique contributions. This is a *tour de force* in many fields of scholarship. I highly recommend it!'
—Professor Ramon Grosfoguel, University of California at Berkeley

'Adam Mayer has taken up a huge task, which helps to put the rich canvas of the Nigerian Left in sharp historic relief, for a global audience. Considering the breadth and depth of its hitherto largely unexplored subject matter, it is an excellent effort which is concisely articulated.'
—Baba Aye, National Convener, United Action for Democracy (UAD), Nigeria

'Adam Mayer has done something of exceptional importance – he has rescued the history of Nigerian Marxism from scholarly and political oblivion. This first book-length history of Marxism and Marxist thought in Nigeria puts to rest some of the more pervasive Cold War assumptions, which often cast the "giant of Africa" as a "communism-free zone". Mayer's source base is rich and spectacularly diverse, his commitment to the subject of his study in all its overwhelming complexity is worthy of praise. As a former citizen of a socialist state Mayer is well-positioned to recognize and analyze the transnational nature of Nigerian Marxism. Nigeria's maddening neoliberal contradictions, its deep rifts of class and economic inequality also generated an intense intellectual critique of global capitalism and brought to life several generations of Marxian thinkers and political activists whose massive work has finally found its historian.'

—Maxim Matusevich, Associate Professor of World History,
Seton Hall University, author of *Africa in Russia, Russia in Africa:*
Three Centuries of Encounters (2006) and *No Easy Row for a Russian Hoe:*
Ideology and Pragmatism in Nigerian-Soviet Relations, 1960–1991 (2003)

'This is the first major book on the Nigerian Left, carefully revealing the socialist ideas of Marxist movements, along with their achievements and failures, all set in the larger context of a troubled country. Part learned and part inspirational, it successfully provides the historical and epistemological foundation to understand a powerful ideology that remains alive today, as well as the intellectual orientations and practical efforts of the consistently committed comrades. It pushes counterculture to the critical centre, thereby supplying scholarly leadership that promises to unleash vibrant dialogues and even new forms of action.'

—Toyin Falola, Past President, African Studies Association,
Jacob and Frances Mossiker Chair in the Humanities and University
Distinguished Teaching Professor, University of Texas at Austin

'*Naija Marxisms* provides a comprehensive and accessible introduction to the history of Marxist thought in Nigeria. If you are angry about the current state of society in Nigeria, you should use this book to learn important lessons from those who struggled against similar challenges. As Isaac Newton said, we can see further because we stand on the shoulders of giants. This book provides you with access to the thoughts of the giants of Nigerian Marxism.'

—Andy Wynne, Senior Lecturer at the University of Leicester, researcher in Nigeria

'Three-plus decades in the aftermath of post-colonial euphoria and a quarter century after the implosion of the Soviet Union, Adam Mayer's work on Nigerian "marxisms" is a much welcomed contribution to the study of Africa's largest country. One doesn't have to agree with all of Mayer's conclusions to recognize that his work is an important step in the direction of recognizing, understanding and even resuscitating an often ignored tradition.'

—William Hansen, American University of Nigeria, Yola

'Adam Mayer's *Naija Marxisms* is a compelling exploration of leftist/Marxist ideas in Nigerian economics, political history, unions, social development and the arts. The scope and depth of the work is simply astonishing. In a style that is both informative and witty, Mayer's work gives us deep insight into the forces that have shaped Nigeria into the state it is today.'

—Professor Michael Erickson, Webster University

Naija Marxisms

Revolutionary Thought in Nigeria

Adam Mayer

First published 2016 by Pluto Press
345 Archway Road, London N6 5AA

www.plutobooks.com

British Library Cataloguing in Publication Data
A catalogue record for this book is available from the British Library

ISBN   978 0 7453 3662 6   Hardback
ISBN   978 0 7453 3657 2   Paperback
ISBN   978 1 7837 1788 0   PDF eBook
ISBN   978 1 7837 1790 3   Kindle eBook
ISBN   978 1 7837 1789 7   EPUB eBook

Typeset by Stanford DTP Services, Northampton, England

Printed and bound by CPI Group (UK) Ltd, Croydon, CR0 4YY

To Ida, with love

the poet is tired of visiting and revisiting
the frozen imagery of patriotic villainy and violence
and the otiose accretion of neocolonialism's imperialistic
exploitation
but
the poet cannot afford to remain tired
a matter of chance and choice?
a question of submission or subversion?
the only viable choice is the word the rhythm and the
rhyme even where nothing rhymes
the word hard and harsh as the retribution against
nationalist nincompoops and
soft and sweet as the lullaby welcoming to the world
children of hope
and the rhythm of life and love
of duty and desire
of rights and responsibilities
it keeps stirring the people's souls into action
it keeps arousing defeated dreams into a new day of
determination and faith.

Femi Ojo-Ade*

*   Femi Ojo-Ade: 'poets and poetry (for Aimé Césaire)', in: *Gorée's Unwavering Songs* (Poetry), Amoge Publishers, Lagos, 2014, p. 28. Reproduced by kind permission of Professor Ojo-Ade.

Contents

Acknowledgements

Many people helped me with ideas, criticism and also in the practical sense, while I did research and prepared the manuscript. The *urtext* was my PhD dissertation, submitted to the Department of Contemporary International History at Budapest University (Eotvos Lorand Tudomanyegyetem), under Gabor Bur's supervision. Professor Bur is a doyen of African Studies in Hungary and our early discussions back in 2010 were instrumental in my finding this topic. My PhD committee members Professor Gyozo Lugosi, who is at the heart of Marxist theory in Hungary, and Professor Colonel Janos Besenyo, the leading specialist on African security in East-Central Europe, both furnished me with very important ideas. I wholeheartedly thank all three of them, specifically Professor Bur for his myriad ways of giving practical help, Professor Colonel Besenyo for drawing my attention to security-related issues, and Professor Lugosi for leading me not only to a crucial passage in Lukács's *oeuvre* but also for drawing my attention to the debate that has centred on the Asiatic mode of production in Marxist African Studies.

I thank friends and colleagues Alvin Lim, Alex Chirila and Steve Devitt for reading parts or all of the manuscript. I also thank friends and comrades Abiodun Olamosu, Baba Aye and Drew Povey for the same, and Leo Zeilig for directing me to them in the first place. I thank Kingsley Orighoye Ashien for his friendship and for his entertaining stories that had triggered my interest in Nigeria in 2006. Walter Rodney wrote that positing an author's ultimate responsibility for her/his text is 'sheer bourgeois subjectivism', but nonetheless I would still stress that there is no one else than myself to blame for the shortcomings of the text. I thank Edwin Madunagu for spending time with me and for his important ideas. I thank Professor Femi Ojo-Ade for his excellent tips and advice. I thank Professors Bill Hansen and Kimberly Sims for their encouragement and information they provided. I also thank the American University of Nigeria for a sabbatical in 2013 that allowed me to do important research. I also thank Budapest University's Department of Russian Historical Studies and, specifically, Professors Gyula Szvak and Tamas Krausz, for some crucial insights into Soviet policies, and also their practical advice. I also thank Eszter Bartha for the same. I thank Ognyan Nikolov for drawing my attention to Ana Pauker. I thank Pluto Press and especially my wonderful editor David Shulman for taking on this project and for being subtle, compassionate and firm at the same time, during the entire academic review process and also in the course of editing. This book gained very much, and I also learned a lot personally, from his dedicated advice. I thank Stuart Tolley for his marvellous cover design. I thank my anonymous reviewers as they corrected a number of misconceptions that I had entertained.

Given the social, political and economic regression ever since the early 1990s in my native Hungary, I became in the mid 1990s a serial scholarship student for many long years. I still have reason to thank Professor John Welfield of the International University of Japan and Franziska Raimund of the United World College of the Adriatic in Italy, and also Nakajima Holdings Ltd, George Soros's Open Society Institute, and the Salgo-Noren Scholarship, for help in hard times. I also thank my own students at the American University of Nigeria and also at Webster University Thailand, especially Hassan Mustafa, Lobsang Dhundup Sherpa Subirana, Nathan Tran and Nishant Upadhyay for their stimulating ideas.

I thank my wonderful in-laws Babou and Awa Touray in London, who helped me in every conceivable way with research in that city. My parents Zoltan Mayer and Eva Pollagh, my grandmother Irene Plutzer, and my brother Benjamin Mayer provided me with crucial financial and emotional assistance. That said, no one assisted me more than my wife Ida Jallow and our daughter Aisa, especially while our young family stayed in Nigeria, at Webster University Thailand, and also in Gyor, Hungary.

I thank Webster University Thailand for their contribution to an online initiative that Drew Povey and I have initiated: a website dedicated to the publication of Nigerian Marxist originals. Our budding collection is available at https://www.scribd.com/Nigeria.Marx.Library. We welcome new submissions and readers.

1

Introduction

When I decided to write this book on Nigerian Marxist thinkers with a survey of the Nigerian socialist movement, both my academic, and my lay friends were startled, whether in Yola or in London, in Jeddah, in Hungary or in Israel. Is this not an arcane subject in the extreme? Is there, really, such a thing as Nigerian Marxism? Does this topic have any relevance in the 21st century? A friend in Jeddah advised me to tackle the issue of the new wave of Nigerian Islamism instead. Multiple others opined that I should focus exclusively on Boko Haram. I am grateful to all of them for their well-meant caveats, but the more I delved into the world of the Nigerian left, the more fascinated I became, and the more determined I felt to pursue the topic.

My interest in the subject was strengthened by a number of factors. First, I knew that Nigerian Marxism was far from dead. Indeed, as a Lecturer in Politics at the American University of Nigeria (AUN), I was fortunate to meet Gramscians such as Usman A. Tar (he was responsible for our department's mock accreditation) and the fiery Trotskyite Edwin Madunagu of *The Guardian* (Nigeria), who in Calabar opened not only his private library for me but the world of the Nigerian left. My old friend at AUN, Bill Hansen (a hero of the civil rights movement in the US,[1] now an expatriate professor in Adamawa state and a lifelong Marxist) had known Yusufu Bala Usman, one of the best Marxist historians of Northern Nigeria – I was to devour Bala Usman's works in the course of my research for this book. Still, I was less surprised by all this since Marxism as an intellectual pursuit is a stock feature in many countries that refuses to wither away. What really struck me was the fact that Nigerian labour leaders evoked ideas and images of class warfare very openly, as in the January 2012 fuel subsidy strikes, when 4–5 million women and men blocked the arteries of Nigerian commerce, while I was stranded in Yola because aeroplanes did not fly during the strike. Many Nigerian labour leaders still refer to themselves as 'Comrade', and labour personalities such as Dipo Fashina of the Academic Staff Union of Universities and Hassan Sunmonu, formerly of the Nigeria Labour Congress (NLC), or the indestructible Femi Aborisade continue to be Marxists, along with feminist socialists such as Molara Ogundipe-Leslie, Ifeoma Okoye or the expatriate thinker Amina Mama. The 'Occupy' movements in the West drew inspiration from the well of Marxian, socialist and communist traditions. But in Nigeria, the connection between the anti-capitalist counterculture and its 20th-century antecedents is even more visible to the naked eye. Marxist-inspired movements are still to be found in the country. The late Chinua Achebe's party, the People's Redemption Party, the oldest political party in existence in the country, with roots in 1978 Kaduna, is still in operation, and it proudly displays its Marxian inspirations. Adams Aliyu Oshiomhole, former leader of the NLC, has been the governor of Edo state since 2007, elected on the platform of the Action Congress (which is allied with his own Labour Party, a social democratic party with links to the NLC). There are a number of diehard Marxist parties, such as the Democratic Socialist Movement and its Socialist Party of Nigeria (associated with the Committee for Workers' International under Segun Sango's leadership), the Socialist Workers' League (Femi Aborisade, Baba Aye) and the National Conscience Party with a left-leaning progressive agenda. Two major newspapers, *This Day* and *The Guardian*, are sympathetic to the cause of the left. Party 'hard-core' membership also reads periodicals such as the *Workers' Alternative*[2] and the Democratic Socialist Movement website[3] (both also issue pamphlets, booklets and leaflets).

Their core message is not *passé*. On the contrary, it seems to be one of the possible answers to the problems posed by the Nigerian condition itself to the country, to Africa and to the world at large: most especially, unhindered corporate tyranny. The idea that militant Marxism is dead also smacks of Eurocentrism in the case of Westerners, and Slavophilia in the case of Russians and other Eastern Europeans; in large sections of the world outside Europe, militant Marxism is clearly on the rise. It is the second biggest 'security threat', in the form of the Naxalite movement (with Maoist inspirations) against the Indian state. It is the single strongest political force in Nepal. Marxism, through especially Istvan Meszaros' works, has influenced the late Hugo Chávez's policies in Venezuela, and a host of other Central and South American countries beyond Cuba. It still influences the policies of the Chinese Communist Party, especially in matters such as China's unique refusal to do away with the peasants' 'right to land' that manifests in the ban on capitalist private land ownership and that is celebrated by thinkers such as Samir Amin.[4] The mainstream view on China and its institutional relationship to Marxist theory is that in that country an organisationally Leninist vanguard party is less concerned with Marxism as an ideology with actual policy implications[5] than with Leninism which provides an organ-isational methodology for rule in the technical sense. General-Secretary

Xi Jin-ping, however, is thought by some to be orchestrating a conscious return to Marx in the country and there are indications that the Chinese state might even engage with some aspects of foreign, including Western, Marxist thought.[6]

The Nigerian condition presents some very difficult questions to the observer. An entire subchapter of this book is devoted to a survey of that general condition. Every researcher of Nigeria ends up doing so, because the 'Nigeria *problematique*' is simply inescapable for anyone who spent time in the country and knows how bad its condition really is. When I suggest that Marxist-inspired analysis and Marxian answers might be part of the solution, this is not so easily chalked up to a left-wing agenda on my part. Indeed, it was none other than John Campbell, former United States ambassador and currently Council on Foreign Relations Fellow, the single most important US expert on Nigeria, who aired the view that Nigeria might well still produce a Fidel Castro.[7] *Nota bene*, he did not say that Cuban, North Korean or any other saboteurs, agents or spies might produce just such a leader: he thought that the Nigerian condition itself might. Obviously, for John Campbell and for United States foreign policy, the emergence of a Castro in Nigeria would be a very unwelcome development.

It would be foolish to discount the Nigerian socialists' many and varied works, their movement, their toil and their thoughts, on the sole ground that they and their activist friends have not captured political power in Nigeria historically – if for no other reason than for the fact that they still might. In May 2013, for the first time since 1967, the Nigerian air force conducted attacks on home territory as part of the government's continued fight against Boko Haram, their Islamist menace. What is happening in the north-east of Nigeria might very well bring unexpected developments in this decade, and a social revolution is arguably the only one among them that offers any hope of change for the better.

This book, first and foremost, is a history of socialist ideas and of left-leaning thinkers, and in it the history of the socialist movement is presented as the larger milieu that those alternative ideas grew out of. I devote a chapter to the movement to provide the necessary framework for understanding the works themselves. This is more than has appeared in the literature on the subject so far, but hardly a complete narrative. There is a technical reason for this relative silence: writing the detailed academic history of the movement would necessitate multiple trips to all Nigerian states, a focus on oral history and on personal archives (as public archives are so random in Nigeria), and an altogether different methodology. But it was not only for those negative reasons that I opted to write on Nigerian thinkers more than on Nigerian strikes. First, it was because these works outline alternatives to the existing grim reality endured by millions. Second, because those books were so well written, so entertaining, so stimulating, dense, humorous, witty, apt, and so singularly clever. The world has discovered literary giants such as Chinua Achebe, Wole Soyinka, Ben Okri, Cyprian Ekwensi, Ken Saro-Wiwa, and the new wave of Helon Habila and Chimamanda Ngozi Adichie, but the world has *not* discovered (or has not rediscovered anyway, since the 1970s/1980s) the prolific Mokwugo Okoye, the fiery Edwin Madunagu, the heterodox Eskor Toyo, and so many others such as Bene Madunagu, Ola Oni, Bade Onimode, Tunji Otegbeye, Niyi Oniororo, Ikenna Nzimiro, Yusufu Bala Usman, Igho Natufe, Wahab Goodluck, or the early Adebayo Olukoshi. To some extent even radical young Toyin Falola[8] and Biodun Jeyifo leaned towards Marxism in the 1980s, and so did many more Nigerian Marxian authors who discussed and still discuss vital social, political, economic and cultural issues in their works. In the 1990s, a new cohort appeared, with Claude Ake, the feminist poet Ogundipe-Leslie, the socially committed writer Ifeoma Okoye; and others simply continued their work well into the 1990s and beyond. This book aims to be a testimony to their eloquence, their acumen, their analytical prowess when it comes to the problems of Nigerians. It is also one of the aims of this book to familiarise the Western reader with the frames of references that might make reading those authors somewhat difficult. Their books have all been written entirely in English. At the same time, most of them were written for a readership that claimed a close familiarity with Nigeria and West Africa, including even those that were published by Zed Books or other publishers in the West. It is with that in view that this book has introductory chapters on the literature, on Nigeria's history, on the Nigerian independence movement and especially Zikism, the labour movement and its international aspects, including African Marxism in general, before embarking on the detailed study of Nigerian Marxists' oeuvres.

Beyond the intrinsic intellectual value of these works, the countercul-ture they sustained had a very visible presence and shaped both social resistance and Nigerian mentalities in a major way. More than that, in this work I shall argue that Marxism was seen as a major legitimising factor even as it was exploited or co-opted by military and civilian governments. Conditions of illegality, and even military rule, did not succeed in eliminating Marxism in Nigeria. Very often, mainstream politicians also felt a need to co-opt it precisely because of its perceived legitimising potential among the African masses. Edwin Madunagu was enticed by Ibrahim Badamasi Babangida to serve on his Political Bureau, Ebenezer Babatope was practically forced to join Sani Abacha's government, Hassan Sunmonu of the NLC was carefully cultivated by the corrupt plutocrats of the second republic and the military governments of the 1980s. The Marxian counterculture groups at universities, the NLC, illegal party circles and even village communes, were subjected to constant pressure to incorporate into the existing power structures. When formal democracy was reinstituted in 1999, Marxism continued to underpin the NLC's efforts, and it is making a comeback today with the Socialist Workers' League, the Movement for Democratic Socialism, Calabar groups, Usman Tar, Amina Mama and literary author Ifeoma Okoye (the author of the novel *The Fourth World*) in the 2000s. This counterculture, beyond exhibiting the most varied versions and understandings of Marxism, has consistently been intellectually inclined, committed to ideas of honesty and authenticity, and artistic in its tastes.

Finding most Nigerian Marxist writings today is very difficult. Not even an introductory reader has ever been published. As Nigerian libraries routinely cleansed these works from their shelves in the 1990s, it is now easier to find a tome by a Nigerian Marxist in a public library in Wales than it is in Nigeria! Many of the books reviewed were available only from small libraries in Wales. Edwin Madunagu's fantastic private library in Calabar, Nigeria, was also among the most important places to find original articles and books. When Nigerian Marxists were still viewed with suspicion and curiosity in the United States, libraries even in places like Missouri bought their books. Via online retailers, I had the opportunity to acquire volumes that had been withdrawn and sold from those US libraries. I have been privileged to be able to read these works that represent for me the best in Nigerian social, political, cultural and economic thought, and that are as entertaining as they are enlightening, while offering analysis and alternatives for the future.

These books are works of African political thought, African economic thought, African feminist thought – indeed, of African philosophy. African thought is being recognised more widely in the West as a valuable field of study in the last 20 years or so. Indeed, it has been a trend to decipher African philosophy from every possible source, including folklore – even Henry Odera Oruka's 'sage philosophy' and 'philosophic sagacity' can be traced back to such an effort. Such projects were emancipatory in their intentions. But Africa is not frozen in time, say in the 1920s. African philosophy may also be found in more recent works on political theory, written by Africans.

The works of Nigerian Marxists demonstrate the falsehood of the witticism commonly repeated by expatriates that 'In our Naija there is no abstraction,' where 'Naija' is simply another word for Nigeria used by Nigerians and expatriates alike. (The word is used as a noun and even as an adjective in spoken Nigerian English.) The statement, however, is false in the extreme, as the careers of brilliant Nigerian intellectuals in the UK, the US, the UN, or the World Bank, have demonstrated. And Nigerian talent of other kinds is being recognised as well. A recent study focused on how Nigerian 'tiger moms' are among the most successful of all immigrants in the United States at inculcating in their progeny the skills for mainstream success.[9] Nigerians have made notable contributions, not only in literature and the arts but also in intellectual production. And the works of their Marxist thinkers go far beyond day-to-day abstraction to achieve the aesthetic, descriptive and analytic richness of truly great works which merit much closer study. This is the central claim of this book. In this sense, it is only an added bonus that many of these works might be considered definitive, or, at the very least, relevant and profound, regarding many subjects that concern Nigeria, Africa and the world. One need only think of radical Islam, Boko Haram, and the current low-intensity civil war. There have appeared many academic and popular works that expound on the Boko Haram phenomenon and its possible implications for the West. At the same time, most of those articles focused exclusively on how to tackle Boko Haram as a security threat, and propose solutions that will come mainly by way of one or another security apparatus – an impossible task as Boko Haram is a social problem, created by the conditions that prevail in feudal and criminally governed Northern Nigeria. I suspect that the best analysis of the Boko Haram movement by extrapolation is still Yusufu Bala Usman's *The Manipulation of Religion in Nigeria*, written about another Islamist movement, that of the Maitatsine, but which has historical parallels with Boko Haram and was crushed with military force in 1982–85.[10] Religion itself may be a force for good or for bad, but kowtowing to obscurantist feudal quasi-religious wisdoms will create an explosion in Nigeria, says Yusufu Bala Usman in this slim book with an orange cover that appeared in Kaduna in 1987. At the same time, today not everyone is blind to the nature of the Boko Haram threat, even in the world of Nigerian periodicals. *Workers' Alternative* has published an editorial about the 2013 state of emergency in the north-east:

> The concrete truth about *Jama'atu Ahlis Sunna Lidda'awati wal-Jihad*, which in Arabic means, 'People Committed to the Propagation of the Prophet's Teachings and Jihad', aka Boko Haram, is that it is nothing but a set of foot soldiers of sections of the Nigerian ruling class that went berserk. It is an arch-reactionary organization that was and is still doing the bidding of sections of the Nigerian elites.[11]

So writes the editor, who actually names Senator Ndume as someone that has been charged for terrorism in connection with Boko Haram, to prove his point beyond speculation.

Unbeknown to the West, the thinkers of the Nigerian radical left are known in Nigeria, even though their works are often discarded from public libraries. Representations of Marxist intellectuals even appear in popular 'home videos' produced in Nollywood.[12] The otherwise quite marvellous film *Waterfalls*,[13] featuring Tonto Dikeh and Van Vicker in the lead roles as college sweethearts, features a USSR-returned professor who speaks in Marxist truisms but who is too ignorant to know the difference between metaphor and simile. Enter brilliant freshman Tonto Dikeh, who swiftly corrects our Marxist buffoon's mistakes with feminine charm and gusto, winning a smile from heartthrob Vicker, the most eligible bachelor on campus. This representation of the Marxist professor as uncommonly ignorant at least does not rob him of his African extraction, as the *Gods Must Be Crazy II* does, where the clumsy communist revolutionary in Angola, is actually a Cuban (who were of course present in the country, but by no means constituted the only driving force behind Angolan communism).

It is not hard to see why Nigeria's mainstream entertainment industry, which is obviously a business before being anything else, treats the subject of Marxist intellectuals in precisely this manner. What is harder to understand is how Nigerian intellectuals themselves, positioned in the pinnacles of Western learning, have sometimes disregarded the trains of thought that I call Naija Marxisms. Biodun Jeyifo was the editor of the *Oxford Encyclopedia of African Thought*,[14] a towering intellectual and, as a matter of fact, Edwin Madunagu's personal friend and the editor of one of his essay collections. At the same time, in his two-volume encyclopaedia, he included no entry on Marx, or on the one time Muscovite communist turned Pan-Africanist George Padmore, nor on Black Marxism, African Marxism or Afromarxism, or even on Edwin Madunagu himself. Lest we think that he did not want to appear biased towards his old friend, he also omitted Mokwugo Okoye, Ikenna Nzimiro, Yusufu Bala Usman, Tunji Otegbeye and Ola Oni, while including entries on Joe Slovo (the leader of the South African Communist Party), Fela Anikulapo-Kuti, Amilcar Cabral and Ngugi wa Thiong'o (who were all communists but retain popularity in the West for other reasons), and also on Awolowo and Azikiwe (who were not communists at all, of course) and even (non-Marxist) 'African socialism' of the pro-Western variety. It is not controversial to suggest that Jeyifo's omissions must have been conscious ones. Jeyifo had shown Marxian tendencies in his early career; he was in fact the head of the Academic Staff Union in the turbulent Nigeria of the early 1980s,[15] and it is unfortunate that he chose to commit to oblivion everything to do with Nigerian Marxism in the important study that he co-edited. His omissions are symptomatic. Guy Martin in his recent *African Political Thought* introduces novel categories such as 'socialist-populist ideology' and 'populist-socialist ideology' to avoid explicit mention of the Marxist content that many thinkers he deals with so obviously exhibit.[16]

In this book I do not intend to engage in cheerleading instead of analysis. Indeed, there are many reasons to worry for Africa, and even more reasons to worry specifically for Nigeria (unless we deliberately confuse the petro-fuelled growth rate of the country's economy with genuine development). We cannot disregard Patrick Chabal's bleak view in *Africa Works: Disorder as Political Instrument*,[17] based on the meagre premise that oil well owners, luxury chocolate bar importers and road construction companies are doing better now than they did under Sani Abacha. Where I would disagree with Chabal's Afro-pessimism is not with respect to the immediate future of Africa. Rather, I take issue with his conviction that in Africa absolutely everything is ruled by crude instrumentality, by instant gratification, ultimately, by the power of money. If it were so, then all the thinkers of the Nigerian Marxian left would have turned to neoliberalism or tribalism when China stopped financing revolutionary movements and the USSR fell. Some indeed did, and that was inevitable – think of how many Communist-turned-nationalists one finds in Eastern Europe and ex-Soviet Central Asia today. But people such as Usman A. Tar, Edwin Madunagu, Bene Madunagu, Femi Aborisade, Abiodun Olamosu, Baba Aye, Amina Mama, Laoye Sanda, Bamidele Aturu, Chima Ubani, Funmi Adewunmi, Niyi Osundare, Omafume Eonoge, the writers Ifeoma Okoye, Molara Ogundipe-Leslie and Festus Iyayi, perhaps the majority of labour leaders at the NLC, the celebrated lawyer Tunji Braithwaite and others, have not only maintained their political allegiances and Marxian analytical frames of mind but, even more importantly, most of them chose to stay on in a country that is hostile to its intellectuals like few others. Many of them have effectively sacrificed what might have been cushy careers in Western academic institutions to work within Nigeria, to understand Nigeria better or to help Nigeria. Anyone who has ever stayed in Nigeria outside the confines of the Abuja Sheraton knows very well what this entails. Many of these authors have been more than just good academics: they have lived lives that were positively heroic. Many have known the insides of jails, some have been beaten and tortured; some endured hiding, some prosecution. Many had difficulty getting published. All had to fight the hegemonic culture maintained by the criminal, comprador, bureaucratic bourgeoisie that rules Nigeria: a class bereft of taste, a class that oozes vulgarity. If it is not politically correct from a European to call it that, then let Chinua Achebe speak: it is 'dirty, callous, noisy, ostentatious, dishonest and vulgar'.[18]

This book, the first monographic study of Nigerian Marxism, had to be written sooner or later. It is reasonable to ask, however, why exactly a Hungarian researcher should have undertaken the task. Indeed, it is – or it should be – humbling to write on a history that is not one's own. However, without trying to gloss over the obvious difficulties of being a foreigner (and someone who does not hail from a Commonwealth country at that), there may be some advantages resulting from my standpoint. I spent my formative years in socialist Hungary. Linkages between Eastern Europe and the Nigerian socialist movement abounded from the 1940s until 1989. Some authors discussed below were actually schooled in Eastern Europe: Eskor Toyo studied economics in Poland, and even had a book published in Polish. Labour leader Michael Imoudu, Tunji Otegbeye, Wahab Goodluck, socialist feminist Olufunmilayo Ransome-Kuti and others travelled regularly to Moscow for conferences and for funds to support the socialist movement and labour initiatives, including strikes. The Eastern Europe–Marxist Nigeria link has been recognised and partly documented by the eminent Nigerian historian Hakeem Tijani[19] (whose eminence is matched by his allegiance to the political status quo), but the connection is still awaiting a historian to unearth the exact details in the Russian language in Moscow. At the same time, to reduce Nigerian Marxism to an acolyte movement, funded by Eastern Europeans would be a very erroneous proposition. Even Tunji Otegbeye, leader of the Moscow-sanctioned Marxist party (Socialist Workers' and Farmers' Party), made frivolous remarks about the land of the Soviets in his books, not to mention heterodox thinkers such as Niyi Oniororo or Edwin Madunagu, who condemned Soviet leaders nearly as often as they did Americans. Two Nigerian Marxists, Peter Ayodele Curtis Joseph and Olufunmilayo Ransome-Kuti were the recipients of the Lenin Peace Prize along with Nasser, Nehru, W.E.B. Du Bois, Angela Davis, Salvador Allende, Pablo Picasso and Nelson Mandela – a sign that the USSR recognised the potential of the Nigerian Marxist movement. I devote a chapter to the international links of the Nigerian Marxist movement: mainly British, East European, Ghanaian, and South African. Indeed, the multifaceted nature of the Nigerian left's international links reminds us that there is more to the international flow of ideas than the metropole–colony relationship.

Through the essays, articles, treatises, analytical tomes and pamphlets written by Nigerian Marxists, a subaltern of sorts spoke, and she spoke with the voice of a Black Jacobin. Most of their aims stood for radical equality in the vein of veritable levellers. Although one could claim to be, say, a Marxist labour organiser in the 1970s if one had read only the classics of Marxism, it was inevitably of interest for leftists to get acquainted with Marxian takes on issues that more directly concerned their own lives. The tomes discussed in this volume were printed in editions of thousands, often reprinted just months after their first publication. Northern Nigerians such as Yusufu Bala Usman were read and appreciated in the South; Southern Igbos such as Madunagu were inspirations in the North as well as their home constituencies; men read feminists such as Ogundipe-Leslie; women read rugged labour-oriented organisers such as Oniororo. Some, like Imoudu, had the most obvious working-class pedigrees, others were second-generation literates (or, like Ransome-Kuti, fourth-generation literates) but their focus was the same: liberation for ordinary Nigerians. In more than one way, the authors I deal with all belong, many out of choice, to the subaltern class in neocolonial Nigeria.

Capitalist Nigeria is a crime against its own people, say Naija Marxists, with convincing force. The ostentatious Nigerian leadership of the 1980s was one of the first, globally, to introduce structural adjustment programmes (SAPs), ostensibly to revive the country's ailing economy. SAPs in the end deindustrialised Nigeria, forced upon it the worst kind of militarisation of politics, sucked the blood out of its veins and turned it into a barren land of no production, no middle class, few medical doctors (more Nigerian medical doctors practise in the US than in Nigeria!),[20] no oil refineries (four of these stand idle while compradors re-import refined petrol!), two hours of electricity a day for most people, very little indoor and no outdoor plumbing, no operational water towers (except in Calabar), no sewage system to speak of, and cities filled with filth that would startle even Engels.

It is not hard to see why a Nigerian academic friend of mine, who had studied in socialist Hungary in the 1980s but who had no socialist political leanings whatsoever, once said over coffee: 'What Nigeria needs is a touch of communism.' For Nigeria today is a sad parody of democracy, a petro state where indecent individualism reigns supreme; a country where every driver uses high beams after dusk, effectively blinding each other, and maiming and even killing innocent bystanders. What is possibly the most dangerous country on earth not involved in a conventional war, however, is full of talented, warm-hearted, open people, people who deserve better from their leaders and honest analysis from their intellectual class. The authors I discuss in this book appear to me to represent that kind of honesty: their voice has not been bought, their reasoning, along with their sympathetic hearts, is evident to all those who care to read them. They offer hope that in Nigeria the status quo might one day be overcome.

Everyone knows that Nigeria is famous for fraudulent emails and internet scams. What is less known is that this fraud is the fifth biggest sector of the Nigerian economy.[21] What is central here is that, as David Harvey warns, 'a serious case can be made that the extralegal forms are fundamental rather than peripheral to capitalism (the three largest sectors of global foreign trade are in drugs, illegal guns, and human trafficking).'[22] When we discuss Nigeria, we have to understand that it is Western companies such as Royal Dutch Shell, Agip, Chevron, Julius Berger, Standard Chartered Bank and others that make money there on a daily basis; in conjunction that is, with Nigeria's predatory elite.

Nigeria shows to the naked eye that accumulation is indeed oft by dispossession. In Yola where I lived, on the local hills (lovingly nicknamed Beverly Hills, rather aptly too as we shall see), a shining new development was crowding out local mud huts in an extralegal way. Anyone who had no written title deed to a given area was promptly evicted by the governor. Fulani herdsmen rarely had title deeds for their huts to hand. As the property was on the top of a hill in a major flood-prone region, its commercial value was very high and still rising. Accumulation by dispossession in Nigeria is not something one reads about in left-leaning periodicals but something one observes as a matter of indisputable fact right in front of one's gate. That is the reason why I believe that learning about Nigeria not only tells us about Nigeria but, equally importantly, it tells us about ourselves, about the 21st century, about global capitalism.

The most important authors covered here will be Edwin Madunagu, Mokwugo Okoye, Bade Onimode, Yusufu Bala Usman, Ikenna Nzimiro, Molara Ogundipe-Leslie, Bene Madunagu, Amina Mama, Eskor Toyo, and a number of others. Claude Ake was a Marxist political scientist of global renown, the only author discussed in this book whose oeuvre has invited a monograph so far – but he also ventured far from Marxism, or rather utilised Marxist thought to show why revolution was irrelevant to Nigeria; hence I am disinclined to deal with him in detail in this work. Edwin Madunagu is a mathematician and journalist, a combination of a Trotskyist rebel who founded a rural commune while hiding from the police in the 1970s, and a Nigerian *Aufklaerist* who opened his private library to the public in Calabar. When 1989 came, he did not take the mantle of any petty ethnocentric cause, but set up a non-governmental organisation (NGO) instead to conscientise adolescents about gender. His oeuvre spans four decades and is massively voluminous even discounting his journalistic contributions. While I have tried to avoid treating this book as a *Festschrift* to Madunagu, my personal appreciation of his contributions will be apparent. I also owe him much for offering me his invaluable help at the time when I started this research. Bene Madunagu, Edwin's wife and a professor of biology and a Marxian feminist, argues for women's emancipation as part and parcel of a community-based future in her works, some of which have been published by Zed Books in London. Other Marxists I deal with have been less heterodox. Tunji Otegbeye was a hero of the Marxian left in the 1960s and 1970s, especially as the general-secretary of a Soviet-backed Marxis-Leninist party. Otegbeye wrote interesting autobiographies but he was not what one might call an independent Marxian thinker in theoretical terms, so his contributions will not be discussed in chapters on Marxian thought. Reviled by the Trotskyists, Otegbeye loved ballroom dancing and street politics. After the fall of the USSR, he became a member of the Yoruba Council of Elders, a feudal institution – a curious move even in Nigeria. Mokwugo Okoye, a writer, was one of the most colourful characters in the Nigerian Marxist movement: a liberation fighter and Zikist hero who knew the inside of jails; accused of plotting for political assassinations of British colonialists (of this there is no proof as I shall show); an accomplished belletrist who wrote 20 books, eminently readable and very fashionable in his time, both in Nigeria and abroad. Almost forgotten abroad in 2014, Okoye's style was influenced by one of his favourite light hearted essayists, the Chinese Lin Yu-tang. Unfortunately for him, he was also a Marxist (albeit in a very broad sense), and this may account for the fact that the Nigerian *Oeffentlichkeit* excludes his texts from the national canon. Completely non-sectarian, funny, witty, with a fantastic erudition that he acquired without recourse to a university education, Okoye enchants the reader with his beautiful, Proustian sentences. Ikenna Nzimiro was a professional anthropologist who, while teaching at Cambridge, produced a meticulous analysis of the running of Igbo royal houses. An Igbo himself, he later participated in the Biafran war on the side of Biafra, and was in charge of ideology and propaganda efforts to strengthen Ojukwu's secession. Nzimiro later broke the self-imposed silence of the socialist left on the matter of Biafra and wrote a peculiarly interesting book in which he argued that the Biafran conflict was primarily a class conflict, and not an ethnic one. Others, such as Ola Oni, Bade Onimode, Adebayo Olukoshi and Okwudiba Nnoli, were political economists with left-leaning convictions, strongest in the case of the outright Marxist Oni and Onimode. Their doyen was Eskor Toyo,[23] nicknamed Mao Toyo by Niyi Oniororo, who had Maoist as well as loosely Trotskyite, leanings. Niyi Oniororo advocated for a radical foreign policy, especially after Murtala Muhammad's assassination. Yusufu Bala Usman was a professional historian and an adviser to the People's Redemption Party; he was a Fulani aristocrat by birth but one who sided with the *talakawa* ('the common people' in Hausa) following a moral imperative. Bala Usman poured criticism on the modus operandi of the Nigerian elite, especially in how it abused religion and ethnicity. As such abuses provided the core of Nigeria's bloody conflicts and unending physical violence, the class that fuels them, demands our close attention. Molara Ogundipe-Leslie, Bene Madunagu, Olufunmilayo Ransome-Kuti and Amina Mama have been Marxian democratic socialist feminists. The only version of Marxian thought that seems to be absent from Nigeria has been 'left communism', with its emphasis on direct action.

Generally, we can say that the ruling classes of Nigeria, the common enemy of these thinkers, are effectively an illustration of David Harvey's pessimistic dictums. They have successfully privatised profits and socialised risks.[24] Wages are repressed to extremes in the country (when there are wages paid at all, that is), prices unbelievably high. I have been offered in Yola a living turkey for $100, and this did not surprise as a boney backyard chicken goes for $25. At the highest socioeconomic level, privatisation of parastatal companies finished the job of dispossession. That came with democracy in the post-1999 scenario, celebrated in the West as a return to good governance and decency. Thievery, fraud and robbery are rampant in today's 'democratic' state, as in Central Europe during the Thirty Years War, and traditional systems that had once put limitations on ostentatious personal consumption and greed have been made to look ridiculous by the mainstream media. Indeed, when someone with a conscience is confronted with Nigeria, he/she is forced to think like a radical.

This book concentrates on authors and works that deal with political, economic, feminist and historical theory. It provides analysis and criticism of literary works only when and if those have immediate theoretical implications (Mokwugo Okoye), or when a writer also engages in theoretical work (Ogundipe-Leslie). I do not go into specifically literary questions, such as possible Marxian influences on Achebe's works, which are discussed so well in Bjorn Beckman's and Gbemisola Adeoti's excellently edited volume,[25] or the nature of Festus Iyayi's 'proletarian novels',[26] Fela Kuti's left-leaning songs, or even Ifeoma Okoye's robust novel *The Fourth World*. It would be wonderful to see a scholar deal with these works from an angle that is at least informed by critical theory, or, even better, one that explicitly explores their Marxian dimensions and how those relate and compare to each other. However, that is a task better left to a literary critic who is similarly inclined.

For such a rich and varied topic as the intellectual movement of the Nigerian Marxian left, my review of existing secondary literature will be relatively short. The reason for this is simple. Scholarly research and the production of secondary sources on these authors are not just incomplete: in fact, these tasks have only just been started on. It is not that books do not appear on the subject of Nigeria from a Marxian standpoint: indeed, many do even today. Orike Ben Didi's *Comrade Che at 80*,[27] Abayomi Ferreira's *Savagery in Politics*,[28] Igho Natufe's *Soviet Policy in Africa*,[29] along with Usman Tar's, Amina Mama's and Edwin Madunagu's recent books all recently appeared and they are still in print. However, those works are part and parcel of the very intellectual tradition that we are trying to understand: for our purposes they are mostly treated as primary sources, dealt with in the body of this book, and *not* secondary sources that constitute a scholarly treatment of the subject. London-based refereed journal *Review of African Political Economy* (*ROAPE*) has been very committed to publishing short essays by Nigerian Marxist and radical leftist authors, but none of those authors has so far undertaken the task of narrating in sufficient detail and analysing the branch of social inquiry to which they themselves belong.

African Marxism, the African worker and his labour struggle, and student unrest over the continent has received careful attention lately, through especially Leo Zeilig's magnificent studies such as *Class Struggle and Resistance in Africa*,[30] *Revolt and Protest: Student Politics and Activism in Sub-Saharan Africa*,[31] inspiring works in their scope and breadth of analysis. Zeilig's crucial contribution to the subject is his hard earned and sparklingly intelligent explanation of how workers' resistance flourished in Africa, even after deindustrialisation, a counter-intuitive but nonetheless empirically valid phenomenon that calls for a nuanced class analysis in the Marxist sense – a task that Zeilig executes elegantly and convincingly. I will make use of Zeilig's findings especially in my concluding chapter, 'Analysing Nigerian Marxism'. While Zeilig does service to African resistance movements and African Marxism perhaps more than anyone else globally in academic circles, I disagree with his analysis. Based on the experience of 'really existing' African Marxist-Leninist states, Zeilig dismisses the African Marxisms of the Cold War era, thus joining mainstream analysts in their dismissal of the value of African Marxisms. The same may be said about Zeilig's take on the 'Marxist content' of Soviet socialism, which according to him was apparently negligible. At the same time, Zeilig completely abandons the methods of silence regarding African Marxism so characteristic of mainstream scholars. Indeed, he writes: 'For almost forty years, the ideas of Marxism were seemingly omnipresent in Africa. They dominated every serious intellectual debate on the continent and occupied the minds of those who sought independence.'[32] Indeed, one might say that when Zeilig wants to challenge the historical links of the USSR to African Marxism and resistance, he follows a very honest and well-meaning political imperative, that is, to allow space for African resistance to flourish without the burdens of a failed empire. This is laudable. Also notable is Bjorn Beckman's *Intellectuals and African Development* and *Trade Unions and Party Politics: Labour Movements in Africa.* Carlos Lopes' *Africa's Contemporary Challenges: The Legacy of Amilcar Cabral* is also available. Malachy Igwilo's *A Philosophical Analysis of Claude Ake's Idea of Development* was written on the basis of the realisation that a (recently deceased) Nigerian Marxist thinker may deserve a monograph and closer attention to his search for alternatives for Africa.

The situation is happier when it comes to Nigerian history in general and labour history in particular. Our state of knowledge is well served when it comes to general Nigerian history, the Nigerian labour movement itself (especially up to the late 1970s) and, in particular, the Marxist thread in Zikism (the left wing of the national independence movement). Toyin Falola,[33] John Campbell[34] and Karl Maier[35] have written celebrated general histories of Nigeria. Robin Cohen,[36] Ananaba Wogu,[37] Richard L. Sklar,[38] Ehiedu E.G. Iweriebor[39] and Hakeem Tijani[40] wrote the best-known works on Nigerian labour and on Zikism.[41]

Marxist political activism in Nigeria is discussed by our primary authors too. Tunji Otegbeye's *Turbulent Years*[42] is an obvious source. Niyi Oniororo wrote a comic rebuttal of his own movement, useful in its comic characterization of our protagonists (*Who Are the Nigerian Comrades?*).[43] Edwin Madunagu devoted *The Tragedy of the Nigerian Socialist Movement*[44] to the fate of the Marxist left. Sometimes, of course, primary and secondary sources cannot be neatly distinguished from each other for the purposes of this research. The 'Adebiyi trials', designed to outlaw the communist opposition, are best dealt with in economist Bade Onimode's *Dialectics of Mass Poverty*,[45] and not in a book written by a professional historian or in a text with a specifically historical theme. The same is true of Usman A. Tar's *The Politics of Neoliberal Democracy in Africa: State and Civil Society in Nigeria*,[46] which gives virtually the only reliable history of the NLC through the military administrations of Gowon, Obasanjo, Buhari, Babangida and Abacha, although the book's central theme is how civil society is faring in neoliberal Nigeria rather than labour history. I do not give an analysis of Tar's oeuvre in this book, though his works are exciting applications of Gramscian analysis, because he is still very young and maybe the best of his output is yet to come.

Regarding African Marxism in general, I drew on Joe Slovo's *Slovo: The Unfinished Autobiography*,[47] Ruth First's articles, George Padmore's *Pan-Africanism or Communism*, Robert Legvold's legendary *Soviet Policy in West Africa*, Matusevich's *Africa in Russia, Russia in Africa* and *No Easy Row for a Russian Hoe: Ideology and Pragmatism in Nigerian-Soviet Relations 1960–1991*, the Ottaways' *Afrocommunism*, Keller and Rothchild's *Afro-Marxist Regimes*, and Cedric J. Robinson's *Black Marxism*, some of which were more useful than others. I also made use of an Eastern European anthology of Africa's Marxist voices: Andras Simor's 1972 book *Black Howl – Black Africa* (*Neger kialtas – Fekete-Afrika*).[48] I consider Walter Rodney's *How Europe Underdeveloped Africa* a profound introduction to Africa's political economy, and I follow his controversial take on the concept of African feudalism.

There seems to be in the literature much confusion about the term 'African Marxism', sometimes called Afrocommunism, and its relationship to Black Marxism. The most widely known book on the subject, the one that actually introduced the very term 'Afrocommunism' to the discourse, was David and Marina Ottaway's *Afrocommunism*,[49] which appeared in New York and London in 1981. The Ottaways' view is summed up by the following quote about African Marxist regimes: 'ideology was re-elaborated continually by Lenin, Mao, and innumerable forgotten ideologues, including those squabbling over fine points in African universities'.[50] A comment as patronising as this can only stem from ignorance. Indeed, the Ottaways, who wrote a celebrated book about *Afrocommunism*, knew so little about communism and Marxism that they thought that 'serving as the vanguard of the revolution' was 'a minor role' in the political life of a socialist country (they were referring to Boumedienne's FLN [Front de Libération Nationale] in Algeria).[51]

This book thus aims to establish a workable history of the Marxist movement beyond the trade union movement itself, including illegal parties and clandestine organisations, whenever our sources permit. It also aims to present Nigerian Marxisms as coherent schools of thought that flourished in Nigerian academia and intellectual circles at universities, in newspapers and in the NGO sector, existing in the intellectual space that organised against officialdom. I also claim that Nigerian Marxism was the single most effective alternative worldview that informed not only the Nigerian labour movement but academia and the public at large, including voices in feminism, historiography, political economy and even literature. In my view, Naija Marxisms have produced so many excellent works and made such an important imprint on the Nigerian imagination that it is negligent to keep ignoring their history. In subsequent chapters, I will focus on many primary works that constitute the history of ideas: those of Naija Marxisms in all their richness and variety.

This book was written from a somewhat unusual perspective of a young Eastern European historian who experienced sub-optimal 'really existing socialism' in its Indian summer, but whose life came to be defined by the barbarity of the region's new capitalism that turned his country into a rather soulless semi-periphery and its inhabitants into disgruntled and under-represented *new poor,* including the author. Only thanks to scholarships in Italy, Japan and American universities in Kyrgyzstan and Bulgaria, was I later able to work in international NGOs in the global South (Afghanistan) and then at American universities in Nigeria and in Thailand. My method has been to treat the history of ideas, including socialist ideas, at the intersection of speculative and empirical fields. I find it impossible to discuss workers' self-government without directly referring back to Yugoslavia's practical experience with this method, to Giovanni Arrighi's findings on the Chinese experience with workers' self-government,[52] to Venezuelan attempts at meaningful democratisation, and even to British workers' cooperatives or to Herend Porcelain's unique workers' ownership structure system when I read some of today's speculative Marxist literature on the subject – but I also find that mainstream histories of both Eastern Europe and of the South often neglect the importance of ideas produced in those regions themselves, and I find that wanting too; in fact I find it to be shallow empiricism. Political history and the history of ideas should ideally be discussed together, and putting the 'historical' back into 'historical materialism' may be one of the most important tasks for today's socialists.

Southern radical epistemologies are celebrated today by thinkers such as Ramon Grosfoguel, but Eastern Europe's new role as a *bona fide* capitalist semi-periphery has so far mostly nurtured fascists of various persuasions, occultists and 'perennialists'; so much so that Eastern Europe today seems like an empty shell, an epistemological no-man's-land – still unable to digest that its 1989 revolts have been stolen from the people. Eastern European art, especially writers like Pelevin and Krasznahorkai, and the films of Bela Tarr provide a glimpse into the post-apocalyptic psychology of most sensitive Eastern Europeans. That said, despair in the long run might preferably be overcome, not just savoured. My wildest hope is that radical Nigerian voices, including Marxist ones, among many other catalysts, may have a role in fostering socialist thinking in newly subjugated capitalist regions such as mine. Beyond that, of course, I hope that an exposition of the history of Marxist thought may be useful to the Nigerian movement itself, and that it may be interesting to the general reader.

On a theoretical note: the definition of Marxism in this book is intentionally wide and inclusive. It is not even posited as a necessary antithesis to conservatism (in my view, capitalism conserves very few things of value). I choose caution when considering Mokwugo Okoye's way of discussing traditional African village life with nostalgia, or discussing the work of Niyi Oniororo, also a Marxist, who treated cultural conservatism with the disdain of a Maoist cultural revolutionary. I also do not enter the debate on whether Marxism should allow space for religion in a way that would be unconventional for 19th-century Marxists. Bade Onimode became religious as he aged, Tunji Otegbeye maintained his nonchalant silence on the subject to his death, the labour leader Michael Imoudu sported *juju* regalia all his life, and Edwin Madunagu is an agnostic with respect for all religions, animist or monotheist. I have not yet come across doctrinaire atheism among Nigerian Marxist thinkers, but rather compassionate analyses of why religions can so effectively be manipulated in the soulless world of suffering that most ordinary people inhabit in that country.

2
The Descent

Once a patchwork of traditional kingdoms, merchant states and acephalous village communities, postcolonial Nigeria since 1960 has been cut and torn by its brutal elites, allies of the 'free world' led by the United States. Since the mid 1980s, the IMF's SAPs refashioned the state and made it a vehicle for resource extraction *par excellence*. The political-economic condition in which Nigeria now finds itself has virtually rewoven the very fabric of Nigerian society.

The Nigerian Condition

Nobody knows how many people live in the Federal Republic of Nigeria. This is the result of the reigning budgetary distribution method whereby the constituent states of the federation receive federal assistance according to the size of their populations. State governors simply lie about their population data. One may come across aggregate numbers for the country's population as a whole that vary as widely as between 120 million and 180 million in scholarly publications and educated estimates. After the 1963 nationwide census, religion disappeared from the subsequent census enquiry sheets, as numbers of adherents seemed to have been the cause of the turmoil that brought down the first republic in 1966. When oil incomes reached government coffers in the 1970s, the politicking with numbers became worse. Thus Nigerians have no knowledge of how many they are. Neither do they have data on the religious distribution of their own populace. Any public statement that champions the numerical majority of a given religion or the numerical plurality of a given ethnic group is a political statement, effectively laying claim to the relative superiority of one identity group over another. This has huge implications for discussion of the role that religions and tribes play in Nigerian life. This failure to come up with reliable figures has been recognised even by *The Economist*. In an article entitled 'We Happy Few – Nigeria's Population has been Systematically Exaggerated', the magazine's editors exhort the usefulness of satellite imagery for trying to determine what real population numbers are: a sure sign of scientific desperation.[1]

What Nigerians do know very well is the world that surrounds them, the social landscape that they have to navigate in order to survive. Arguably, a person needs what might be called criminal skills to survive in the long run in Nigeria. Michael Peel in *A Swamp Full of Dollars* claims that old money is often crucial to doing business in Nigeria.[2] That is probably so. However, it is harder to keep old money in Nigeria than it is elsewhere. Rich Nigerians most often have to take their property's title deeds to their London lawyers because they cannot trust a Nigerian law firm. What is true for multimillion-dollar petro-mansions, is also true for the title deeds of a run-down 40-year-old Peugeot – one needs to hide the papers, in London or in the mud hut. One needs fairly developed skills to hold on to just about anything – sometimes life itself. This is not the problem of the businessman per se. All is open for negotiation, especially for the petty market trader woman and for the wheelbarrow man, who need to elbow their way among all the others who have no formal employment – the bottom 70 per cent of the nation.[3]

Nigeria, not long ago the fifth biggest oil supplier of the United States and the tenth biggest crude oil supplier worldwide in absolute numbers, an OPEC member nation and a country that defines West Africa, shockingly managed to squander $280 billion by the early 2000s.[4] After spending so much, Nigeria lies at 154th on the list of the world's nations according to the Human Development Index.[5] Its infant mortality rate is startling: nearly 200 children die, per 1000 births in the country.[6] It is a hotbed of polio, malaria, meningitis, cholera and yellow fever.[7] With 8.6 per cent HIV-positive, an AIDS epidemic of 'catastrophic proportions' looms on the horizon.[8] There are known reasons for these alarming health data: Northerners resist polio vaccinations because there is a widespread belief that they are a Western plot to make Muslim women infertile. If that were not bad enough, clean potable water, or even water that is fit for taking showers, is a luxury in Nigeria that only the lucky few can afford.

Digging a proper borehole costs $2000 even in a village compound, an amount that is beyond the dreams of most villagers. Pipe-borne water runs, as a rule, within, and only within, a given compound in Nigeria – there are no municipal pipes. With the notable exception of Calabar, operational water towers that serve a given district are non-existent. The rich and their family servants have access to clean water in the form of bottled table water. To shower they use filtered water that runs from their compound's small private water tower. In the villages and slums where the majority of Nigerians live, people have only small petrol barrels on the roofs in lieu of water towers. Villagers walk kilometres to a well as a matter of course. While expatriates are forced to give bottled water to their cats to avoid feline diseases, the vast majority of Nigerian women and men make do with contaminated water that is the direct cause of human ailments and the carrier of dangerous microbes. Water from boreholes usually mixes with rubbish and sewage as there are no piped municipal sewage systems except private concrete sewers that serve a given private compound. The roadside dumping grounds and illegal trash heaps, where local goats feast on the poisoned vegetation, are a common sight everywhere. People are also denied their right to privacy. Often they have no other option but to defecate in public, right next to the rubbish heaps, goats and the ubiquitous sheep. Nigerians are a very resilient people and they laugh at problems when others would cry. But even their hearty laughs stop, when they, their husbands, their wives and children die, under these conditions. Life is very short in Nigeria. Life expectancy is 45 to 46 years.[9]

The number of doctors practising in Nigeria is lower than the number of Nigerian doctors practising in the United States (the latter standing at 21,000).[10] This would be bad enough if many of those practising in Nigeria had not bought their diplomas in the diploma mills of the country, as is the case. Everyday medical emergencies necessitate trips to the capital – for those that have the ability to pay for services of foreign doctors there. Others simply die at home or in their local health centres where medical skills are lacking to a startling degree.

Life, death, health and survival are basic human concerns anywhere. So is, in a capitalist economy, money. In Nigeria, money is not simply a means of exchange. It has acquired near-magical attributes in the sad, peripheral capitalism of the country. Mike Davis, in his *Planet of Slums*, claims that in war-torn Kinshasa (Congo), 'money is a fantastic entity bearing no relation to production and labour'.[11] The same is true for Nigeria, the petro-state that is 'a country because outsiders interested in its resources decreed so'.[12] Formal job creation virtually ceased to exist[13] with SAPs in the 1980s and privatisation at the turn of the millennium pounding at the salaried middle class. Deindustrialisation (a continuous process since the 1980s) has been eroding the class of industrial labourers: all four petrol refineries stand idle, and the Ajaokuta steel plant (the country's first steel plant) never commenced production. Railways that the British laid in the early 1900s have all fallen out of use (one single line was reopened in early 2013 in the vast country). It is a shocking paradox that 'urbanization has marched on even in the years of no nominal economic growth and even contraction' in Nigeria.[14] The kind of economy that grows in monster cities like Lagos is one of gangs, slumlords and the sex trade, and a pervasive capitalist ethic where wheelbarrows are rented out as beds for the homeless.[15] If the reader thinks this is an urban legend, then one has to learn that the same happens in front of Yakubu Store in rural Yola, where this author for three years bought his daily bread. Communal spaces are hectic and crowded in cities to the point of choking. As a result, anyone with money will want to privatise space to cut herself off from the hustle and the dangers of a brutalised, impoverished community. The compounds of the rich are now surrounded by 4-metre walls with barbed wire and electricity running through metallic fences. In a vintage travelogue from 1967, the reader is shocked, retrospectively, by a photo of Apapa, where the then *nouveaux riches* erected modern houses in tropical chic style: those houses had barely any walls around them, they were simply styled and of moderate size.[16] Today, *the architecture of fear*[17] defines Nigerian urbanisation: the buildings are huge, drab and ugly as a war camp. The Nigerian rich fear for their lives with good reason, as private jet accidents, burglaries that go wrong, armed robberies and hit men often kill them in their prime. Nonetheless they engage in 'hallucinatory levels of conspicuous consumption'[18] in search of social prestige and instant gratification.

The propensity of the Nigerian rich to waste wealth on ostentation has barely a global equal. Rich Nigerian brides do not think it proper to dress only their bridesmaids in matching garments: they provide these for every single female guest, which may mean 800 or 2000 dresses that are used only once.[19] Parvenus from the armed forces shame the Ottomans and the emperors of Cathay with the number of their concubines.[20] It is deeply saddening for most Nigerians and the country's observers to see how the capitalist ethic permeates and debases human life in the country. Ultimately money cannot buy security in Nigeria, as probably nothing can at the end of the day. But it can buy every luxury. There is a Porsche dealership in Lagos. In the capitalist narrative, this is a good thing.

As money cannot buy anyone security in Nigeria, people hope God will step in just to execute the task. Religion is big business in the country: perhaps the second biggest after oil. Religion in the 1980s, according to Edwin Madunagu, was as deregulated as the economy, with a proliferation of different churches.[21] Handicrafts have long disappeared as a viable branch of production, and agriculture has been crowded out by investments in the petroleum sector. What do people busy themselves with in the deindustrialised urban wastelands of Nigeria? As Michael Peel puts it, 'A huge amount of time is spent pursuing people with cash.'[22] The cash is there – and many are prepared to shoot, sleep with, swindle, or harass the people who carry it in order to get it. '*The money*' acquired near mythological status, a resonance of its own in Nigerian pidgin. (The famed Nollywood actor Olu Jacob has a way of rolling it like no other with his melodic baritone: 'monney', 'Where is the monney, my dear?' in his Nollywood dramas.) And the way to get it is not to 'earn' it: the term in pidgin, is 'to chop'.

Inter-city roads are so unsafe to travel even during the day that expatriates rarely, if ever even try. Night-time driving outside city parameters is unthinkable: everyone knows that the roads are in the hands of armed robbers. Even petty trades people consider setting up operations in Ghana instead. Corruption, according to the most famous Nigerian historian Toyin Falola, 'has become a normal aspect of life'.[23] According to many observers, corruption is the wrong word, as the very term corruption still presupposes a rational system. Instead, Nigeria operates by methods of 'prebendal' clientelism: politicians distribute sums that they expropriate directly from the federal budget. They also obtain kickbacks from government commissions. The concept of 'ten percenters' has become outdated and outmoded long ago. Currently, the kickbacks are larger than the original payment for a given job; sometimes many times larger. Democratically elected politicians win elections with the help of 'godfathers'.[24] The Kaduna mafia, the Babangida Boys grouping, the Abacha Boys, and Buhari's Northern network were arguably stronger even than former president Jonathan in designing ways to feed their respective clienteles.[25] The most infamous among these is Ibrahim Badamasi Babangida, former dictator and currently billionaire kingmaker, one of the most influential men among Nigeria's officer corps.[26] It is often said that he enjoys his nickname 'the evil genius'. But beyond Babangida, Jonathan and the current president Buhari, there are other *ogas* (bosses/politicos): their competitive condominium, with the blessings of the West, constitutes the bedrock of the Nigerian political system.[27]

When eminent Nigeria researcher Karl Maier first entered Nigeria, he was struck by the sight of a wrestling match at the airport.[28] This is an excellent analogy for how the country works: a brawl with almost no rules. The country ostensibly operates according to the US presidential model since 1979, with breaks of military rule.[29] But in reality, Nigeria is a parody of the American political system. This 'bastard child of imperialism',[30] according to US analyst John Campbell, may undergo in future a regional cantonisation in the same way as the Congo.[31] Nigeria is already crossing the line to become a 'felonious state', a state that criminally preys on its own people.[32] Max Weber's famous *Gewaltmonopol des Staates* barely holds in the country, as several people seem to have more influence in the armed forces than the president, and legality matters little anyway, especially for the police and the army, whose forensic methods focus almost exclusively on torture as a means of obtaining evidence.[33]

Nigeria is a petro-state that suffers constant fuel shortages[34] – truly a unique exercise in failure. The state that appears to its own civil society as 'strong, domineering and authoritarian'[35] is an unholy edifice for private gain. It is clearly a vehicle of self-enrichment for generals-turned-oil well owners, politicos, con men and simple 419-ers (those violating Article 419 of the Nigerian criminal code: fraudsters), who regard it as their theatre of operations, not their home. For the researcher, the Nigerian polity and its economic workings seem almost paradoxical. Nigeria is so corrupt that a burglar enchants the observer with the relative simplicity and honesty of his trade. Yet in private life Nigerians are generous, giving, warm-hearted, devoid of classism and snobbery, patient, witty, humorous and uncommonly kind. Even the Nigerian bourgeois, vile and crooked when earnings are at stake, will sit with his guard and often eat rice from his bowl – a quaint but deeply human habit that shames many an expatriate with a realisation of their own subconscious classism.

Patience Ozokwor, popularly known as Mama G, often plays a kidnapper in her Nollywood films: in one of them, she collects full ranges of original Louis Vuitton bags from the proceeds of her trade (her character kidnaps children to sell them abroad). Nigerian dailies are full of horror stories that go beyond Nollywood fiction, of money-making sacrifices that involve beheadings of old men, kidnappings of youngsters for ritual killings, exhumations of corpses for ritual purposes, the offering of babies to spirits through rites, campus cults, political cults, evil brotherhoods, and the blood oaths that especially politicians enter with each other.[36] Secret societies that at the time of Ja Ja of Opobo in the 1820s still carried a very positive connotation as the providers of intercommunal trust, a common worldview and authentic culture, clearly degenerated and have become a security problem within Nigeria and beyond.

All the more remarkable, then, that the human spirit claims incredible triumphs in Naija. Nigerian writers are among the best in the world: from Soyinka to Adichie, we witness a stream of global literary genius. As if recreating 19th-century Russia, where the politics of autocracy forced so much talent into literature, Nigeria has produced far more than its share of world-class writers. The Nigerian film industry too, alien as it might seem to non-Nigerians in its forms of representation, is undoubtedly an inspiration to Africans and Black diasporas in many parts of the world. Nigeria's traditional culture lives on in its dances, oral traditions and arts. Along with these, Nigerian Marxist thought, and Nigerian Marxian thinkers constitute a reason for hope for the country's future.

The History of Nigeria

Nigeria's morbid condition appeared as a result of the historical forces that have shaped the regions that in time became the country. I will attempt to provide a sketch from ancient times, but especially following European penetration. I will examine Nigerian history in some detail in order to understand the forces that have defined the country and delivered its contemporary ruling class.

The first known human settlement in the lands that constitute today's Nigeria, was the Iwo Eleru rock shelter, dated around 9000 BC. Hunter-gatherer societies gave way to agriculture first, with regional variations, between 4000 and 1000 BC.[37] Pottery appeared by about 3000 BC. Animal husbandry was introduced probably by Sahel immigrants between 3000 and 2000 BC. The Stone Age gave way to the Iron Age directly in Nigeria: by the 7th century BC representatives of the Nok culture smelted iron at Taruga. Copper and bronze *objets d'art* date from the 9th century CE (found first at Igbo-Ukwu). Interestingly, this means that the Iron Age came to Nok much earlier than to other parts of West Africa,[38] and significantly earlier than to Central-East Africa.[39]

The earliest political systems in Nigeria, as far as we can tell, were acephalous village community systems where political leadership was provided by elders, age grades and by secret societies. A prime example of those acephalous communities, until recently, was a segment of ethnic Igbos – but, surprisingly, royalty and feudal titles have become fashionable among them in the last 30 years. The monarchical system, together with true urbanity, came with the Yoruba of Ile Ife and their *ooni* (king). Ile Ife was built first in the 9th century CE, and became the centre of an empire in the 12th century.[40] Roads in the holy city were strengthened with potsherds, and elaborate bronze sculptures were made. The city remained powerful until the 15th century. Later other Yoruba and Edo cities wrestled primacy from Ife: the first was to be ancient Benin with its *obas*, who became important regionally from 1440 onwards.[41] In the North, centralised states appeared with Kanem-Borno with its *mais* (rulers) in the 12th century: a Kanuri-dominated empire in ethnic terms. Hausa states surfaced when Mali and Songhay lost their grip on their areas in the 15th and 16th centuries: Kano, Katsina, Zaria and Gobir were each governed by a *sarkin*.[42] Islam made inroads into Kanem-Borno first: Idris Aloma *mai* converted[43] and in 1250 Kanuri students set up a dormitory in Cairo. Wandering *ulema*, together with Fulani merchants, impressed the Northern rulers with Islam's usefulness in outdoing their rivals' *juju*. At the same time, Borno tradesmen made use of the Quranic attitude towards slavery when it came to *kafirs* (infidels):[44] they preyed on their rural neighbours and set up a flourishing trans-Saharan slave trade.[45] Livestock, leather, pepper and kola nuts were also important trading items initially, before the arrival of the transatlantic slave trade that connected the Nigerian coast to world markets and the region to the world economy.

From the 16th century, slavery influenced political and economic relationships in what is today Nigeria. Slavers became kings, and most kings had to become slavers if they wanted to survive as royals at all. The selling of slaves paid for war *materiel* and for luxury goods from abroad. Traditionally, slavery was similar to domestic pawnship, a patriarchal institution in the region. Slaves often ended up marrying into their owners' families.[46] By way of trans-Saharan routes, it is estimated that 3000–8000 slaves per year were sold to North Africa and beyond. Borno exchanged them for Ottoman Turkish guns, horses and European renegade musketeers, perhaps the earliest expatriates in Nigeria. In Yorubaland, the Oyo empire (powerful between the 17th and 19th centuries) was especially famous as a slave trading state.[47] To Oyo's south lay the Bight of Benin – the Slave Coast. 'Beware, beware the Bight of Benin, where few come out, though many go in,' says the old British rhyme, impressing upon us the impending doom that awaits many expatriates who brave the journey to the country, even today.

Dangers did not prevent the Europeans from making contact with the coastal states both in the Bight of Benin and in the Bight of Biafra, the main gulfs on the Nigerian shore. The first were the Portuguese: their trading post was set up at Gwarto (Ughoton) in 1480. Up until as late as the early 16th century, pepper, gold and textiles were still more important than slaves in Portuguese trade. The slave trade quickly spread and by 1550, the *oba* of Benin had to restrict the sale of male slaves – because slaving starved his realm of men. The Dutch and the British elbowed out the Portuguese from the main slave ports in Grand and Little Popo, Ouidah, Offra, Jakin, Epe, Apa, Porto Novo, Badagry and Lagos (Bight of Benin), Elem Kalabari (New Calabar), Bonny, and Calabar (Old Calabar) (Bight of Biafra). From 1600 to 1800, nearly 2.5 million slaves were sold from those ports, usually to the Americas where they were used as plantation labour. Although the French Revolution actually outlawed slavery before the British Empire did (1791/1794 and 1807, respectively),[48] the latter's move carried more practical weight globally, as the British started to patrol the high seas to stop slave shipments.

Inland areas were regularly victimised by coastal states that geared their political economies entirely towards slaving. Not only prisoners of war and criminals were enslaved now but also simple villagers who were kidnapped. The religious oracle at Arochukwu (the heart of Igbo influence and power) was instrumental in setting the code for slaving. The coastal states also restricted access to the European traders for hinterland states – the classic gatekeeper/comprador method. In the Niger Delta, especially in the Ijo areas, the (war) canoe house was the centre of political and economic power: war canoes were of course used for capturing slaves along river shores.[49] This 'house system' was the quasi interstate system of the day in the delta. In both the delta and in Calabar (Efik ethnic area), the Ekpe secret society provided the common legal and moral code, especially to the wealthy, which meant mostly slavers.

Brutalising the weak did not end in the South, where aggressive militarised polities that Walter Rodney would call 'more advanced' in terms of both state formation and in terms of approximating feudalism, transformed members of less organised and more communitarian polities into human cargo destined for the Americas. In the North, a full blown, and, Rodney would say, *bona fide* feudal Fulani elite brutalised and subjugated many independent Hausa polities in the name of the purity of Islam, trying to ensure their inhabitants' route to heaven by military force.[50]

The Fulani are a minuscule ethnic group in Nigeria but some Fulani are extremely wealthy and powerful thanks to their association with the army, even today. Muhammadu Buhari, the current president, hails from this group. The Moroccan wife of a Nigerian Fulani minister, when I asked her whether her husband was black, answered me, 'He is Fulani, not black,' indicating a sense of Northern-Berber self-identification. The Fulani of course are typically 'black' in their physiognomy – their self-image however, is that of the Saharan invader, the cultured Northerner, the custodian of Islam in the wider Soudan. In 1804, a Fulani *shehu* (sheik), Usman don Fodio launched a jihad against the Northern Hausa states in the name of Islamic purity. Don Fodio was not as dogmatic and fundamentalist as today's Saudi-inspired Salafi and Wahhabi leaders who abhor Sufism; he was the member of the Qadiriyya Sufi brotherhood that believed in a relatively more open interpretation of Islam than that of ibn Wahhab.[51] At the same time, Fodio's *jihad* did achieve the establishment of a centralised umbrella empire – the Sokoto caliphate – and organised a number of tributary Hausa emirates around its north-western core.[52] *Kofa*s, emissaries of the caliph in Sokoto, were sent to the Hausa emirates to collect tribute and guide foreign policy (as British Residents would later do). Royal courts, however, were the only thoroughly Islamised elements in Northern Nigeria throughout the 19th century. Islamisation of urban centres, and especially the rural hinterland, would begin only under the British and would finally be accomplished only in independent Nigeria, where the *grand kadi* of the North, Abubakar Gummi, would oversee sweeping Islamisation campaigns as late as the 1960s/1970s. Gummi would be given the King Faisal prize by Saudi Arabia for embedding the Saudi version of Islam in Nigeria.[53] (Gummi, a right-hand man of Northern feudalists in the vein of Sir Ahmadu Bello, acted with full Western connivance in bringing *niqab*s to Northern villages where more convenient fashions had earlier proliferated. He died in 1992.) Usman don Fodio's jihad was thus successful but incomplete, and his caliphate would succumb to the British in 1903.

The Fulani first made inroads into the Nigerian Middle Belt in 1823 when Abd al-Salam incorporated Ilorin (Yorubaland) into the Sokoto caliphate as an emirate. However, in the south-west, the power of Oyo remained supreme. Oyo, Bonny and Calabar slowly reoriented themselves towards legitimate trade in palm oil instead of slaves: a change that took four decades from 1807.[54] In the meantime, slaves were made useful locally, in palm oil production. Kurumi, a famous Yoruba warlord who took Ijaye in 1829, employed over 1000 slaves and his very own 300 wives, in palm oil production.[55] Ja Ja, the legendary self-made king of Opobo, built up his seat as one of the most important ports for palm oil export.

In the South, Christian missionaries from the UK and the US became very active after 1840. Re-captive slaves (that is, slaves freed by British anti-slavery patrol ships) were especially receptive of their new creed: Samuel Ajayi Crowther was the most famous example. He became Bishop of the Niger in 1862. The biggest obstacle that prevented Europeans from penetrating the hinterland in the early 19th century was still malaria. Mungo Park travelled from Timbuktu to the Niger in 1805. Clapperton and Lander followed in his wake. In 1854, Dr William Balfour Baikie's expedition to the Niger Delta used quinine as a prophylactic against malaria with success, proving that Europeans could survive in the 'native interior' – and this had a major effect on the military occupation of those areas.[56]

In the late 1870s, France too began a serious push from Senegal to the Niger. In 1880, Germany, a newcomer in the league of active colonisers, sent expeditions to the Benue River in regions that are currently partly in Cameroon, partly in Nigeria. The British sensed encroachment on their sphere of influence and were unnerved. Direct interference by the British dated back to the dethroning of the king of Lagos in 1851. The first major British offensive in the hinterland was in 1886 when they intervened in the Ekitiparapo war. The British colonisers, having achieved easy victories with their vastly superior guns, made attempts to root out human sacrifice and the killing of twins – with more success in the case of the latter than the former, as cults still perform human sacrifice in Nigeria in the 21st century.[57] In 1884–85, treaties of protection had to be signed by local rulers that effectively gave suzerainty over their kingdoms to the British crown.[58] Ja Ja of Opobo grudgingly signed but when he failed to act as a British stooge he was quickly deported to the West Indies. The Niger Coast Protectorate was established in 1893. Most of the Niger was run by George Goldie's National African Company (NAC), which was granted a royal charter in 1886. A ruthlessly monopolistic machine of exploitation, the NAC had control over the political administration of territories, beyond its trading monopoly. Goldie brought together the three largest British firms operating on the Niger: Holland Jacque, Miller Brothers and James Pinnock, and he also bought out three French competitors by 1884. Whitehall had to revoke Goldie's charter in 1899, after a decade and a half of cut-throat business practices which took no account of the suffering of Africans. The Brass tribe were prevented from carrying on their ancient trade, and were starving as a result, when they resorted to kidnapping and ritually eating NAC employees in 1894. Joseph Chamberlain, who became colonial secretary in Lord Salisbury's conservative administration, revoked the company's charter. Chamberlain bypassed Goldie and created the West African Frontier Force under Frederick Lugard instead. On 1 January 1900, the new Protectorate of Southern Nigeria was set up to replace NAC rule and the Protectorate of Northern Nigeria was also established. The very term 'Nigeria' comes from Flora Shaw, Frederick Lugard's then girlfriend.[59] In 1903, the British brought down the Sokoto caliphate, killing the last caliph, Attahiru[60] – most of his elite Fulani warriors and *ulema* fled to eastern Sudan over the Sahara desert. Finally, in 1914, the British amalgamated Northern and Southern Nigeria into one single protectorate, giving shape to the future independent country at most borders except in the north-east.

Nigeria as a British colony (1914–60) left a major imprint on Nigerian (under-)development. The colonial economy raised cash crops and set up mineral production for export (to the *metropole*), and introduced the importation of finished goods (from the *metropole*). A new, English-speaking, literate class emerged in the South. Lugard emphasised that, according to the 'Dual Mandate', colonial rule was to serve both coloniser and colonised – barely even a smokescreen if we actually examine the political economy of colonial Nigeria. The British tried, wherever possible, to rely on the traditional ruling class, with the most terrible consequences especially in the North. As in India with the *zamindars*, they ended up creating quasi-nobilities where there had been none before, introducing the system of 'warrant chiefs' in hitherto acephalous societies. The emirs' rule in the North was even set in stone by the British, with British Residents advising Hausa rulers on vital matters. An ugly dichotomy appeared: in the South, a Medical Department and a Public Works Department were created as early as 1898, but in the North, expenditure on modern social services was forbidden.[61]

British confluence with the Fulani feudalists went so far as forbidding Christian missionaries from entering the North, effectively enabling the subsequent Islamisation of Hausa areas. The British made use of indirect rule in the North. More than the North however, the South made profits for the British: first through customs duties and fees, later by direct taxation (introduced in most parts of the South by 1926). Cash crops included groundnuts (peanuts) and cotton in the North, cocoa and palm oil in the South.

The first railway line opened in 1900 between Ibadan and Lagos. Such minor improvements (washed away quickly after independence) came at a terrible price: by 1939 seven European firms controlled two-thirds of all Nigeria's export trade. Unilever alone controlled 80 per cent of the total export trade of the country.[62] The new sectors of the economy needed miners, freight haulers, dock workers, road builders, people for the ports, rail workers. Forced labour was a common solution. However, to solve the problem, the British banned traditional forms of monetary exchange (cowry), and British paper money and coins became the only legal tender, but direct taxes had to be paid: Nigerians had to take up employment. In 1926, there were 26 secondary schools in Nigeria; none in the North.

Africans started to put up resistance first in the field of spirituality: new African-led churches appeared in the South. Then came the press: before the Second World War, already 50 different newspapers were printed in the Nigerian colony. Herbert Macaulay, Bishop Crowther's grandson, the 'father of Nigerian nationalism' was a journalist too. Street riots against the British started in 1908 in Lagos against the water rate. In 1929–30, the 'Women's War' was fought against direct taxation and many other grievances. Women's activism remained central to fighting the British even later. Olufunmilayo Ransome-Kuti organised the Abeokuta Women's Union in 1946.[63] In 1936 the Nigerian Youth Movement was launched. By 1945, unhappiness with the colonial administration produced a general strike. Parties were formed. First the National Council of Nigeria and the Cameroons (later renamed the National Convention of Nigerian Citizens, NCNC) founded by Nnamdi Azikiwe (1904–96), an Igbo. Azikiwe (or Zik, or even 'the great Zik of Africa') studied in the United States, where he became active in the pan-African movement. He quit the Nigerian Youth Movement in 1944 to establish the NCNC.

Azikiwe was the first black governor-general of the then British-run Nigeria in 1959, and its figurehead president in 1963 (ousted in 1966).[64] It was in his name that Zikism, a radically inclined independence movement was launched, but he chose to dissociate himself from their more radical demands, most especially their Marxism and their East European sympathies. Zik was a politician with very few scruples: he feigned an assassination attempt on his own life.[65] Chinua Achebe said of him that his self-definition indicated a self-made billionaire rather than a politician.[66] Azikiwe's party quickly became an Igbo-dominated ethnic party vying for political influence in the south-east of Nigeria. Its ideology centred on political democracy in the Anglo-Saxon liberal form.[67] The NPC (Northern People's Congress) came second in line. The NPC represented the interests of the Northern ruling classes: in the words of Sklar, the 'modernization of traditional political authority'.[68] Third was the Action Group, Chief Obafemi Awolowo's Yoruba party that ran on a Yoruba cultural platform (Oduduwa). Awo (1909–87) became the champion of radical and progressive causes as a result of his position (leader of the opposition) under the first republic but to call him a Marxist would be a misnomer. He did not condemn socialism as such, but understood it rather as the Senegalese did – a beautiful word devoid of meaning.[69] He also came to stand for universal free education and health care in time, and made use of Marxists like Ebenezer Babatope as propaganda experts.

The British strengthened centrifugal forces in Nigeria by dividing it into a federation of three regions with elected governments in 1954.[70] Each of those regions was dominated by a given ethnic group (the one that had majority, or at least plurality, in the specific region). Ethnic groups with smaller numbers were sidelined even in their own regions. At the federal level, their lot got worse and worse, prompting the political radicalisation of many of those ethnic groups (especially the Tiv). In the North, the Northern Elements Progressive Union appeared as an opposition force against the feudal status quo under Mallam Aminu Kano that later operated as the People's Redemption Party.

Nigeria faced tremendous difficulties at independence. The terms of independence were set by the British. The NPC won the first election in 1960, and set out to dominate the government and the entire political economy. Alhaji Sir Abubakar Tafawa Balewa became prime minister in the Westminster political model. Tafawa Balewa was a teacher and not a rich man by birth, but he chose to represent the vested interests of the Northern elite. The Action Group was sidelined,[71] the Igbos became restless. In 1963, a census brought widespread violence and intimidation.

In the 1965 elections, the NPC won with an absolute majority (a numerical impossibility achieved only via fraudulent practices).

The Northern feudalists, who, of all Nigerians, most lacked the necessary skills and qualifications, decided to swallow Nigeria – but it was more than they could chew at first. In January 1966 the Igbo officer Major General Johnson Thomas Umunankwe Aguiyi-Ironsi (1924–66), a well-travelled diplomat, officer and UN peacekeeping force commander, seized power.[72] Ironsi was killed in July 1966, in a counter-coup that was launched by non-Igbo ethnic groups. Northerners saw to it that their front man was this time a non-Muslim, Yakubu Gowon (sometimes spelled Gowan) (b. 1934), who was born in Plateau State and was a Christian but who was friendly to Northern feudal interests. By July 1966, Nigeria was aflame: everywhere, pogroms and lynchings against Igbos were organised by local thugs and politicians. In these years, Igbos started to compare themselves with *galut* (diasporic) Jewry, and came to see themselves specifically as 'the Jews of Nigeria'. Igbos had to flee all other regions except their own. In 1967, a brutalised and cornered East under Colonel Chukwuemeka Odumegwu Ojukwu (1933–2011) declared independence under the flag of Biafra. Ojukwu, a product of Oxford, oversaw Biafran secession. In 1970 he fled to Côte d'Ivoire. In 1982, Ojukwu returned to Nigeria. The civil war for Biafran independence cost between 1 million and 2 million lives.[73] Federal forces won due to a miscalculation in Soviet foreign policy-making: the USSR chose to side with the federal government that had barely recognised it before, and decided to sell it weapons that the West had denied it.[74] France stood openly on the side of Biafra, in the hope of dismantling much-too-large Nigeria in the middle of France's West African sphere of influence. The US and the UK were not steadfast in backing the federal side either. Not long after winning the civil war, federal Nigeria abandoned completely any pretensions to a Soviet foreign policy orientation.

Gowon, wisely, decided to grant a universal amnesty and oversaw a national reconciliation. The oil boom started in 1973–74. Corruption skyrocketed among army officers, contractors, gatekeepers, politicos (*ogas*) from 1973 onwards. High-ranking officers and their wives started their London shopping sprees in these years. Food imports grew 700 per cent from 1970 to 1978, showing a near-complete collapse of agribusiness.[75] On 29 July 1975, General Murtala Ramat Muhammad (aka Murtala Muhammed) (1938–76) staged a coup. A Royal Military Academy Sandhurst (UK) graduate, he managed to force Nigerian public servants to turn up at their workplaces in the morning; this was such a towering achievement that, to this day, it is remembered by everyone in the country.[76] On 13 February 1976, Muhammad was assassinated by men loyal to Lieutenant Colonel B. Suka Dimka. Dimka's coup proved abortive. Muhammad's second-in-command, General Olusegun Obasanjo (b. 1937), the officer who had accepted the surrender of Biafra, became military head of state. In 1979, according to schedule, he ceded power to a democratically elected government. (Obasanjo would later become a born-again Christian and a civilian executive president from 1999 to 2007.)

In 1979, the political system of the country was changed to a presidential one, copying the US system. The first executive president was Shehu Shagari, head of the National Party of Nigeria (NPN, successor to the Northern-run NPC). In 1983, amid a major economic slump that resulted from declining oil prices on world markets, the NPN won again, but its rule was unpopular and corrupt to the bone, despite the economic slump. On 31 December 1983, Major General Muhammadu Buhari (1942–present), a soldier of soldiers, became military head of state. The UK-educated Fulani leader with strict Islamic views has an austere personality,[77] with simple tastes and pleasures like many a successful war leader. Less apt at leading a country than a war camp, Buhari launched the 'War Against Indiscipline'. When Samuel Ikoku, a Marxist thinker, sent him a memorandum regarding governance issues, he asked: 'Why is this man Ikoku still out of prison, so that he may write memoranda to me?', and had him incarcerated.[78] After 20 months, on 27 August 1985, a counter-coup toppled Buhari. That coup was led by General Ibrahim Badamasi Babangida (IBB; b. 1941) who would take the title of president.[79] Babangida toppled Buhari but chose not to kill him. This curious fact, according to John Campbell, is directly connected with how the *oga* system works at the very top of the Naija hierarchy.[80]

Babangida was, and still is, a charmer. He included in his advisory team a broad range of perspectives, including Edwin Madunagu, a Trotskyist, until disagreements forced the latter out. However, Babangida's government proved to be more business friendly than any before or after: he made use of quasi-fascist corporatist ideas and when the Nigeria Labour Congress stood up to him, he simply sacked its leadership and replaced it with his pawns.[81] In June 1986, the nefarious Babangida instituted the SAP, one of the first in Africa. Some debt rescheduling occurred but the SAP's effect was so negative that there is complete agreement in the literature on its devastating effects irrespective of political allegiance. Staff were laid off. Devaluation of currency brought inflation to levels never seen before.[82] Government subsidies for fuel were drastically reduced. Electricity supply became erratic. The infamous NEPA (Nigerian Electric Power Authority) came to mean 'Never Expect Power Always'. Government expenditure was cut, state-owned enterprises privatised. As government institutions declined, people took their children out of state schools and started to frequent traditional (*juju*) doctors again. In 1988, Babangida started his privatisation drive – still ongoing in the 21st century despite the obvious lack of any positive effect for the average Nigerian. Even mainstream historian Toyin Falola recorded that suffering reached such proportions in Nigeria that fundamentalist Islam and Pentecostal Christianity claimed easy converts. In 1986, IBB signed up Nigeria as a member of the Organisation of the Islamic Conference (OIC).[83] After a popular outcry, this move was shelved. In the late 1980s, violence erupted and became normal between Christians and Muslims. The brain drain started, robbing Nigeria of important skilled workers. Nigeria now has a very serious skills deficit: its graduates are barely literate, its school certificates faked, its mechanics working by trial and error. Falola reports that, by 2000, 25–50 per cent of all Nigerian university graduates were living abroad, an almost unbelievable figure.[84]

The skills deficit is of such proportions that it cries out for a convincing explanation. Contrary to Patrick Chabal's opinion, it is not that 'Africans refuse any rational approach to organization'.[85] Rather, it has been the Washington Consensus that confined Africa to its role as a provider of raw materials: Nigeria as essentially a petro-state. Bad organisation is obviously also a result of the startling lack of skills within the country while skilled people move abroad. Indeed, repairing a car with chewing gum is something this author has personally witnessed – but one is mistaken if one blames only the mechanic for such methods. Deskilling, as Walter Rodney reminds us, had happened already, when the British destroyed the textile industry of Kano, and when foreign scrap metal substituted for locally smelted iron. SAPs had a comparable devastating effect on skilled labour in the late 20th century.

Babangida faced more and more protests as the late 1980s gave way to the early 1990s. His answer was brutal repression, including, possibly, politically motivated murder.[86] On 13 June 1993, democratic elections took place. Chief Mashood Kashimawo Olawale Abiola (aka Moshood Abiola) (1937–98), a Yoruba Muslim businessman, won. Election results were simply annulled by a displeased Babangida. Babangida then installed his handpicked civilian president Ernest Shonekan, but Defence Minister General Sani Abacha (1943–98) soon launched a coup and seized power. Abacha's rule was similar to that of Mobutu Sese Seko, or the early Charles Taylor. Under Abacha, an introvert and a very troubled man, it was sometimes safer to leave the Murtala Muhammad International Airport in Lagos with military escort.[87] Abacha stole approximately US$3 billion directly from the budget.[88] He also threw his opponents in jail, including Abiola and Obasanjo. He killed Ken Saro-Wiwa and the Ogoni Nine for inciting revolt in the Niger Delta. In 1996, he created six new states (bringing the total number to 36), adding to ethnic fragmentation. Committees of labour unions were simply dissolved. Sani Abacha died in June 1998, reportedly while cavorting with two Indian prostitutes. Maier believes he died of natural causes ('the coup from heaven'), John Campbell suggests that he was murdered; Falola speaks of an 'apparent heart attack'.[89] It is improbable that the public will ever know the truth.

General Abdulsalami Abubakar succeeded Abacha. Abubakar presided over a transition programme. Running on a PDP (People's Democratic Party) ticket, Olusegun Obasanjo was voted into power in 1999, together with his Northern running-mate Atiku Abubakar (as vice president). He was sworn in on 29 May 1999. Obasanjo's rule won the coveted prize of a US presidential visit to the country, a stunning feat for the Nigerian elite. The PDP is not a Northern-only party, as the NPC had been – but the acquiescence of the Northern Fulani feudalist elite is a *conditio sine qua non* in the party. The Niger Delta under Obasanjo degenerated into chaos. Parastatal companies were sold in a frantic drive to loot. Following Zamfara in 1999, one after another the Northern states adopted sharia (the only exception in the North is Adamawa). Obasanjo set up the Economic and Financial Crimes Commission, but its proceedings were marred by questions over political motivations.[90] After Obasanjo had served two terms, in May 2007 Alhaji Umaru Yar'Adua (1951–2010) became president. Yar'Adua's brother Musa had been Obasanjo's second-in-command in the late 1970s, and he himself had been thrown into prison by Abacha during the 1990s. Yar'Adua's death in 2010 brought his vice president, Goodluck Jonathan, a zoologist by training, into the presidential seat. Jonathan, who hails from the delta, managed to calm down (some say buy off) the insurgents, but he had to face a serious threat in the north-east: Boko Haram. An Islamist organisation, Boko Haram was so successful in attacking the representatives of the Nigerian state that in May 2013, Jonathan declared a state of emergency in three states (Borno, Yobe, Adamawa). For the first time since 1967, the Nigerian airforce in 2013 bombarded home territory, while Boko Haram was burning schoolchildren alive for learning in government schools instead of *madrasas*. The secular left, after a long slumber, is also reappearing as a vehicle of protest, especially in the South, as evidenced by the January 2012 fuel subsidy strikes that mobilised millions. Finally, in late May 2015, Muhammadu Buhari was sworn in as president after a peaceful transfer of power, while Boko Haram's insurgency claimed more victims than ever.

3

Leftist Movements in Nigeria

This chapter discusses the progression of leftist movements in Nigeria. After general remarks, it is organised in a roughly chronological fashion. It first deals with the most significant threads of anti-colonial resistance, especially Zikism, a radical nationalist group loosely connected with first-president-to-be Dr Azikiwe in the late 1940s, before discussing the central role that Nigeria's juggernaut labour unions have played in the country to the present day. It outlines the fate of the Marxist-inspired socialist movements and also classical Marxist-Leninist parties and groupings in Nigeria, including somewhat esoteric intellectual circles and currents. Marxism was *the* defining factor in Eastern European-style vanguard parties such as the Socialist Workers' and Farmers' Party of Nigeria (SWAFP), but it also guided post-1968, New Left communes in the virgin forests of the country, away from the watchful eye of the military dictatorship. There is also an introductory account of the left-leaning feminist movement: part and parcel of the Nigerian modernisation drive in the fight against a patriarchal, archaic order. The discussion addresses one major peasant revolt (the Agbekoya riots), inasmuch as it was class driven, and did not degenerate into an inter-ethnic feud at the behest of mainstream plutocratic politicians, as many other such revolts did. The narrative also recounts a long succession of student revolts: a major force against military dictatorships and for meaningful democracy, prominent from the 1970s onwards. There is then a brief description of the NEPU–PRP political parties' continuum (Northern Elements Progressive Union, People's Redemption Party). Comprising Chinua Achebe's intellectual hinterland, these have been Northern-based political parties that stood (and in the PRP's case, still stand to this day) for social justice in Nigeria, against all odds. The PRP, of which Achebe was once deputy president in the 1980s, is a party that maintains a broadly Marxian platform with an emphasis on the peasantry, sustainable agriculture, and building a liveable and all-inclusive (tribally blind) nation state.

Since the 1940s, these movements, separate but interconnected, have fought a very formidable hydra: pre-modern-style male chauvinism, classical British imperialism and, later on, the Nigerian polity itself (dominated by a semi-criminal comprador class). They fought against exploitation by foreign corporations continuously. At one time or another, all these movements were illegal; militantly Marxist movements technically still are, in 2016. The question of legality may have influenced the availability of literature on these movements: while excellent works have been published on Zikism (Iweriebor, Tijani),[1] NEPU–PRP (Feinstein)[2] and on the Nigerian labour movement (Wogu, Cohen, Tar, Beckman, Zeilig),[3] no scholarly work has appeared to date on the socialist movement itself (with the partial exception of Tijani), not very much has appeared on Nigerian leftist feminism or Marxian political economists or Marxist historiography (except a very recent short article by Fatou Janneh),[4] and not even its participants have made many written references to illegal communes that were set up by students and academics in the 1970s in Nigeria.

It would be a misrepresentation of Nigerian history, however, to ignore the ever present socialist, and often openly Marxian, thread in the history of the country's multifaceted struggles for emancipation. The history of leftist movements has always clearly included a socialist element. There have been Marxist trade unions (especially the Nigerian Trade Union Congress [NTUC] but its predecessors and successors too), and Marxist political parties in Nigeria – both the orthodox Eastern European, and the heterodox, Maoist or Trotskyite variety: the Socialist Workers' and Farmers' Party of Nigeria, the Nigerian Labour Party, the Calabar Group of Socialists, the Democratic Socialist Movement, the Socialist Party of Nigeria, the Socialist Workers' League, the National Conscience Party. There were (are) also partly Marxian, peasant-oriented plebeian parties (the NEPU and the PRP). Richard Sklar, in the 1980 edition of his celebrated *Nigerian Political Parties*, lamented that there was still 'a need for a systematic history of the role of socialist political groups in Nigerian politics'.[5] This void has not yet been filled, and this chapter is an attempt to partially do so in a systematic manner.

Among other historical questions, this chapter will try to address whether Nigerian Marxism was violent. According to the literature, especially in the 1950s Nigerian Marxists planned and attempted political assassinations *à la* Red Army Faction of West Germany. This topic reveals as much about Nigeria, as about theoretical and activist Marxism: I will aim to demonstrate that there was no violent Marxist group in Nigeria that would have advocated terrorist methods, nor do we find any Nigerian Marxist thinkers who embraced 'left communism' and its theories. The research was made considerably harder because, in Nigeria, left-wing movements and parties were strictly illegal in the periods 1946–60, 1966–78 and 1983–99 (the periods of military rule), and, even when legal, they often operated according to the rules of clandestine political organisations, not as mainstream parties.

It is important to note that all major left-leaning movements sprang from the modern segments of Nigerian society. Unionism was a product of wage labour, a modern phenomenon. National liberation and Zikism came from the native 'lawyer-merchant class'[6] and its most enlightened and educated members. The Marxian socialist movement was made up of both unionists and highly cultivated professionals and academics (sometimes educated abroad). The feminist thinkers of Nigeria were also a markedly intellectual group, with international relationships that spanned the globe. These movements did not deny modernity: in fact, their relationship to capitalist modernity has been a dialectical one.

In this narrative, movements based on ethnic separatism, communalism or ethnic secession do not figure in their own right, and that is intentional. Tribal conservatives and communalists rarely became Marxian thinkers of the sort that this book ultimately is about; whereas labour leaders, Zikists and other national liberation fighters, student organisers, feminists and pro-democracy campaigners under military rule became Marxian thinkers very frequently in the last 80 years.

General Framework, Examples and Caveats

Before we narrate chronologically the movements of the left in Nigeria, it is necessary to examine the forces they have been poised to fight, to fully appreciate the enormity of their task. Among all their formidable adversaries, one group towers above the rest: the strongest foe since the mid 1940s have been Western corporations, powerful beyond measure, in operation in the country since the late 19th century. Certainly corporations have been more formidable, more effective and more powerful than the post-Second World War crumbling British colonial state or later the inept federal government, military or civilian. Fighting the former is the single most important task that Nigerian leftist movements identified for themselves.

At the systemic level, the question of whether radical movements are fighting capitalism, quasi-feudalism, outright thuggery or a 21st-century proto-feudal state is a very contentious theoretical matter. Whether the Nigerian political economy as such is fully capitalist today or not is a challenging problem in Marxist discourse within the country and, as such, it is far from settled; Aminu Kano and his friends in NEPU posited that Nigeria was more feudal than capitalist. That said, capitalism is obviously *present* in Nigeria by way of representatives of the global economy. Apart from its role as a producer of crude oil, Nigeria links with the world economy from a very peripheral position: it is chronically underdeveloped, not only in terms of its national wealth and assets, but, more importantly, in the routine processes that define its political economy. Whether Nigeria's politico-economic system is textbook-capitalist may be questioned on theoretical grounds, but the country does not exist in isolation. The way the global economy visibly penetrates Nigeria is by way of global, primarily Western, corporations that operate there. Much has been written about the ecological devastation to the Niger Delta, caused by petroleum drilling in that region. By crowding out investment, the foreign-dominated petroleum economy has all but destroyed Nigerian agriculture. The same economy ensured that foreign industrial goods have also crowded out Nigerian handicrafts. Today, in the wake of neoliberal deindustrialisation, an army of urban lumpenproletariat, 'infantilized by lack of work', 'unemployed and retired' swarms in Nigeria's monster cities.[7] The role that foreign corporations play in Nigeria is still crucial and structurally central amid the deskilled and lumpenised populace of shanty dwellers and the rural poor.

Indeed, in 2016 Nigeria still, or once again, lacks many basic managerial, vocational and professional skills, while its professionals flee abroad. Most recently, it lacked the organisational capacity to issue identity documents for its citizens. Typically, the solution of government was to agree in 2013 with MasterCard Inc. 'to issue 13 million debit cards in Nigeria which will also act as identity documents'.[8] The stupefying lack of concern for human rights notwithstanding, a core governmental organisational function has been farmed out to a foreign corporation *en masse*. Nigeria has expatriate quotas for every nook and cranny of its economy, but foreign companies find their way around them as a matter of course, using bribery or other means. Many managerial positions, and even more professional jobs, are done almost exclusively by foreigners. In the especially skills-deprived North, this extends to skilled worker positions. As discussed in the previous chapter, deskilling is a consequence of the neocolonial status quo.

The struggles of the Nigerian left against classical British imperialism, or against Nigerian military dictatorships or crooked 'democrats', are political struggles that are specifically Nigerian, but the tyranny of monopolistic global corporations might define the future worldwide. One thread that runs through this chapter is that of resistance against transnational corporate capital as it has manifested in Nigerian history. It would be a mistake to discuss one resistance movement without the others that give it context, to discuss heroes of the anti-capitalist struggle without their anti-imperialist, anti-male-chauvinist, anti-feudalist brethren. In the course of the last 70–80 years, these struggles have reinforced each other constantly. It was not possible for Nigerian patriots to fight the colonial state without the labour movement, and it was not possible to maintain an effective labour movement without Marxists who attacked the bourgeois polity, military or civilian. This is why it makes sense to discuss these interrelated threads of resistance as they really have always appeared and fought – together.

It also makes sense to include the feminist movement as an integral part. Fela Kuti, a singer and a rebel, was Olufunmilayo Ransome-Kuti's son, and his thought was heavily influenced by his mother's Marxian feminism. Trotskyite intellectual Edwin Madunagu's wife, Bene Madunagu, wrote books on women in Nigeria in the 1970s that were published by Zed Books in London. Feminism influenced and informed especially Edwin Madunagu and Gramscians such as Usman Tar from the 1970s to today. Molara Ogundipe-Leslie presented a wholly original synthesis of Marxism and feminism in the country. Women fought for their own rights as women, as well as against the politico-economical hydra of neocolonialism and corporate rule.

Before considering the history of the Nigerian left in more detail, it is perhaps worthwhile to present two examples that illustrate the near-un-hindered power of corporations in that country. One comes from colonial times, the other from the independence period. Monopolistic company rule has been the guiding principle of the Nigerian political economy since the days of Sir George Goldie in the late 19th century. However, the British Empire created a textbook case of monopolistic capitalism by the late 1930s in Nigeria.

> By 1939 a mere seven European firms controlled over two-thirds of all Nigeria's export trade. The largest was the United Africa Company (UAC), which was a branch of the larger Anglo-Dutch consortium Unilever. The UAC controlled 40% of Nigeria's export economy by 1939, while the parent company, Unilever, controlled 80% of the total external trade of Nigeria.[9]

Nduka Eze, who was first a firebrand journalist and then a famous labour leader,[10] a Marxist pamphleteer[11] and also field-secretary of the Zikist movement,[12] decided to confront this behemoth. His 1949 article 'UAC: An Octopus and How it Treats its African Workers'[13] exposed the company's methods towards its black employees. The UAC took Eze to court, and stressed that it would not conduct any negotiations with the labour union (Amalgamated Union of UAC African Workers; UNAMAG) that had Eze as its general-secretary. Eze defied them and organised a strike to improve the labourers' wages and living conditions. Company executives warned that striking workers would be laid off with immediate effect. Nevertheless, 300 workers decided to continue opposing the company. The dispute was then brought before a labour conciliator at the colonial Labour Department for settlement. However, Eze was not accepted as a representative by the UAC management, who withdrew from the negotiations on the grounds that Eze was not acceptable due to the fact that he had been made redundant by the company. On 6 May 1949, a strike ensued by UAC's African workers. Some improvements to the wages and to the cost of living allowance (COLA) were won, but in May 1950 the conflict resumed. On 2 August 1950, another strike started that ended nine days later. During the strike, Eze was arrested and was taken to court. He was charged with inciting unlawful assembly and inciting people to assault unknown persons. When UNAMAG called for a general strike in the entire mercantile sector to bolster opposition to UAC, companies reacted by simply laying off striking personnel.[14]

UAC did not stop short of calling the colonial police, on 21 June 1947, to shoot at workers who demanded wage increases.[15] In a related incident, on 7 November 1949, a go-slow action was organised at the coal mines of Enugu[16] by the Colliery Workers Union there. On 18 November, members of the armed police arrived to remove explosives from both the Obwetti and the Iva Valley mines of Enugu, lest workers use them against management. Evacuation of the Iva Valley mine failed because of the workers' resistance, but the striking workers were shot at, killing 21 and leaving 51 others severely injured.[17] The Iva Valley massacre proved too much even for mainstream Nigerian nationalists, who initiated protests all over Nigeria to push for workers' rights and national liberation.[18] Communist MPs in the British House of Commons organised a hearing on the matter, such was the international outrage caused by the incident.[19] Eze was detained (probably imprisoned), and with him the Nigeria Labour Congress lost most of its backing. (Eze himself went on to study law and resurfaced in the 1970s as a prominent lawyer; later he set up the Great Nigeria People's Party.)[20]

Obviously, the relative strength of the formally independent Nigerian state vis-à-vis foreign capital increased when Nigeria became a petro-state in the 1970s, but far less than one might perhaps think. Notwithstanding its status as an OPEC member nation, because of skills deficiencies and organisational problems, Nigeria is still very much the weaker party compared to representatives of international capital even in the 21st century. We only have to consider the case of the delta uprisings to see how the interests of foreign oil companies are safeguarded in independent Nigeria (under military rule as well as under civilian 'democracy'). The famous case of Ken Saro-Wiwa is an illustration of the confluence of interests between Royal Dutch Shell and the hated military dictator Sani Abacha. Saro-Wiwa, a writer and a rebel, along with eight friends, was executed in November 1995 on trumped up murder charges, because they had stood up for the economic, environmental and cultural rights of their own minority Ogoni people of the Niger Delta.[21] Saro-Wiwa was not a Marxian socialist, and his demands were anything but radical: he wanted a part of the region's oil wealth for the people who actually inhabit it, and whose cultivation of the land was made impossible by oil spills. The Ogoni didn't have hospitals or schools, and they had lived in poverty like that of the dark ages, amid a post-apocalyptic, oil-spill-defined landscape. Sani Abacha established a kangaroo court to sentence the Ogoni Nine, so that he might continue making personal use of the region's oil income, and to allow Royal Dutch Shell, Chevron and BP easier operations. This did not slake the anger of the populations of the delta, however, and post-Abacha democracy inherited a full blown insurgency, this time mostly led by the Ijaw ethnic group.

It was then that simply stealing crude oil (bunkering) ceased to be the local villagers' only occupation. A 'Mad Max world of roving bandits'[22] emerged, where livelihoods were built on kidnapping and murdering expatriates and extortion. Theft, bank robberies, armed robbery on the roads, guerrilla warfare and sabotage came to characterise especially the operations of MEND (Movement for the Emancipation of the Niger Delta). Regionally 6 billion naira a month was still being lost to theft in 2010.[23] Beyond illegal bunkering, MEND[24] and other groups that vandalised the pipelines of Royal Dutch Shell and BP, came to abandon the most brutal aspects to their *modus operandi* (notably kidnapping and murder) only after Goodluck Jonathan came to power in 2010. Jonathan hails from the same Ijaw ethnic group as many members of MEND, and this might have made it easier for him to negotiate with them. MEND was given the opportunity to disarm in exchange for a general amnesty, while their members received governmental compensation that amounted to billions of naira.[25] MEND is an elusive organisation. Some utterances by representatives of MEND indicate that they had a general 'Robin Hood' agenda against the foreign corporations and the Nigerian state; indeed, that some of their men had adopted a quasi-socialist worldview. Socialists in Nigeria tended to see MEND as a sympathetic plebeian rebel force precisely because they were hell-bent on ending corporate tyranny over their ancestral lands.

Labour and Early Women's Revolts, 1800–1945

In what is today Nigeria, wage employment probably began with European 'explorers', who had a constant need for guides and carriers. Mungo Park was reported to employ one Amadi and another Isaac, whom he reportedly paid in the village of Yauri. At this point, even in the more urbanised Yoruba regions, a subsistence economy flourished that had no evident need of wage employment.

> People served their parents, family and their village heads for free. Especially farming was done on a co-operative basis. On a given day, people went and worked for a particular individual. Throughout that day the man they served was responsible for their food and drink. On another day the man returned the service, and so it went until everybody in the group was served.

Thus Wogu Ananaba explains how traditional West Africa did without wage employment.[26] By 1871, 2500 Europeans and Africans were employed in the delta (the economic heartland of the region then and now).[27] When, in 1898, the British decided to create *ex nihilo* a colonial infrastructure geared towards the business needs of the oligopolistic British and other European companies, they laid railways, built harbours, established telegraph lines and built some intercity roads. Along with infrastructural betterment, there appeared a new and ever growing need for local manual labour. First came carriers, as, due to the lack of roads, expatriates of the day were physically carried around in palanquins,[28] like the imperial Chinese mandarins of old, or the pope at Easter prior to the second Vatican Council.

Carrier jobs must have been onerous, but digging roads, laying railways or excavating coal in mines was doubtless even worse. The inhabitants of Nigeria had no desire to take up these menial and low-paying jobs. In the beginning, European employers solved the problem by hiring Kroo labourers from the Gold Coast, Liberia and Sierra Leone. Companies then turned to local chiefs to supply labour. The chiefs evaded this nuisance by picking and sending off to the British slaves, people in traditional 'pawnship', or 'the offspring of hated wives'.[29] The same happened when the British recruited young children to be sent off to school: most often, the sons of slaves or outcasts were sent, proxies for the progeny of the powerful. Careers were launched this way: the first prime minister of independent Nigeria, Abubakar Tafawa Balewa, a political reactionary from the North, came from a slave lineage, and was sent away for school in lieu of his princes. To solve the ever more serious labour shortage, from 1901 to 1907 Lord Lugard brought Indians to Nigeria.

Pushing peasants into industry presented a serious problem for the authorities. William L. Blackwell, a historian of Russian industrialisation, noted that: 'Industrialization is a process that in most societies has involved the suffering, sacrifice, and waste of millions of lives.'[30] In all cases the problem is the same: how to compel members of self-suffi-cient traditional economic units, who were also very locally minded and extremely traditional in outlook, to uproot themselves, sever themselves from their families, and work the rest of their lives for a pittance at an emerging industrial site of filth, dirt, uncertainty, disease and human suffering? The less industrially developed a country was, the more technical difficulties this presented. The British were relatively subtle: local currencies were banned and direct taxation was introduced. Nobody could pay taxes without earning British banknotes or coins by business, by theft or extortion, or by paid employment, creating at once a modern criminal class and a modern labouring class. In 1915, Baron Lugard added forced labour camps to the colonial state's arsenal.[31] For a while, bewildered labourers (in fact, captives) did not know what had hit them. The first strike, 17 years before trade unions became legal, was organised in 1921 when artisans on the government railroad, together with technical workers of the mechanics' union, organised and won a strike against a threatened reduction in wages.[32, 33]

It is notable that in Nigeria, we frequently read of wage reductions even very early on. These have been central to neoliberal SAPs from the 1980s onwards, but they were already attempted in the 1920s. Wages generally are very inelastic, that is, they do not tend to decrease easily. Usually decreases are achieved only piecemeal and by stealth.[34] In Nigeria, corporate brutality is such that wage reduction is part of the open arsenal of bourgeois class warfare against employees, and always has been.

A well-known example of resistance against direct taxation was the Women's War, also known as 'Aba Riots' in British imperial parlance, in 1929–30. The civil unrest spread beyond Aba to Owerri and parts of the old Calabar province. It successfully delayed the introduction of direct taxation for a time.[35] We shall see more below how women's movements have consistently been at the forefront of the fight for rights in Nigeria.

A little earlier, in 1920, there was the first, almost forgotten step towards modern Nigerian nationalism: the founding of the National Congress of British West Africa, with sections in the Gold Coast, Sierra Leone, the Gambia and Nigeria.[36] The nascent nationalist organisation was set up at the Accra Native Club in the Gold Coast (today's Ghana). It included prominent members of the Nigerian lawyer-merchant class, such as the Reverend Patriarch Patrick Campbell, the newspaper editor Thomas Horatio Jackson, the medical doctor Richard Savage and Prince Bassey Ephraim of Calabar.[37] A proto-party, like the Indian National Congress at its own inception, this regional organisation carried on only till 1933, when more narrowly defined organisations appeared on the scene.

Trade Unions 1912–45

The first unions were so aristocratic that they never threatened to strike,[38] as they belonged to the exclusivist colonial civil service. The Southern Nigerian Civil Service Union was inaugurated on 19 August 1912, two years before Nigeria was unified as a single colony.[39] Henry Libert, a Sierra Leonean, was its founder, and in the beginning it seems to have had purely social (and perhaps recreational) functions. Native civil servants, however privileged, were at the receiving end of racism, treated 'like indentured apprentices' according to Wogu.[40] Racial discrimination was quite openly built into the system they worked under. Higher grades were altogether closed to Africans, and even at lower grades an African could only receive 75 per cent of a white civil servant's salary.[41] They were mercilessly fined for lateness or absence. The Great War added to their problems, bringing inflation. The union agitated for a war bonus from 1916 up to 1919.

Unions became more outspoken with the arrival, first, of the Nigerian Union of Teachers (1931), then the Marine Daily Paid Workers' Union and especially the Railway Workers' Union. Unionised railway workers, until railways themselves mostly fell out of use in the 1970s due to mismanagement and lack of repairs, were always among the best organised trade unionists in Nigeria. This was perhaps due to the nature of their jobs, but also, to an extent, to their first militant leader, Michael Athokhamien Ominus Imoudu, Michael Imoudu for short. Imoudu, born in Ora-Oke in Benin Province in 1906 into a poor family, worked first in the capital Lagos at the colonial Posts and Telegraph Department as a lineman from 1928. In 1929 he entered the railway as a labourer and then as an apprentice turner.[42] In 1940, he was elected president of the Railway Workers' Union. He constantly fought racist discrimination against Africans on the railway. He led a workers' protest march to the residence of Governor Bourdillon, demanding the introduction of a COLA for railway workers.[43] As a result, Imoudu was dismissed from the railway in 1943, and banished from Lagos, returning for the 1945 general strike. Imoudu, 'labour leader number one' as he was dubbed, had a very colourful personality. He loved showmanship and often appeared before the striking workers and railway executives dressed like a *juju* priest, sporting a horse-tail fan that many believed was the secret of his power.[44]

Some Marxist leaders, especially Tunji Otegbeye, who returned from medical studies in the UK and was later to become secretary-general of the Socialist Workers' and Farmers' Party, later despised Imoudu for his salt-of-the-earth persona and his *juju* tricks. Imoudu had no grasp of English and no education, commented Otegbeye retrospectively.[45] For many Nigerian workers, Imoudu was more to their liking than any other working-class leader (including Otegbeye), as he continued to speak their language and better expressed their own aims. Imoudu came from the plebeian class himself, and conspicuously lacked the will to exit it and to acquire the markers of elite standing – an appealing quality in a labour leader.

Nationalist Parties in the Making, 1923–45

Political parties, founded by the new, English-speaking professional elite, appeared first with the Nigerian National Democratic Party (NNDP) in 1923, founded by Herbert Macaulay, a notable representative of the professional class. Macaulay later came to be called 'the father of Nigerian nationalism' for his role in NNDP and NCNC (National Council of Nigeria and the Cameroons). The NNDP was more active in Lagos than elsewhere, and did not manage to stir up popular feelings at first. At the Yaba Higher College, also in Lagos, a new organisation grew out of student discontent: the Nigerian Youth Movement (established in 1933).[46] By 1938, the Youth Movement produced the Nigerian Youth Charter, standing for unity and against inter-ethnic hatred, and calling for the complete right to self-governance (like that of dominions).[47] Ethnically based associations (Igbo, Yoruba, Hausa) also sprang up. Famously, the NCNC was founded in 1944 by Dr Nnamdi Azikiwe and Herbert Macaulay, and was one of the three most important parties of the pre-1966 period. Not the first Nigerian political party as many, even scholarly, publications assert,[48] it was nevertheless the first one with a broader appeal. The NCNC later changed its name to National Convention of Nigerian Citizens, as Cameroon's borders were defined. The NCNC in the 1940s became an Igbo-dominated party under Azikiwe, while Chief Obafemi Awolowo, champion of the West and the ethnic Yorubas, set up the Action Group, with a regional power base there (1951). By that time, mainstream Northerners had set up the Northern People's Congress (NPC; in 1949), their respective ethnic stronghold. The Northern mainstream meant mostly feudalists and their street thugs, honoured and respected by Western statesmen. These parties, especially the latter NPC, came to define the terms of Nigerian independence vis-à-vis the British, as negotiating partners. Their leaders, especially in the North, counted on British help to secure their undisturbed rule, while modernity was encroaching on their ancestral patrimonies.

The mainstream parties were also affected by the country's increasing radicalism in the mid 1940s. Labour militancy on the one hand and nationalist agitation on the other were fuelled not only by economic changes within Nigeria or by the power of the modern press. Equally important was the fact that Nigeria was an active participant in the Second World War. Nigerian soldiers fought off Italians in Kenya and Somaliland.[49] Returning soldiers were promised jobs but these were not delivered in most cases. Between July and December 1944, 3000 veterans were registered and jobs were found for only 150 of them, which caused discontent.[50]

Changes in the International System 1945–60

The victory of the grand coalition against Hitler ushered in a new international system, in which hitherto major global powers became players of secondary importance. The British by 1946 were unable financially to maintain their naval bases in Aden and elsewhere. Anti-colonial agitation was on the march everywhere in the newly appearing 'Third World', the world beyond the First World (USA, Canada, Western European countries) and the Second World (Eastern European countries). The boundaries of the two Cold War camps remained unchanged until 1989: Berlin's crises were resolved, and internal revolutions were suppressed (such as Greece in the West and Hungary in the East).[51] The Third World, however, as if by tacit understanding between the superpowers (the US and the USSR), was the field where, by methods of proxy wars, the conflict could play out in 'hot' fashion. Nigeria was firmly in the Western fold since its colonial days, and this will be explored further in chapter 4 on the international relations of the Nigerian left. The importance of the Cold War division comes from the fact that the USSR, especially after Stalin's death, would underwrite some of the costs incurred by Nigerian radical movements.

Northern Elements' Progressive Union, 1946–66

NEPU, the antecedent of Chinua Achebe's own PRP, appeared in 1946, pre-dating most mainstream parties. It was in operation until 1966, when it went down together with civilian rule. Its head, Mallam Aminu Kano, fought the ruling NPC and its thugs on the streets in the 1950s and especially the 1960s, but later took part in the Gowon administration as a minister. Later, on 21 October 1978 in Kaduna, the PRP was launched (still in existence, the oldest active party today; discussed later in this chapter). Chinua Achebe was a member and deputy president in the early 1980s. Mallam Aminu Kano, Balarabe Musa and Abubakar Rimi were to be its most prominent leaders.[52] I will discuss especially Aminu Kano and Balarabe Musa in the subsequent chapter, in the section on Yusufu Bala Usman, their comrade with the greatest theoretical output.

Progressive Feminism, 1940s–2016

Feminism appeared in Nigeria with Olufunmilayo Ransome-Kuti (also known as Funmilayo Ransome-Kuti), the Reverend Ransome-Kuti's wife. She reorganised the Abeokuta Ladies' Club in 1944 as a political force. The club articulated the demands of market women, along with those of the minuscule professional class. In 1946 the organisation was renamed Abeokuta Women's Union, and it took up political issues with the traditional ruler, the *Alake* of Abeokuta.[53] A friend of British radical Labour MPs, Olufunmilayo Ransome-Kuti was included in the NCNC delegation to London in 1947 to meet the Secretary of State for the Colonies. While in London, she joined the Women's International Democratic Federation, an umbrella organisation for communists and fellow travellers that was founded by the Soviets in Paris in 1945. In Abeokuta, Olufunmilayo Ransome-Kuti organised a protest against the water rate, as a representative of the National Women's Union that she helped establish in 1952. In 1955, she was denied a passport to travel to Helsinki for the World Assembly of Peace. She visited Beijing in 1956 for a Women's International Democratic Federation meeting.[54] In 1957, the colonial government refused to renew her passport. In independent Nigeria, when Olufunmilayo's world famous Afrobeat star son, Fela 'Anikulapo' Kuti, earned himself the anger of the then Military Head of State Obasanjo, the latter sent a thousand soldiers to burn and destroy their compound, and Olufunmilayo was defenestrated and thus murdered by his soldiers.[55] Fela Kuti later composed a touching anthem against the ruthless elite that killed his mother:

> I go many places/ I go government places/ I see, see, see/ All the bad, bad, bad things/ Den dey do, do, do/ Dem steal all the money/ Dem kill many students/ Dem burn many houses/ Dem burn my house too/ And killed my mama/ So I carry the coffin/ I Waka waka waka/ Movement of the people/ Dey Waka waka waka/ Young African Pioneers/ Waka waka waka/ We go Obalende/ We go Dodan barracks/

Reach dem gattee-o/ And put the coffin down/ Obasanjo dey there/
With him big fat stomach/ Yar'adua dey there/ With him neck like
ostrich/ We put the coffin down.[56]

(Obasanjo was later thrown into prison by Sani Abacha, where he claims
he was born again as a Christian. His subsequent rule, however, fails to
indicate signs of the meekness or moral compass commonly associated
with serious Christian conviction.)

Bene Madunagu and her husband Edwin Madunagu were stripped of
their university professorships for their feminist and socialist political
activism in the 1970s (more of this in chapter 7). Hajiya Gambo Sawaba
(1933–2001) was a prominent politician of the NEPU, and a pioneer of
feminism in Northern Nigeria in the 1950s. A friend of Olufunmilayo
Ransome-Kuti, Margaret Ekpo (1914–2006) set up the Aba Township
Women's Association in 1953. In 1961, she won a seat at the Eastern
Regional House of Assembly, but after the 1966 coup she retired from
active political life. Partial recognition by the establishment came
posthumously when the International Airport at Calabar was named
after Ekpo, after she passed away. An eminent late 20th- and 21st-century
Nigerian feminist (abroad) is Ifi Amadiume, whose works have acquired
global renown. She made extensive use of Engels' concepts in her works
on the family in Nigeria.[57] As opposed to both Amadiume and Kolawole,
Molara Ogundipe-Leslie, a poet and a feminist thinker, is a professed
Marxist. I will analyse their oeuvres in chapter 7.

Marxist and Communist Ideologies and Movements 1930s–1945

Non-metropolitan (that is, not specifically British) intellectual currents
appeared in Nigeria from the early 1940s onwards, and found receptive
audiences in the intellectual circles of the country. Gandhian thought
excited Mallam Aminu Kano, Nehruvian politics fuelled the Zikists, and
existentialism gained adherents at Ibadan and elsewhere. For example,
when in the 1950s a Hungarian journalist (and possibly spy) travelled
to the University of Ibadan, he found an existentialist club there,
engaged in heated debates that centred on that train of thought, over
sumptuous dinners.[58]

Communism first made an imprint on the very elite echelons of the
Nigerian professional class. Herbert Macaulay's son, Frank Macaulay,
attended the International Congress of Negro Workers in Hamburg
in 1930. Together with I.T.A. Wallace-Johnson (a Sierra Leonean), he
launched the African Workers Union of Nigeria in 1931 as a proto-Marx-
ian party. George Padmore was their main inspiration.[59] Padmore had

set up the Hamburg congress under Soviet auspices. An early hero of pan-Africanism, Padmore was lured by Stalin to Moscow and the Comintern from 1929 to 1933, but he was effectively banned from both from 1934. An original and influential thinker, his was a very important voice that moved pan-Africanism to the forefront of radical African thinking, before Nkrumah and Frantz Fanon.

In West Africa, communist agitation was successfully gaining converts even before the end of the war. The Group d'Etudes Communistes formed in 1943 in Abidjan, Bamako, Conakry, Bobo-Diolasso and Dakar. The same young people formed the Rassemblement Democratique Africain in 1946 (later to ally with the French Communist Party for a while). In French Cameroun, the Union des Populations du Cameroun was also learning towards Marxism.[60] The British dreaded communist influence in West Africa, as in places such as Malaya pressures were mounting towards open insurrection by (mostly ethnic Chinese) armed communist fighters, while Mao's People's Liberation Army was marching on Beijing, and Greece was in Marxist-inspired turmoil. In 1944, Sudanese students founded the Sudan Movement of National Liberation in Cairo, a proto-communist party that was almost immediately banned.[61]

In 1943 some Nigerian students sent a letter of solidarity to Moscow. Moscow recognised a need, and sent pamphlets in return. Hakeem Tijani, in his otherwise magnificent work, claims that the Nigerian communist groupings of the 1950s were foreign-induced bodies, produced via the machinations of the Communist Party of Great Britain (CPGB), and ultimately of the USSR.[62] The mid 1940s saw people become receptive to communist agitation for a number of reasons. Old-style European imperialism had weakened considerably. Stalin's forcible modernisation produced an impressive rate of growth in the USSR in the years from 1931 to the Second World War. European colonial powers' growth rates were paltry in comparison. It was true that the United States had an even higher growth rate during the same years, but Africans and other non-Europeans saw a greater similarity between their own socio-economic position and that of pre-revolutionary Russia, than between the United States and themselves. Also, Stalin's international reputation was at its peak: a winner of the war, he enjoyed immense global prestige, even to some extent in the US. It did not seem unreasonable at the time to expect that the East might soon outpace the West in sheer developmental terms.

Peter Ayodele Curtis Joseph, a UAC employee in Okitipupa at the time, was certainly a Marxian radical by 1944.[63] Joseph was not an elite intellectual but a labour organiser, an autodidact and a self-made revolutionary. He campaigned for trade with the USSR. He also engaged in the publication of Marxist literature in the country. His efforts to open up Nigeria for Soviet trade, along with his publishing activities, earned him the Lenin Peace Prize.

Other early examples include Kola Balogun, who wrote in one of the first-ever leaflets of the Zikists (1946) that Nigeria should emulate the Soviet example.[64] By 1947, Nduka Eze, the hero of the anti-UAC demonstrations in 1946–49, praised Russia's 'social democracy'.[65]

Militant Labour Unionism 1945–51

Labour, influenced and strengthened by foreign Marxist literature now available within Nigeria, was on the ascendant. A massive blow to colonial rule, the 1945 general strike was a high point in both labour activism and in anti-colonial agitation in Nigeria. Michael Imoudu, with his horse-tail fan, resurfaced in Lagos to launch direct action after the British let him out of prison. The strike reflected that real wages in Lagos had fallen to just 68 per cent of their 1939 value by 1941.[66] Unions also claimed in 1945 that between 1942 and that year the cost of living had increased by 200 per cent – most probably an exaggeration, but an exaggeration that reflected serious hardships on the part of wage earners. The 1942 General Defence Regulation had outlawed strikes and lockouts, so the strike was technically illegal. Governor Bourdillon had promised yearly adjustments to the COLA in July 1942. From June 1944, the unions started pressing for those adjustments. The acting chief secretary of the colonial government, in colonial-phlegmatic fashion, slapped civil servants in the face by remarking: 'Unless the public is willing to do without or reduce their consumption of commodities which are scarce … no benefit will result from increasing COLA', a remark that still shocks with its arrogance 70 years later.[67]

In 1943, Sir Bernard Bourdillon retired as Governor of Nigeria. His successor was the jingoistic Sir Arthur Frederick Richards (later Lord Milverton of Clifton). Disregarding Bourdillon's promises,[68] when students went on strike at King's College in 1944, Richards ordered the ringleaders to be conscripted into the army; one of the conscripted boys died just a few days later. The public, incensed by Azikiwe's *West African Pilot* articles and given hope by Imoudu's release, ran to march behind the banners of the strike organisers. Iweriebor claims that between 32,000 and 100,000 employees participated in the strike, Coleman puts the number at 30,000, and Padmore at 150,000. The Labour Department's Annual Report estimated 42,951 workers.[69] Of those participating, 41,165 were public employees, others came out in sympathy. With the exception of electricity providers and hospital personnel, everyone else took part: railways and port services came to a halt, telephones were dead (landlines were still in existence in 1950 – they are no longer in 2016). The strike started on 21 June 1945 and lasted for 44 days in Lagos and 52 days elsewhere.[70] The colonial state declared the strike illegal and issued threats of mass dismissal and loss of wages. They brought in prison labour from Port Harcourt as replacement. Ten leaders were arraigned before the court and charged with illegally taking part in a strike. The strike was called off on 4 August 1945, and it established Imoudu as a champion of the working class, a man whose popularity even mainstream nationalists could now exploit.[71] London sent repeated fact-finding commissions (Tudor Davies Commission, Harragin Commission) to report on the situation in Nigeria.[72]

The 1945 general strike reinforced nationalist agitation: labour action and the nationalist press (especially Azikiwe's *West African Pilot* and his *Daily Comet*) reached overlapping audiences in the modern and modernising sectors of the colonial Nigerian economy. A numerical minority at the time, these groups were in an economically central position in Nigeria, and their movements reinforced each other. Anthony Enahoro, the editor of Zik's *Daily Comet*, became a leading voice for anti-colonial agitation.[73] Other main voices were Nduka Eze,[74] Kola Balogun,[75] Osita Agwuna[76] and Habib Raji Abdallah,[77] along with Ikenna Nzimiro (president of the movement's Onitsha branch)[78] and Mokwugo Okoye.[79] Ikenna Nzimiro and Mokwugo Okoye would become very prominent Marxist thinkers, Nzimiro on the side of Biafran independence, championing the Igbo cause. Okoye acquired global renown in the detente years of the 1970s as a thinker, writer and a Marxian belletrist.

Zikism, 1946–50

Zikism was launched under a misnomer in 1946: 'Zik' was Azikiwe's nickname. Azikiwe, a cunning politician, orchestrated a hoax by claiming that the colonial state was intent on murdering him after colonial authorities banned his papers, the *Pilot* and the *Comet* on 8 July that year. Zik ostentatiously hid in his ancestral Onitsha, claiming that his wireless operator had intercepted a message about his assassination. No proof ever surfaced to establish the truth of Azikiwe's claim. Azikiwe also promoted ethnic politics in his own constituency to win a nomination for his man against Ernest Ikoli soon after the assassination hoax.[80] He later ended up in the Privy Council of the UK (1960), and as an Onitsha nobleman of Owelle-Osowa-Anya rank. Zikists were not taking orders from Zik; indeed he later claimed that the connection between him and Zikists was like that between Jesus and Christianity (a remarkably free-thinking line of argument – but then again, Zik had studied in the United States).

Members of the Zikist movement did not end up in the Privy Council of Elizabeth II; they more likely found themselves in prison. The movement was formally inaugurated on 16 February 1946 in Lagos, by M.C.K. Ajuluchuku, Kola Balogun, Nduka Eze and Abiodun Aloba.[81] They had all worked for a Lebanese newspaper, but went over to Zik's papers roughly at the same time. Balogun was the first president of the organisation. In their first pamphlet, Balogun wrote of the 'Himalayan impediments ... of foreign rule' and noted that: 'Nigeria should have taken the path of revolutionary transformation pioneered by Soviet Russia.' After electing officers, the organisation designed its constitution, its insignia, and published ideological tracts. In May 1946, Nduka Eze became assistant/field-secretary. Eze opined that the new Nigeria 'should be fashioned after Russia's social democracy'.[82] Azikiwe's birthday, 16 November, was designated as Zik Day, the day of independence. Ex-servicemen, teachers, workers, clerks, students, journalists, petty traders, artisans and labour organisers joined and, by 1949, the organisation had 2500 members.[83]

The leaders' backgrounds were varied: Balogun's father was a produce trader in Ibadan; after finishing school he joined and then left UAC, the 'octopus' that ran half the country's economy. Ajuluchuku studied on a government scholarship through his high school years, and gained admittance to Yaba Higher College on a scholarship (1944–46). He became a journalist in Zik's *Comet*. Aloba was also a UAC employee before joining the *West African Pilot*. Eze was born in 1925 in Asaba in the delta. A UAC clerk from 1944 to 1946, he became the secretary-general of UNAMAG that fought UAC, the British and the colonial police.[84] Mokwugo Okoye was in the Zikist movement's Lagos branch first; in chapter 5, there is a detailed biography of Okoye and an analysis of his works. He was 'one of the major theoreticians of the movement ... and in the subsequent development of Nigerian radicalism'.[85] These leaders advocated for direct action: strikes and demonstrations against colonial rule. In 1945, Osita Agwuna founded the African Anti-Colour Bar Movement and in 1947, he joined Zik's *Daily Comet*. The North was represented in the Zikist movement by Habib Raji Abdallah.[86] A high school graduate (a major achievement in Northern Nigeria at the time), Abdallah was a devout Muslim but a political progressive and a committed Nigerian radical.

The movement sent out Nduka Eze on a tour to propagate Zikism all over the country. In June and July 1946, Eze toured 15 towns in

Nigeria, travelling in very difficult circumstances. The *West African Pilot*, with its flowery similes, compared Eze to Demosthenes himself. The tour was successful and by 1950 the Zikist movement had offices in 35 towns. Ikenna Nzimiro was the president of the movement's Onitsha branch. Originally 'Francis' Ikenna Nzimiro, he shortened his name in an effort to underline his African pride.[87] In August 1947, after the Arthur Richards constitution introduced in January, a change in leadership meant that Habib Raji Abdallah became president-general, Osita Agwuna his deputy, Ajuluchuku secretary-general.[88] In 1947, India became independent (first as a dominion, and then, by 1950, as an independent republic). India was a serious inspiration, on par with Russia, for Zikist freedom fighters. Okoye praised Gandhi and Balogun wrote a pamphlet with the title *India Is With Us*.[89] Pundit Jawaharlal Nehru and his ally V.P.K. Krishna Menon were the global stars of the day at the United Nations, speaking out against Western domination and the United States.

In 1948, for the first time, the Zikist movement called for a national revolution in the form of direct action.[90] Osita Agwuna and Anthony Enahoro were arrested,[91] and in 1948/49 they were tried for sedition.[92] Azikiwe made sure to dissociate himself from the incarcerated revolutionaries. He publicly criticised the movement, insinuated fraud by imprisoned Zikists, and refused to seek the release of the prisoners.[93] This was a watershed. The last phase of the movement stretched from 1949 to April 1950. In February 1949, Nduka Eze was elected president and Mokwugo Okoye as secretary-general. The movement still did not break its technical affiliation with the NCNC, but it was seeking contacts with the CPGB. The freedom fighters amassed hand grenades, firearms and bullets.[94] Michael Imoudu was also a member of the Zikist movement, and his labour radicalism gradually came to filter through to Zikism. Anti-UAC moves and the Iva Valley massacre came in 1949–50. Incensed by the power of politicised labour, the colonial government ordered the police to descend on the homes and offices of the movement in Gusau, Kano, Lagos, Enugu, Aba and Kaduna. In Yaba they arrested Mokwugo Okoye with 'seditious documents', and at Onitsha Ikenna Nzimiro was searched, arrested and charged. Jail terms were meted out liberally all over the North and South. On 12 April 1950, six weeks after Okoye's incarceration, the movement was officially banned.[95]

Marxian Labour Activism against Reaction 1951–66

Zikism thus melted away, but labour unionism remained very active in the period 1951–66. The overwhelming dominance of British, French and Lebanese capital remained a stable feature of Nigerian capitalism in the period. Adding to them, in Wahab Goodluck's words: 'In 1960, when Nigeria threw off the yoke of British colonialism, like a ravenous pack of economic wolves the US monopolies, the West German capitalists, the … Israelis and a host of others descended on Nigeria's virgin economic field each helping himself to the best pickings.'[96] Needless to say, Lebanese capital was already there to begin with, along with Levantine managers and professionals. These corporate interests are still present in Nigeria 55 years later; the only impediment to their operations is that, over that time, the country has deteriorated to such an extent that it is now nearly unliveable for expatriates.

In the 1950s, labour unionism appeared in the North, with the Northern Native Administration Staff Association in 1957, and later with the Northern Mine Workers Union. The Northern Mine Workers Union was a union of 'marionettes': Alhaji Isa Haruna, a mine contractor, was the president, and Audu Danladi, who was the welfare officer of the Bisichi Tin Mining Company, became secretary.[97] Northern unions were thus organised and controlled by employer interests. No wonder that their representative, Alhaji Adebola, came to abandon genuine labour activism for the safe, government-sponsored variety. Labour activism at this time was clearly split along Cold War lines. The different local, regional and sector-based unions were briefly united by the All-Nigerian Trade Union Federation (ANTUF), commencing in August 1953,[98] with Imoudu as president and Gogo Chu Nzeribe as general-secretary. ANTUF itself was not affiliated either with World Federation of Trade Unions (WFTU; the Soviet-dominated umbrella organisation), nor with the International Confederation of Free Trade Unions (ICFTU; of Western orientation), and many in its leadership were ready to do deals with bourgeois politicians. By April 1956, L.L. Borha, Haroon Popoola Adebola (aka Horse Power),[99] and N.A. Cole, all doctrinaire anti-communists, loosely affiliated ANTUF with ICFTU. In November a formal vote on this was rejected, although Western unions sent hundreds of pounds to influence the process.[100] H.P. Adebola resigned after six days, charging Imoudu with being 'Communist inspired'. They tried to remove Gogo Nzeribe too, but when this did not work they set up a new body, the National Council of Trade Unions of Nigeria (NCTUN), on 17 April 1957. NCTUN was officially affiliated to ICFTU.

In the course of 1955, in ANTUF, Imoudu, Wahab Goodluck and Samuel Udo Bassey became leading personalities. The Trade Union Congress of Nigeria (TUC(N); set up in March 1959) was the result of the merger between ANTUF and NCTUN. NCTUN revoked its affiliation with the pro-Western ICFTU. ICFTU intrigued in the background, and tried to get Imoudu out of his presidential position at TUC(N).[101] In 1959, Imoudu served a prison term. Without him, TUC(N) was led by right-wingers. There was a Ghana link too (see the famous Tettegah story in chapter 4). By 1959, the lines were drawn: the IULC (Independent United Labour Congress; the name was changed to NTUC in 1963)[102] was pro-Soviet, headed by Michael Imoudu, the colourful labour leader, and the TUC(N), headed by Alhaji H.P. Adebola, was pro-American.

Ananaba Wogu, himself a member of the TUC(N) leadership, gives an excellent account of the intrigue, the tricks and the tug of war that ensued between NTUC and TUC(N) in these years. They made it a sport to woo local and sector-based trade unions from each other. These organisations split into two separate entities only in 1960. That year, the Central Working Committee of the TUC convened in Kano (20 April). It claimed to represent 98,000 union members. Amid applause from the British Trade Union Congress and the ICFTU headquarters in Brussels, they elected right-wing labour leader Alhaji Adebola as president.[103] Deposed President Imoudu then convened a counter-conference in Lagos on 21 April 1960. Representatives claimed to represent 184,612 unionised workers. The representatives reconfirmed pro-Soviet Imoudu in his role as president of the TUC. Merger congresses ensued from 1962 onwards, but true amalgamation only happened in 1978, under right-wing leadership, orchestrated by the reigning military.

Leninism and Early Vanguard Communist Parties 1945–62

The first Marxist party in Nigeria was Amanke Okafor's Talakawa Party ('*talakawa*' is the Hausa word for the common people) as early as 1945. Okafor soon left for studies in the UK, and the party itself went into oblivion, while Okafor joined the CPGB.[104] The CPBG certainly had a role in the birth of organised Nigerian Marxism, as Hakeem Tijani shows, based on the meticulous analysis of many primary sources. Tijani, however, takes declassified British secret service reports on the CPGB–Nigeria link too seriously. A document by secret service operatives, or the wishes and whims of CPGB members themselves, reflect their own way of thinking as much as the reality of a complex international relationship. Even Tijani allows that CPGB or WFTU directives were 'not strictly followed'[105] – after all, Nigeria was not in the Soviet orbit.

In the range of actual Marxian movements, first came the Freedom Movement (defunct by October 1951). In the same year, the Communist Party of Nigeria and the Cameroons appeared in Ibadan (a group we know very little about). In February 1951, 'The League' was formed.[106] Samuel Ikoku set up the People's Committee for Independence in February 1952. They were Marxist organisations with a global perspective, and they focused on the major anti-imperialist issues of the day. Ikoku founded the Nigeria Convention People's Party in 1951, and reportedly drew inspiration from Palme Dutt's *Britain's Crisis of Empire*. On 7 May 1952, Ikoku, Ogunsheye, Gogo Nzeribe, D. Fatogun and D. Onwugbuzie set up an avowedly Marxist-Leninist party. In July 1952, the United Working People's Party was set up by returnees from the UK (Onwugbuzie, Anagbogu) and its secretary was Ogunsheye. Samuel Ikoku broke away from the labour leader Nduka Eze. Ikoku was also joint editor with Eze, of the *Labour Champion*. And in February 1952, Ikoku launched the *Nigerian Socialist Review* with Eastern European and CPGB backing.[107]

During the 1950s, the CPGB was concerned about Nigerian Marxist parties because of the ostensible lack of unity. Soviet foreign policy-makers were less concerned, according to Zubok, but this problem awaits a historian of the Soviet archives.[108] N.F. Kolagbodi, a former Zikist, was sent with two students who had just received scholarships to Prague and Berlin. Samuel Bankole Akpata, obtained a Soviet-style doctorate at Charles University, Prague, and later became the Librarian of University College, Ibadan. Nduka Eze, Samuel Akpata, Samuel Udo Bassey and Michael Imoudu were the top labour organisers of the country, along with new entrant Wahab Goodluck.[109] Samuel Udo Bassey became the scribe of the NTUC, and played an important role in torpedoing the Anglo-Nigerian Defence Pact.[110]

The Anglo-Nigerian Defence Pact, according to primary evidence, was not forced on Nigeria;[111] indeed, the ruling circles were happy to stay in the embrace of mother Britannia. Kano and Lagos airfields, and the harbours of Lagos and Port Harcourt, were to be used by British troops. The bill was passed in the Nigerian Parliament on 19 November 1960, by a vote of 149 to 39. The Zikist National Vanguard, the National University Students' Union and the Nigerian Youth Congress attacked the Pact so fiercely that, in January 1962, the Balewa government had to abrogate it.[112] By 1953, the British thought there was a Communist Party of Nigeria (CPN).[113] To be sure, they banned it in 1955. Tijani makes no mention of the CPN, which we may take as evidence that the state organs in the UK knew it to be a hoax. In 1955, in Abeokuta, Chukwudolue Orkhakamalu set up the United Working People's Party (UWPP). Around 1964, UWPP and CPN were both in existence (the latter perhaps as a fictitious body of agents provocateurs).[114]

Marxists and Murder, 1950, 1954

Two of the most important savants of the subject of Nigerian Marxism, Tijani and Wogu Ananaba, allege that the Marxists of the 1950s were guilty of murder. According to them, Nigerian Marxists planned and/or committed political killings in the vein of the Red Army Faction of West Germany. Wogu Ananaba describes what happened in 1954 thus:

> The ANTUF held its second congress in 1954. An event that took place before that congress led to the break-up of the Marxist Group. A two-day meeting was held at Abeokuta, attended by many members of the group and a guest from the British Communist Party. Discussion centred around the stumbling-block which leading and wealthy nationalists constituted to proletarian revolution. The chief theoretician at the meeting and ideological director of the Group later became general-secretary of one of the leading political parties in the country. The first day of the meeting went through smoothly with general agreement on objectives but there was a difference of opinion on strategy. The following day the communist guest attended and addressed the meeting. He advocated the use of force to eliminate the so-called stumbling blocks and quoted extensively from history to support his argument. As in every controversial issue, there were supporters and opposers of the proposal. The supporters saw in it the only way to hasten the achievement of independence and the introduction of a new social order in Nigeria. Those who would not subscribe to it called the proposal a British plot to annihilate Nigerian nationalists. They argued that, if it was not, the advocate and his fellow communists in Britain would have first eliminated men like Churchill and other Tory leaders to demonstrate their sincerity. So outraged were they that some did not disguise their feeling that if plotting to kill fellow Nigerians was the objective of the Marxist Group, then they had reached a parting of the ways.[115]

Wogu makes no reference to any source, and one might conclude that this entire story was false, concocted by the secret services at best, or Wogu himself at worst, to discredit Nduka Eze and the Marxist elements in the Zikist movement.

Tijani's is a more serious allegation, drawing on multiple sources that give it, ostensibly, prestige and credibility. Let us examine Tijani's narrative on the issue of the attempted murder of colonial Chief Secretary Hugh Foot in 1950:

The height of Zikist activities was an abortive attempt on the life of Chief Secretary Hugh Foot in early 1950. On February 18, 1950, Reuters reported that a young Ibo man named Heelas Chukwuma Ugokwe, of the Posts and Telegraph Department, attacked Foot with a knife when the Chief Secretary was entering the Secretariat building in Lagos. Two days later, Ugokwe was charged with attempted murder; on March 13, 1950, Mr. Justice Rhodes at the Lagos Magistrate Court sentenced Ugokwe to life imprisonment.

Then Tijani goes on to explain the background of the story:

> In his report to the Secretary of the State, Governor Macpherson laid full blame for the assassination plan on the Zikist Movement, noting that Ugokwe, a World War II veteran, had joined the Zikist Movement at its inception in 1946. He, along with eleven other youths, was allegedly specifically recruited as an 'assassin' during the Zikist Movement convention at Kaduna in December of 1949 to carry out a nation-wide plot aimed at the forcible seizure of power from the government. It was further claimed that Mokwugo Okoye personally issued instructions for this assignment. Initially, Ugokwe's target was Macpherson himself, but after waiting nine days without finding an opportunity to kill the Governor (Secretary of State for colonies), he shifted his sights to the Chief Secretary. Fellow Zikists and their sympathizers applauded Ugokwe's action ... This incident predictably led to a tightening of security within official circles, and the eventual banning of the movement under the 'Unlawful Societies Act, April 1950.'[116]

The connection between Mokwugo Okoye and assassin Ugokwe is alleged by Tijani here not with the help of original documents or even credible secondary sources, but by reference to Azikiwe's memoir,[117] and to a single academic article on a different subject in which the author notes that he agrees with Azikiwe on this matter. It is reasonable to conclude, therefore, that Tijani fails to establish the incriminated Mokwugo Okoye's fault in the assassination attempt at any stage. He does however shed light on the way in which the colonial establishment exploited this accusation to ban not only Okoye's and Eze's Marxist elements but the entire Zikist movement.

There is no real evidence that Marxists planned, attempted, or committed murder for political purposes in Nigeria. When they amassed weapons in 1949–50, they did so with the hope of inciting a fully fledged armed rebellion against the British, not individual murders of British officials or civilians.

'McCarthyism' in Nigeria Prior to Independence, 1950–60

Nigeria became formally independent on 1 October 1960. Its descent into a neocolonial political economy began immediately. By then, the British had operated a full-scale McCarthyist initiative (even described as such by the conservative historian Tijani) for an entire decade, to counteract what they saw as aggressive Marxist agitation in the country, using secret service methods. The International Federation of Trade Unions sent a major delegation on 15 February 1951, to woo Nigerian organised labour to the side of 'the free world'.[118] Scholarships were given to labour leaders at the Department of Extra-Mural Studies at University College, Ibadan up to 1960.[119] British Prime Minister Attlee had already banned CPGB members from public employment in the UK in 1948,[120] and now a similar purge started in Nigeria. The United States showed a keen interest too, at first because of the presence of uranium and cobalt, but soon it started to displace the UK as regional hegemonic power. For Elmer Bourgerie, director of African Affairs at the US Department of State, Marxist activities in Nigeria seemed dangerous in their own right.[121] The US secretly worked towards bettering living conditions near mines and private companies where Marxist labour agitation had been worst.

Labour in the 1960s

Labour carried on with the fight for justice in the companies, on the streets, in the mines. The next great workers' revolt, the 1964 general strike, showed again, for a brief moment, labour unity in the country. It was an unusual strike as it did not involve the physical withdrawal of labour. It was a sit-down action: labourers actually claimed their pay because they showed up at their workplaces.[122] Labour made its dissatisfaction known to the government (the largest employer then, and now, of formally employed labour in the country). Sidi Khayam, general-secretary of the National Council of Dock Workers and Seamen, launched the strike, first and foremost against the Preventive Detention Act,[123] but also based on the realisation that the political leadership of the newly independent country had started to behave as an elite 'on mushrooms' (that is, hallucinogens). Naturally, the strike was also a reaction to the serious economic distress of the workers. H.P. Adebola's death was reported prematurely. All government offices and industrial undertakings were affected as in 1945, save hospitals and the electricity company. Unionists introduced the principle of a living wage into the discourse and as a rallying cry. A Joint Action Committee (JAC) was formed between Horse Power and others, plus Wahab Goodluck, Imoudu and Bassey. Later, Alhaji Adebola said:

> When the JAC was formed we of the United Labour Congress thought it was only for the purpose of using it to obtain benefits for the workers of Nigeria, but members of the NTUC took the opportunity to advocate and further the interests of the Socialist Workers' and Farmers' Party.[124]

General Ironsi in 1966 tried to bring labour leaders together to form a unified labour umbrella organisation. The Nigerian Workers' Council, Labour Unity Front, United Labour Congress (ULC) and NTUC were the biggest unions: they belonged to the NTUF (Nigerian Trade Union Federation) and fought wars of attrition against each other. The ULC was particularly preferred by the federal government (Ironsi was Igbo and gave preferential treatment to Igbo-dominated unions). This poured fuel on the fire of anti-Igbo sentiment and Igbos were being massacred all over Nigeria at this time.[125] After 30 May 1967, Eastern unions formed the Biafran Trade Union Federation headed by Ben Udokpora. The NTUC was on the side of the federal government, portraying Biafran leader Ojukwu as a puppet in the imperialists' hands. In 1970, after the war, new wage demands brought the NTUC to the fore.[126] In August 1970, the United Committee of Central Labour Organizations was formed, with equal representation from the major (government-sponsored) unions. On 19 February 1971, the Gowon regime seized Samuel Udo Bassey and Wahab Goodluck, detaining them for 15 months. Bassey was a Marxist fighter who named his children after Marx and Lenin. Imoudu was also banned from labour activity.[127] Political activity by parties was outlawed in January 1966. Marxist parties, especially the SWAFP, were also banned.

Socialist Workers' and Farmers' Party of Nigeria, 1963–66

At this high point in left-wing radicalism, Marxist organisers managed to form a Marxist-Leninist vanguard type party that was to operate in the open for some years. This was the achievement of Tunji Otegbeye, a medical doctor and masterly 'old left' politician. Otegbeye was not, as Tijani claims, a pharmacist,[128] and was not trained in the USSR; indeed, he was trained in the UK. Otegbeye's ignorance of Russian is demonstrated by his confusion of a Russian man's given name and his patronymic.[129]

Otegbeye was trained, after Ibadan University College, in the UK, where he joined the Bevanite Group, who were among the radicals of the Labour Party, before becoming a communist.[130] Unusually for a Leninist he was also a celebrated ballroom dancer.[131] He launched the Nigeria Youth Congress together with Mokwugo Okoye, I.O. Dafe and others. Their aim was to 'work for a socialist Nigeria based on scientific socialism and the attainment of an egalitarian society',[132] 'true democracy' in its Eastern European sense: the rule of the people through the rule of the vanguard party. When Azikiwe became president in 1960, Otegbeye presented him with a gift,[133] but Zik was less amicable to the bearded revolutionary. After Congolese leader Patrice Lumumba was murdered by Belgian secret agents, Otegbeye organised an Action Committee for the Congo (16 February 1961), at a time when anti-British feelings ran so high that a white woman was saved from an attacking crowd only when she showed them her biracial child.[134] Tunji also travelled to the People's Republic of China. The People's Republic of China impressed him profoundly. He noticed how communal taps were established everywhere, and in general 'the Chinese approach was simple, effective and down to earth'.[135] He also met with Chen Yi, the foreign minister. Otegbeye organised Nigerian students to go and study in the USSR, and a Patrice Lumumba Institute of Political Science and Trade Unionism was set up, with Eskor Toyo at its helm.[136]

Marxian radicals came to support minority groups for whom they were the last resort as allies: most notably Tiv radicals in the Middle Belt looked to them for help in the years 1962–64. Otegbeye also met Nkrumah before the latter lost his power.[137] From 14 March 1964, Otegbeye was in prison (as, allegedly with Ghanaian help, his party's youth received military training in Ghana to topple Balewa's government).[138]

In August 1963, they finally managed to establish the SWAFP. A labour-oriented cohort of leaders: Eskor Toyo, Ola Oni, Kolagbodi, Sidi Khayam and Baba Omojola, all wanted Michael Imoudu as leader. They lost out. Tunji Otegbeye became secretary-general, Uche Omo chairman, Wahab Goodluck the vice chairman, Samuel Ukpeme Bassey assistant general-secretary. Eskor Toyo and others then seceded and set up the Socialist Labour Party, but that organisation quickly faded away.[139] The SWAFP was an Eastern European-style vanguardist Marxist-Leninist party that practised 'democratic centralism' in the Leninist sense of the term, with Soviet Embassy backing.[140] The SWAFP even sent a delegation to the 23rd Congress of the Communist Party of the Soviet Union, from 20 March to 8 April 1966 (Tunji and S.U. Bassey went). Tunji and Wahab Goodluck, the two bearded revolutionaries, also attended the 50th anniversary of the October Revolution. Tunji met Potekhin, the doyen of Soviet African studies. The *Advance* newspaper was set up as a party organ.[141] During the civil war, Tunji Otegbeye was on the federal side,[142] all the more so as the federals fought with Soviet weaponry. Nevertheless he was arrested on 30 November 1967, and spent six weeks in Maiduguri Prison (he was dragged from his surgical theatre during an operation to whisk him away to Maiduguri, he claimed).[143] The celebrated human rights lawyer Gani Fawehinmi worked for his release. Mallam Aminu Kano also intervened for him.[144]

According to the Trotskyist faction (Eskor Toyo, Edwin Madunagu), Otegbeye was, all in all, nothing but an opportunist leader. The SWAFP was bureaucratically run. By the end of 1963, Edwin Madunagu implies, it was impossible to mobilise workers 'for purely political action' beyond wage concerns.[145] Otegbeye became 'a secure and comfortable bourgeois millionaire benefactor, holding the purse strings, dictating to the movement and holding it ransom by means of financial power'.[146] It is probable that the money came from the USSR. He also used thuggery and, according to Tijani, was motivated by personal gain.[147] International labour parties and labour movements provided some of the money. The rest was provided by WAATECO, a Soviet-sponsored company that sold Lada cars[148] (notoriously shabby and uncomfortable, inspiring the adage: 'You can with a Nissan, it is harder in a Lada, and you can't in a Trabant').

Soviet estimates of SWAFP's membership put it between 16,000 and 22,000 people,[149] Western estimates at a mere 1000.[150] (The issue of its foreign relations, especially the Soviet role, will be discussed in chapter 4.) Alternatives to the SWAFP existed. In 1961, Gogo Chu Nzeribe and Peter Ayodele Curtis Jospeh set up the Nigerian People's Party; it died out within a year.[151] In 1964, the Trotskyist Nigerian Labour Party was set up by Eskor Toyo and Imoudu. There soon followed a split when in 1964/65 a splinter group led by Ola Oni, Baba Omojola, Jonas Abam and Sidi Khayam formed the Revolutionary Nigerian Labour Party. Information on the latter splinter party is very scarce. Otegbeye himself, in the 1990s, distanced himself from Marxism and became a member of the Yoruba Council of Elders[152] – a move shocking for its careerism, even in Nigeria.

People's Redemption Party, 1978–2016

There were others beyond Tunji and the SWAFP who opined that the Nigerian government should invite Nikita Khrushchev for a visit, and that the *talakawa* should be given opportunities that they had never before had. Chief among them was Mallam Aminu Kano and his friends Michael Imoudu, Samuel Ikoku, Balarabe Musa and Mohammed Abubakar Rimi.[153] On 21 October 1978, in Kaduna, they launched the People's Redemption Party (still in existence as the oldest party in 2016). Chinua Achebe was first a member and then deputy president in the early 1980s. The PRP won two gubernatorial seats in Kano and Kaduna, both in the North, in 1979. Balarabe Musa struggled against being impeached by the mainstream National Party of Nigeria-dominated Assembly, but Mohammed Abubakar Rimi managed to make steps towards social advancement. Rimi made a provincial attempt at modernisation as he abolished feudal dues, but his pioneering experiment ended with Buhari's military takeover in 1983. Much of Rimi's thought derived from that of Yusufu Bala Usman, but he was a political scientist and a coherent thinker in his own right.[154] Rimi abolished the taxes that weighed most heavily on the rural poor, such as the cattle tax. He set up a committee to investigate crimes when the political leadership and the feudalists arbitrarily took away someone's property, contrary to legal procedures and/or local custom (the latter is recognised by Nigerian law as 'the law of the land'). This incredibly modest attempt at rural social justice, stopping way short of land reform, infuriated the elites of Kano and Kaduna to murderous extent; their thugs ransacked government buildings.[155] Samuel Ikoku, veteran fighter of the Marxian left, resigned as secretary-general of the PRP, following the rift between Aminu Kano and Rimi that ensued when the latter introduced some minor changes that affected the trappings of feudal power in Kano, such as carving out new emirates to chop off chunks of the emir's territory. Meek and conciliatory as those steps had been, the old Aminu Kano thought they were outrageous attacks on the intransigent feudalists.[156]

To put this in perspective, one should remember how, in other formally feudalised nations, under more secular and progressive governments, the power of the feudalists ebbed away. In India, by legal trickery, the president in 1970 refused to enlist anyone on the privy purse lists that had hitherto defined who counted as recognised royalty in India, among the *maharajas, rajas, nizams, nawabs, sardars* and other quasi and real royals. India did not take their family jewels and palaces away, but the government did abolish their legal prerogatives. In Nigeria, feudalists were perhaps less sophisticated than the Maharaja of Jaipur, but they employed (and still employ in 2016) more thugs. Their intermarriages with the criminal comprador class ensure that they have, to this day, retained a stake in the Nigerian socio-political system that has never had a parallel in the United States, and which they had brought to an end in France in 1789, in Russia in 1917 and in India in 1970.

Eskor Toyo urged leftist politicians and intellectuals to rally to the cause of the PRP and join the organisation in 1983 (see chapter 5). Many doctrinaire Marxist-Leninists, however, thought that the PRP's focus on the peasantry was a revisionist deviation from the Soviet line and kept their distance.

Agbekoya Riots 1968–69

In 1968–69, the Agbekoya Revolt stirred up Western Nigeria, Yorubaland. The Agbekoya riots were a peasant revolt, but displayed notable similarities with working-class movements.[157] 'Agbekoya Parapo' in Yoruba means 'the union of farmers who reject suffering'. The association was heir to the traditional peasant work cooperatives. Commodity depots that had been established earlier by the British were hijacked by depot officialdom in the 1960s. The peasants' original grievance under the British was the flat tax, but later they developed other distinct demands, such as an increase in the cocoa price, ending forced tax collection, better roads, the removal of government officials who engaged in graft, as well as keeping the old focus on the reduction of the flat rate tax. Their leaders were Mustapha Okikirungbo, Tafa Popoola, Adeniyi Eda, Adeagbo Kobiowo, Rafiu Isola and Mudasiru Adeniran, some of them university educated. Peasants killed many officials and burned state buildings during the course of the riots. Finally, Chief Awolowo, in opposition to the government but still the most important voice in Yorubaland, was let out of prison (partly for this purpose), and he managed to negotiate with them and end the uprising, meeting many of the peasant demands.[158] Political economist Ola Oni (University of Ibadan) was deemed a security threat in connection with the revolts.

Labour Tamed, 1970s to 1999

In the 1970s, under the military rule of Yakubu Gowon, Murtala Muhammad and Obasanjo, there was a marked change in the character of organised labour: unions were tamed, and they had to kowtow to the ruling officers simply in order to survive. According to Usman A. Tar, the military realised that 'throughout the post-independence period, the labour movement has been at the forefront of workers' struggles and anti-state movement – a key rationale for the military state to intervene in the reorganization of labour'.[159] In 1978, the Obasanjo military dictatorship issued a decree, amalgamating every labour union into a single federation, the Nigeria Labour Congress (NLC). This new labour movement was cleansed of its most radical elements: Michael Imoudu, Wahab Goodluck, Samuel U. Bassey and other Marxists were expelled. The curious effect of this purge was that they ushered in a new generation of labour leaders who might have been more acceptable to the authorities at first, but who came to display the exact same Marxist leanings as their predecessors. The founding president of the new NLC was Alhaji Hassan Adebayo Sunmonu. Sunmonu had been an engineer in the Federal Ministry of Works, actually a civil servant.[160]

In February 1980, Sunmonu aired his wish for a national minimum wage and a minimum pension. A major strike broke out on 11 May 1981 under his leadership. President Shehu Shagari personally negotiated with NLC at this juncture. Despite its intended pacification of Marxists, the NLC was still 'one of the most persistent opponents of military rule in Nigeria'.[161] Sunmonu did not even hide his convictions: on May Day 1980, he said

> Workers will not achieve anything except through struggle, unity and solidarity. Our objective is to ensure that class and property will be wiped out of our society once and for all … In the final end of the struggle, there should be no property because there will be no capitalism.[162]

Sunmonu later published together with Bade Onimode on SAPs from a decidedly Marxist angle.[163] The entire movement retained some labour traditions, such as addressing each other as 'Comrade', up to 2016. The NLC's stated mission is radical:

> to organise, unionise and educate all categories of Nigerian workers; defend and advance the political, economic, social and cultural rights of Nigerian workers; emancipate and unite Nigerian workers and people from all forms of exploitation and discrimination; achieve gender justice in the work place and NLC; strengthen and deepen the ties and connections between Nigerian workers and the mutual/natural allies in and outside Nigeria and lead the struggle for the transformation of Nigeria into a just, humane and democratic society.[164]

Over 1000 national industrial unions are represented within NLC. Its membership in 2015 was 4 million, that is, 10 per cent of Nigeria's estimated labour force. Twenty-nine affiliate umbrella unions make up the organisation.[165] In 1993, when the presidential elections were annulled, NUPENG, the National Union of Petroleum and Natural Gas Workers, and PENGASSAN, the Petroleum and Natural Gas Senior Staff Association, were at the forefront of the NLC's struggle for democracy. There are limits to the NLC's inclusiveness however. Trade union decrees have excluded military and paramilitary personnel, and 'essential services' personnel, from forming unions. The Essential

Services Decree of 1977 states exactly which kinds of sectors fall into that category. Teachers were banned by the Teaching Decree of 1993, along with all of academia (the ASUU, Academic Staff Union of Universities) – the latter only temporarily. Oil workers are considered 'non-essential' – a surprising fact. The NLC has been subjected to other measures as well as the sacking of its old guard Marxist personnel. Its funding derives from member contributions (collected by employers), and the government itself, whenever NLC is in financial distress – which is quite often. The latter fact was a recipe for regime takeover, according to Tar. 'Sole administrators' were frequently appointed, especially by military regimes. In times of industrial action, employers may legally withhold membership fees.[166] Still, even though cleansed of the most notorious old left Marxists, the unions that together formed the NLC were viewed as a radical and a socialist force: there remained many radicals in the movement, as obviously their best organisers remained committed socialists. The dictator Buhari promulgated anti-labour decrees along with his discipline campaigns.[167] His successor, Babangida, after wooing Labour and part of the Marxian ultra-left such as Madunagu, Paschal Bafyau and Halilu Ibrahim, abolished Buhari's decrees and claimed he would expand workers' freedoms and improve salaries. Yet his IMF-sponsored SAPs did more than anyone had anticipated: they deindustrialised Nigeria, and lumpenised its labourers. Also, they destroyed the ethos of wage employment as such. Edwin Madunagu writes: 'after the oil boom, everybody hoped to escape from the slavery of wage labour into the freedom of business life'.[168] Worse, in October 1985, the dictator Babangida declared a National Economic Emergency for 15 months. He cut public sector pay by 2–20 per cent, as if the country were at war.[169] The difference was paid into the National Economic Recovery Fund, a neoliberal war chest. Babangida, sitting on that war chest, became a billionaire, while labour was decimated and state-paid professionals flocked abroad *en masse*. In 1986, Babangida orchestrated Madunagu's ousting from his Political Bureau.

In 1987, Babangida made the first attempt to remove the oil subsidy for the retail price of gasoline in the Nigerian petro-state. The naira fell swiftly as a result of deregulation. Living standards were so hard hit that they have not recovered since. The NLC stood up against SAPs, cost of living indices, salary deductions, education policies and the regime's appalling human rights records. In 1988, in an effort to solve the problem, Babangida tried to decapitate the NLC. His candidate, Takai Shamang, was defeated, and Ali Chiroma won. Babangida then declared a National Economic Emergency, dissolved the NLC leadership by decree, and appointed a sole administrator.[170] On 30 December

1987, Paschal Bafyau, Babangida's personal friend, was elected in a vote administered by the regime. Edwin Madunagu claims that he himself was also instrumental in facilitating Bafyau's candidacy.[171] However, protests grew. When Babangida finally resigned in 1993, the NLC wanted the Interim National Government's leader Ernest Shonekan (a Babangida loyalist) to hand over power to the Senate, according to the 1989 Constitution.[172] In 1994, following the pro-democracy general strike that followed the annulled elections of the preceding year, Bafyau was thrown into prison.

Civil sector donors prepared to give donations to unions were few and far between. After 1999 a different situation arose and, during the 2003 elections, the NLC's Civil Society Pro-Democracy Network was granted funds by the EU, the United Nations Development Programme (UNDP), and the National Endowment for Democracy. According to Tar, the NLC remained very much an old left-type organisation, inasmuch as it did not care much for social inclusivity, most especially that of women.[173] (I will challenge this view in chapter 7 on Marxian feminisms.) The heroic and colourful personalities of the 1950s and 1960s were long gone with their horse-tail fans but also with their honest sacrifices for the common good. From 1 to 8 July 2003, a major fuel subsidy strike was organised because the price of domestic-purpose kerosene increased by 70 per cent and petrol (gasoline) by nearly 100 per cent. Nwugo Chimere Nwungo, secretary-general of the National Association of Nigerian Nurses and Midwives (NANNM), was arrested. Christy Edwards, vice president of the National Association of Nigerian Students (NANS), was thrown into prison. Obasanjo replied to the strike by pounding the NLC, granting power over it to the Minister of Labour and the Registrar of the Trade Unions.[174]

Student Radicalism in the 1970s and 1980s

In the 1970s and 1980s student anti-state action was the single most radical force in the country, arguably even more so than labour unions. Student movements were born outside the traditional working-class movement.[175] The concept of student 'vanguardism' appeared.[176] The King's College strike of 1944, in which Governor Macpherson sent striking students to the front to die, was the first. Student riots accompanied the Western Regional Housing Bill in 1959, the Eastern Regional Pension Bill of 1959, the Sharpeville shootings in 1960, French nuclear tests in the Sahara in 1960, the Anglo-Nigerian Defence Pact in November 1960, Patrice Lumumba's deposition in 1961, the sending of Peace Corps into Nigeria in October 1961, the Preventive Detention Act of 1963, the Census in 1962/63, and civil war-related unrest.[177] After that, student activism acquired a more clearly Nigerian focus. Foreign policy ceased to be a major concern. The Gowon administration's murder of Adepeju, a student rebel, in 1971, the introduction of the National Youth Service in 1973, the Adepeju Memorial Revolt in February 1974, the Gowon-induced detentions of 1974/75, army promotions in 1975, the Dimka 'show' in 1976, school fees in 1978, all sparked student demonstrations and campaigns. Gowon, Muhammad, Buhari and Babangida all banned organised student activism in the form of the National Union (later Association) of Nigerian Students.[178]

Edwin Madunagu comments on student revolt and protest in Nigeria thus:

> We can therefore conclude at this stage that though students are formally divorced from material production, they cannot be divorced from ideological and political struggles. Precisely because ideology and politics have a dialectical influence on material production, students can be said to have one leg in material production and one leg outside it. This ambivalent location in social reproduction in general lies at the root of the limitations of students' role: and it is at the same time the objective cause of the ambiguity of this role.[179]

During military rule, the National Union of Nigerian Students was banned. Students did harbour some illusions: they saw themselves as the leaders of tomorrow (instead of legions of future unemployed and unemployable by globalised capitalism, as is now the case in Africa and in many countries of the EU). Their movements did have a certain elitism that, according to Edwin Madunagu, amounted to false consciousness.[180] Students also sometimes terrorised campus workers and other underprivileged personnel.[181] Quite apart from that, many students have been badly influenced by cultism in Nigeria. Campus cultism is occult in form, criminal in content and is the direct ante-room to the corridors of power in criminally governed Nigeria. Leading campus cultists who engage in ritual sacrifices, black magic, drug dealing, trafficking, smuggling, extortion, pimping and other nefarious activities, have open shoot-outs on university campuses in the country, and prompt security services to round them up until, sometimes, their political godfathers get them out of prison.[182] They routinely become politicians themselves. In the pre-1989 era, most students on Nigerian campuses had other concerns than the cults designed as money making enterprises. Some of them paid a heavy price for their idealism. Kunle

Adepeju, a student union leader, was shot dead in front of the University of Ibadan by Obasanjo's men. Kunle Adepeju's death in 1971 prompted Madunagu to write one of the best Marxist theoretical works in Nigeria: *The Philosophy of Violence*. In 1978, in the 'Ali Must Go Riots' at the University of Lagos one student died; at Ahmadu Bello University, more students. Colonel Ahmadu Ali, education minister, gave his name to this campaign which fuelled student unrest. Student activism served another purpose too, furthering the careers of participants: while young, many were in the Nigerian Youth Congress of Tunji Otegbeye and later entered mainstream political parties (NCNC, NEPU and even the NPC).[183] This phenomenon was called *entryism*, or dispersion of leftists into bourgeois political parties, and it was understood as a conscious political strategy. S.U. Bassey was an NCNC candidate in 1965. NYC Marxists such as Ade Thomas, Tunde Lawrance and Femi Okunnu also became NCNC members.[184] Marxist Kunle Oyero entered the House of Representatives in 1979 on the ticket of the Unity Party of Nigeria (UPN). Osita Agwuna, Marxist hero of the Zikist movement, actually became a traditional ruler in Anambra state.[185]

Tunji Otegbeye himself ended up in the ruling UPN too when his SWAFP went down, together with Samuel Dada, a teacher at Patrice Lumumba Labour Academy.[186] Samuel Ikoku entered bourgeois politics too. Sometimes entanglements with mainstream politics ended badly, as when Ikoku wrote a letter to Buhari in 1983 (a memo on good governance), who promptly threw him in prison as a result. In post-1999 Nigeria, it was the Marxian Democratic Alternative that was most often abandoned for the People's Democratic Party (PDP) and other parties.

Olusegun Osoba (Segun Osoba) was a Marxist author who published his essays with New Beacon Books.[187] His namesake Olusegun Osoba was elected into governorship on a Social Democratic Party platform in 1992; he was removed from office by Sani Abacha in 1993. After the reinstallation of formal democracy in 1999, he served for four years as the governor of Ogun State (he ran on Alliance for Democracy platform). In 2004, Osoba was heavily implicated in inciting students to attack a sitting governor (Oloye Gbenga Daniel), which seems to point to 'thuggery' and 'godfatherism' – the scourges of Nigerian politics. Ebenezer Babatope, another Marxist, went so far as to enter Sani Abacha's government itself. Left-wing credentials, especially those of a public thinker or a labour organiser, were seen as giving legitimacy to Nigeria's ever deficient rulers who lacked public legitimacy more than anything else. In many instances, they practically forced leftist politicians to serve on their boards and in their governments.

Marxian Currents at Universities, 1970-2016

Hardly a political movement in itself, but much more important than usually recognised, was the appearance of Marxian thinkers at Nigerian universities. Ola Oni, Ebenezer Babatope, Bade Onimode, Yusufu Bala Usman, Edwin Madunagu, Bene Madunagu, Usman A. Tar, Adebayo O. Olukoshi and Okwudiba Nnoli, and many who belonged to the circle of the *Review of African Political Economy* (London) were all at various Nigerian universities both in the South (especially Ibadan, Calabar and Nsukka) and in the North (especially in Kano, Kaduna and Zaria). Olukoshi (of the Nigerian Institute of International Affairs) and his circle of Marxist political economists formulated answers to SAPs at Ahmadu Bello University, Zaria (together with Yusuf Bangura, Bjorn Beckman, Akin Fadahunsi, Jibrin Ibrahim, Abdul Raufu Mustapha and Shehu Yahaya), at Bayero University, Kano (Attahiru Jega), as did Okwudiba Nnoli's circle at the University of Nigeria, Nsukka (H. Assisi Asobie, Chuku A. Umezurike, Ugochukwu B. Uba, and Okechukwu Ibeanu). Femi Aborisade (Socialist Workers' League) was dismissed from his position at Ibadan Polytechnic as a result of his political activities – prompting an international show of solidarity (by Leo Zeilig, Drew Povey and others).

Some of these academics experimented with markedly New Left, post-1968 methods of social organisation, such as communes (Edwin and Bene Madunagu). Ola Oni, Bade Onimode (Ibadan), Bene Madunagu (Calabar), Claude Ake and Eskor Toyo (Calabar) were followed by a host of other Marxist economists, such as Adebayo Olukoshi and Okwudiba Nnoli and their respective schools, who stood up against SAPs in the 1980s and beyond. (Many of their respective oeuvres will be examined in chapters 5–8.) It is important to see that although these intellectual movements were nurtured in 'ivory towers of learning,' in some cases they did have genuine working-class revolutionary ties (such as in the case of Madunagu, Eskor Toyo, Ola Oni, Bade Onimode and Hassan Sunmonu), and they were seen, up to the 1990s, as intellectuals who carried a lot of weight, in the public relations sense of the word, in the country. It was not a coincidence that Ebenezer Babatope and *Guardian* owner Alex Ibru were forced to join Sani Abacha's government;[188] or that Edwin Madunagu was to sit on Babangida's Political Bureau panel, or that Pascal Bafyau was used by the military. This reflected the popular legitimacy and genuine working-class popularity of the leftist intelligentsia that ordinary people were familiar with, from TV broadcasts, radio, daily newspapers and even their theoretical works that had considerable circulation in the country and among the Nigerian diaspora. Universities also came to be the last strongholds of autonomy under military governments with neoliberal economic agendas. They allowed for the survival of Marxist and radical thought in adverse circumstances in the country.

New Left in the Making: Illegal Rural Commune 1976–77

Professors Edwin Madunagu and Bene Madunagu were in detention in 1975, for opposing the military government's educational policies in Lagos. In their flight to Calabar, and away from the police, they decided to stay 'in the bush' from June 1976 to June 1977, until relative democ- ratisation allowed them to leave. There they built a radical commune among rural villagers. Another lecturer and his wife (a returnee from the United States who wishes to remain anonymous here) also participated. Others wanted to join, but participants opted for the smallest possible membership and kept security protocols so that the commune would not be raided by the police, who were actively searching for them. Men went outside but women stayed in the communal dwelling area. They also stood constant guard, especially at night. The group engaged in subsistence agriculture, planting their own crops. They also organised educational groups for villagers in what would today be called 'capacity building' in NGO parlance. Villagers protected them from the eye of the police and the army, a serious feat. In Madunagu's own words:

> At the end of June 1976, a group of young Nigerian socialists – male and female – gathered at some location in the rural part of what is now Osun State. At the end of the all-night discussion the group decided it was time to extend their conscientisation from Nigerian cities to the rural population at whose core is the peasantry.
>
> In the sense it was understood then, and even now, to conscientise is to lead the masses, through dialogue, to perceive the roots and nature of social contradictions and their exploitative and oppressive elements. What the masses do with this new perspective and consciousness is left to them. It was also decided that to make this conscientisation credible, and to earn the trust of the rural population, the headquarters of this revolutionary enterprise must be located in a rural area and that most of the young idealists must relocate to the headquarters immediately and reside there permanently. And, in order to maintain existing links with the urban masses, especially workers and students, it was decided that some members of the group would remain in the cities but regard their city enterprises as secondary to the rural project.

The rural conscientisation enterprise was engaged vigorously and seriously. The language of discourse was, of course, the local language not English. Vigorous efforts were made to translate difficult concepts into the local language and find local illustrations. World history, including its revolutionary segments, was rendered in the local language. The group lived the way their hosts lived: they rebuilt their acquired house and fences with no external labour; they farmed and reared animals for food; they cooked their food themselves; they sourced water in various ways, including the creation of a new branch for a nearby stream; they organised and executed their security needs. Male and female members were equal, fiercely so.

To underline this fact, a baby girl delivered by a female member just before the group came into being was taken care of, in turns, by members of the group – male and female. Thus, the mother was free to undertake her revolutionary duties like the other members. A male member of the group (am I the one?) would later recall, with pride and joy, that he learnt to baby-sit, feed and change nappies not with his own child (since he had none then), not as a house boy, but as a member of the group. That baby girl is now a graduate, working in Nigeria. One day the history and experiences of that group will be published for the benefit of the younger generation and in honour of the host peasant communities.[189]

Marxian Parties Since the Late 1970s

In 1976, the Adebiyi trial signalled a new resolution on the part of the Obasanjo administration to strangle Marxist forces in the country. Bade Onimode describes the trials thus:

the Adebiyi Tribunal was appointed on 12 February 1976, to investigate the trade union movement as a prelude to its reorganization. The Tribunal Report led to the dismissal of such radical trade unionists as Chief M.A.O. Imoudu, Wahab O. Goodluck, S.U. Bassey, etc. from such socialist-oriented trade unions as the Nigerian Trade Union Congress, Nigerian Workers' Council and the Railway Workers' Union of Nigeria. Following upon Gowon's detention of over 50 political opponents, this purge of progressive trade unionists marked a new phase of overt anti-socialism in military dictatorship in Nigeria. Earlier, in 1973, the Trade Union Decree had prohibited unions from using their funds for political purposes, in anticipation of civil rule in 1976. The Trade Dispute Decree of 1976 imposed compulsory arbitration before recourse to strike action. Later, in August 1978, several radical intellectuals and students were also sacked from the universities.[190]

Babangida established a regime-manufactured labour party that was to serve the purpose of *simulating* democracy. The Social Democratic Party was manned by Ola Oni, Eskor Toyo, Edwin Madunagu and Aboyomi Ferreira, who served on Babangida's Political Bureau, led by S.O.Z. Ejiofor.[191] This party soon ceased to exist. During and after the military regimes, Marxists in Nigeria tried many times to set up umbrella organisations or a real Marxist party again. Bassey Ekpo Bassey established the Calabar municipal council's work on a labour platform from 1989.[192] The first All-Nigeria Socialist Conference took place in Zaria in July 1977. When, in 1978, Olusegun Obasanjo lifted the ban on political parties and political activity, two embryonic new socialist parties emerged: the Socialist Working People's Party led by Dapo Fatogun and Ola Oni's Socialist Party of Workers, Farmers, and Youths.[193] These small parties were banned by Buhari in 1983. The Second All-Nigeria Socialist Conference was convened for the same purpose of unification, along with the Movement of Progressive Nigerians and the Calabar Group of Socialists. In the 1990s, the air around these organisations became thinner and thinner.[194]

In Nigeria, the global events of 1989 which brought an end to the Soviet Union and the Cold War coincided with one more failed attempt at socialist unification in the domestic sphere. Madunagu explains the multifaceted meanings of the year 1989 for the Nigerian left in his *History and Tragedy of 1989*:

I consider the year 1989 a tragic one in the history of post-independence Nigeria. Coincidentally, the year was also significant in the history of the Nigerian Socialist Movement. Beyond that, it was a tragic year for the world socialist movement. For the avoidance of doubt, by history, I mean, the actual movement of society through a continuous chain of contradictions, and resolutions of these contradictions. History is not the official records of the deeds of rulers, or the sanitized accounts of events rendered by victors. Although the deeds and pronouncements of rulers and the state over which they preside and the classes whose interests they represent may, in certain periods, be significant, even decisive, the point I am making is that they alone do not constitute history.

My concern in this piece is limited. I wish to present, in chronological order, and as logically as possible, and without analysis, some critical events which took place in our political history in 1989. I want to put the records straight, as the saying goes, so that researchers and analysts, and Nigerian youths, in particular, can have a reliable compass. And I am restricting myself to the political actions of the military government of General Ibrahim Babangida and the responses of a fraction of the socialist movement. I am compelled to undertake this unusual exercise because I have heard, and read, certain accounts that amount to a gross and dangerous distortion of history. Nigerians who are 25 years old today were merely 12 years old in 1989, 2 years old in 1979, and unborn in 1975. In a country where history is not accorded a respectable status in school curriculums and where what is given by the media is often eclectic, youths are placed in great jeopardy when they are required to act from the premise of our history.

Let me begin this account with the main political deeds and actions of the military government in 1989. On February 28, 1989, Professor Eme Awa was removed as Chairman of the National Electoral Commission (NEC) and replaced with Professor Humphrey Nwosu. A month later, on March 31, 1989, the Prohibition Amendment Decree (1989) was gazetted. The decree stipulated that 'banned' politicians would not be allowed to 'canvass for votes for, or on behalf of, themselves or others'. Violation would attract a five-year jail term or N250,000 fine. A few days later, on April 3, 1989, the Guidelines for the formation and registration of political parties were approved by General Babangida's Armed Forces Ruling Council (AFRC). A month later, on May 3, 1989, the ban on party politics was lifted. By 6.00pm on July 19, 1989, 13 political associations, including the Nigerian Labour Party (NLP), had submitted their applications for registration as political parties. On September 29, 1989, NEC recommended six political associations, including the Labour Party, for registration as political parties. Eight days later, on October 7, 1989, the AFRC turned down NEC's recommendation, banned all the newly formed political parties and announced the formation, by government, of two political parties, the Social Democratic Party (SDP) and the National Republican Convention (NRC).

Now to the Socialist Movement. I shall mention only a few names that are absolutely necessary for the account. More than half of these Nigerians have passed away; others are alive. In February 1989, the Directorate for Literacy, led by Comrade Bassey Ekpo Bassey, who was then the Chairman of Calabar Municipal Council, and Comrade Eskor Toyo, a professor of economics at the University of Calabar, organised a Conference in Calabar. It was a successful political gathering of the Nigerian Left. In early April 1989, a four-day (April 4–7) national workshop under the auspices of Nigeria Labour Congress (NLC) was held in Calabar. The theme of the workshop was Workers and the Political Transition. In attendance were leaders and representatives of the NLC, leaders and representatives of senior staff associations, professional groups and mass organisations as well as radical intellectuals, workers and students organised under the NANS.

The NLC Workshop was the first outing of the Labour Congress after the lifting of the nine-month ban placed on its leadership by the Babangida's regime in March 1989. Together with Kayode Komolafe of *THISDAY* newspaper, I played a crucial role in producing the unified force that ensured the emergence of the new NLC leadership under Comrade Paschal Bafyau. The new NLC president and his team were given a Hero's Welcome to Calabar by crowds which literally took over the Calabar Airport and later 'seized' the ancient city. The event was organized by the Calabar Group of Socialists in conjunction with the state branch of NLC. Among the socialists were Bassey Ekpo Bassey, Eskor Toyo and myself. The Calabar Workers' Workshop passed a resolution asking the NLC to sponsor a Workers Party as soon as the ban on political activities was lifted.

The Nigerian Socialist Alliance (NSA) was formed on Wednesday, April 5, 1989 in a room on the ground floor of Metropolitan Hotel, Calabar. As NSA was being formed, the National Executive Committee (NEC) of NLC was holding a meeting in the Conference Hall of the hotel. The meeting ended with a resolution to sponsor a Workers' Party. The meeting national secretariat made up of two Coordinators was set up for NSA. I was one of the Coordinators, the other being a comrade of Akwa Ibom extraction, a close associate of late Comrade Dapo Fatogun. The night before, on Tuesday, April 4, 1989, Bassey Ekpo Bassey and I organised and hosted a meeting of veterans of labour – socialist struggle – who had been invited to the workshop. The meeting was held in Bassey's house in Calabar. It was a coup, as none of them knew what was being planned; some believing it was a dinner. Known antagonists were conveyed in different vehicles. The gates were locked as soon as the buses entered the compound. Although reporters were barred, an Oyo State Television crew managed to enter the compound. Unable to persuade them to leave 'empty handed', I granted an interview in Yoruba language on the prospects of the proposed Labour Party.

Veterans who were 'captured' for the meeting included Wahab Goodluck, M.E. Kolagbodi, Mokwugo Okoye, S.G. Ikoku, Eskor Toyo, Dapo Fatogun and Ola Oni. The veterans agreed to keep the veterans' forum alive and support the Labour Party whenever it was formed. Bassey and I were appointed conveners of the forum. On its part, the inaugural meeting of the NSA agreed to draft a Programme and a Constitution for the proposed Labour Party and put these forward for the consideration of the labour leadership. I took part in drafting the two documents, which later proved unacceptable to the labour leadership. The rejection of the socialists' documents by the labour leaders effectively ended the joint 'sponsorship' of the Labour Party. From then on it was NLC's show. The Labour Party was launched in Lagos on May 20, 1989. Socialists, though excluded from the leadership, opted to play the role of giving the party the needed credibility, colour and justification.

The inaugural meeting of NSA ended about 4.00am on Thursday, April 6, 1989. I got to my house about 30 minutes later. I had slept for less than two hours when I was awakened by a comrade sent by Bassey Ekpo Bassey. I was asked to come out and help save the agreement which we reached less than three hours earlier. What happened was that as soon as the inaugural meeting of NSA ended, a number of comrades re-assembled at the same venue to reverse the decision earlier taken. Bassey and I rushed to the venue and took our seats. It was about 7.00am. The reason provided by the 'rebels' was that they were not comfortable with working with some of the veterans because of what these veterans did in the past, before and during the First Republic (1960–1965). We listened to them and patiently re-presented the case for NSA, the Veterans' Forum and the Labour Party as elements of the same political strategy. After about seven hours, the earlier agreements and decisions were confirmed.

On September 9, 1989, some members of NSA met in Kaduna and removed me in my absence, as a National Coordinator of NSA, accusing me of taking unilateral actions. No replacement was made. On September 19, 1989, NSA members and some labour leaders attending an executive meeting of the Labour Party in Calabar held a joint meeting with Calabar-based socialists and overturned the decision of the Kaduna meeting. On October 7, 1989, as the AFRC was meeting in Abuja over party registration, a meeting of NSA, convened by me, was taking place in Lagos. The NSA meeting broke up shortly after it opened because one of those who took the Kaduna decision insisted that I had been removed.

This was the last meeting of the NSA. Later that day the AFRC announced the proscription of the Labour Party and the other 12 parties that had applied for registration. Thus, in one day, the Nigerian Left, or a fraction of it, lost both its core organisation, the NSA, and its electoral ally, the Labour Party. It was also about this time that the communist regimes in Eastern Europe were falling, one after the other, as if obeying the domino theory. 1989 was indeed a tragic year.[195]

In 1989, the Nigerian left lost its most important external backer, the USSR, and its Communist Party. Whatever the crimes of the Communist Party of the Soviet Union within the USSR itself (and those were many), in the non-socialist abroad it had been a friendly superpower for workers, for their unions and for socialist movements all over the world. The USSR, even in its decay in the 1980s, still provided material help for striking workers globally, from the UK to Nigeria. It had been, for so many years, a focus of the left's hopes and aspirations. Now many of those aspirations seemed to have failed.

The Marxist critique of the USSR, and the quasi-Marxist futurology of dissident intellectuals such as Rudolph Bahro, proved wrong in the end. *Die Alternative*[196] in Eastern Europe was not what Bahro thought it would be, before he left the GDR (German Democratic Republic) himself. Bahro himself later joined a mystical cult, after resettling in the West. His world, the world of Eastern Europe, faced an even more bitter future: impoverishment and shock therapies that created conditions as bad as during a world war, a criminal wave, and the disappearance of the USSR as the ultimate 'help' for organised labour everywhere in the world. The year 1989 altered the conditions of the Nigerian left too.

In 1987, still under Babangida's regime, the Democratic Socialist Movement was set up illegally, first referred to by the then name of its publication, *Labour Militant*. Until recently, it worked together with the National Conscience Party (see below), but not long ago these again parted ways. The movement's leader, together with the Socialist Party of Nigeria (SPN), is the Lagos based Segun Sango as of 2016, who affiliated SPN with the London based Committee for a Workers' International. The Labour Party, a social democratic party, was set up by Sylvester Ejiofor in 2002, as the political wing of the NLC. Ezekiel Izuogu's Progressive Liberation Party was founded in 2001.

On 1 October 1994, the National Conscience Party of Gani Fawehinmi and Femi Aborisade was established. It still maintains the periodical *The Masses* and, as of 2015, the party was led by Dr Tanko Yinusa. The National Conscience Party was headed by Femi Falana, distinguished human rights lawyer and a political radical, for a while after 2011.

Also in 1994, Marxist veterans Mokwugo Okoye and Anthony Enahoro set up the Movement for National Reformation.[197] Enahoro developed a concept of carving out 70 ethnic groups within Nigeria – essentially, to make Nigeria a federation of federations, where many ethnic nationalities would have their states, autonomous states and so on.[198] This concept owes a lot to the USSR model, and most Nigerian leftists reject it precisely for that reason.

On 4 June 1994 the Democratic Alternative was launched by young people such as Chima Ubani, Lanre Ehonwa, Glory Kilanko and Ademola Azeez.[199] The year 1994 truly seemed to offer a plethora of new, exciting revolutionary options.

The Movement for Democracy and Justice under M.D. Yussuf is another left-leaning radical party today.[200] In 2003, 2007 and also in 2015, all these parties – the Democratic Alternative, the National Conscience Party and the Movement for Democracy and Justice – were kept out of elections by fraud. In February 2003 in an All-Nigeria Socialist Conference was organised, trying again, in vain, to unify the country's socialist movement.[201]

In the year 2011, the Socialist Workers' League formed from some former members of Democratic Socialist Movement (DSM) such as Femi Aborisade and the 'May 3 Movement' of the early 1990s that had organised illegal guerrilla cells against the Babangida dictatorship (Baba Aye, aka B. Adebola Ayelabola Jr)[202] and Abiodun Olamosu. The Socialist Workers' League maintains close relations with the Socialist Workers Party of Great Britain.

Major Marxist periodicals include the DSM's *Socialist Nigeria,* and the *Workers' Alternative.* From more mainstream newspapers, *This Day* and the *Guardian* allow Marxian columnists to explain their views and publish on the problems of the left in the country. *Sahara Reporters* is another news service that serves as an outlet for socialist views (especially to Chido Onuma and his 'Occupy Nigeria' movement).

Unification of leftist political actors, on a social democratic, Trotskyist or Marxist-Leninist basis, has so far failed in the country. What is very interesting is that John Campbell's verdict on Nigeria (that Nigeria as a unitary nation state is most likely doomed) is echoed very closely by the entire Nigerian Marxian left, especially by Eddie Madunagu and Segun Sango, who wrote a pamphlet with the title *Nigeria on a Cliff Edge.*[203] While representatives of the elite ritually claim time and again that all is well, Nigeria faces major challenges, including, today, a major armed insurgency.

'Democracy' and Labour, NGOs, 1999–2016

The contemporary era in Nigeria has been defined by deindustrialisation of cities, lumpenisation of urban dwellers, re-emergence of *juju* witchcraft, and near-total decay. Under these circumstances, socialist movements faced exceptional hardships, while their relative importance in the fight for decency actually increased. If John Campbell is right, and partition turns out to be the fate of the country, then instead of capitalism or socialism making inroads, we will discuss sadder choices, such as in the Democratic Republic of the Congo, where ordinary people reportedly declare their children to be witches and expel them from the family home, compelled by the inability to feed them.[204] Initially, many leftists had high hopes for Obasanjo and the reinstitution of democracy – soon to be bitterly disappointed.[205] In 2009 Edwin Madunagu set up the Congress for Popular Democracy, along with Chido Onumah, leader of the 'Occupy Nigeria' movement. Today, the DSM and the Labour Party in Lagos, the Labour Party and the Action Congress Party in Governor Oshiomhole's Edo state, the Socialist Workers' League in Ibadan, Benin City and Lagos, and Edwin Madunagu's initiatives in Calabar are the strongest advocates in Nigeria for a Marxist platform to define, once again, NLC policies, and work towards social justice with the labour movement as the main vehicle of class action against the criminal comprador class.

They face many hardships. On 1 January 2012, without warning, President Goodluck Jonathan announced that fuel subsidies would be ended. The NLC and the TUC, along with minor actor Joint Action Front, announced a national strike. The strike paralysed Nigeria. Road travel and even travel within cities, along with air travel, became impossible. Jonathan made the usual empty promises about anti-corruption measures in the oil sector. Nigerian TV stations showed images of schools, dams and hospitals that could be built using the fuel subsidy money – that, according to the neoliberal creed, was instead being irresponsibly provided to ordinary people. The fuel subsidy, and with it lower fuel prices, were practically the only benefit that ordinary people still gained from government action. In Nigeria, that was still one step too many in meeting the demands of the people, as opposed to those of the plutocrats. In fact, petrol prices rapidly shot up from 65 naira to 141 naira, prompting widespread anger. It is important to understand that in Nigeria there are no government-subsidised public transport schemes. Through the near-tripling of the price of petrol, the government would have tripled individual transport costs for people, who use scooters and run-down minivans to commute daily. Public outrage was such that, although the military was used on numerous occasions, the strikers stood fast, and the subsidy was only partially removed. Curiously, after petrol prices were set to be 100 naira, petrol disappeared from most stations, prompting a massive fuel shortage. Perhaps naturally for a country that is run like Nigeria, this shortage is partial. Illegally, a number of stations always keep a reservoir of petrol for those who really need it urgently, at about 135–45 naira a litre, while people who want to pay the government price (100 naira) spend entire nights and days in the queues in front of the petrol stations with their vehicles.

Perhaps the single most striking element in the radical left's current and ongoing political activity is the DSM's Education Rights Campaign. As the commercialisation of education since the 1990s eats up their future, with this campaign, children themselves take part in direct actions that press for universal free education. The movement maintains a blog, with children's poems about this topic.[206] One of them, written by an anonymous child poet, laments with great power, the loss of potential at Nigeria's 50th birthday:

BEFORE IT GO DARKER

I was told it was a light
Meant for the outshone illiteracy
To overthrow her ignorance
Gifted to mankind assigning development

Our golden jubilee has passed
But any atom of jubilation?
Seeing the light far from our imagination
And to hope of the few fading away

They said they are the peoples mind
Terminating the intentions of their aces
Hanging their races on an Hyperion tree
Watching their dreams farer than forever

A contemptible assurance
Yet too expensive than it valued
Rendering scholarship
Only to those in high places

Patriots frustrating their scholars
Unable to resist the small from the great
Taking lay down of bribery
I left over the fence stranded

We waved the sun goodbye
The stars not worth a substitute
In haste let rectify the moon
Before the world go darker

Another deeply human effort is Edwin Madunagu's Calabar International Institute for Research, Information and Development (CIINSTRID) that educates male adolescents towards gender equality. Helped by the Population Council, CIINSTRID engages young boys and girls to re-evaluate their conceptions of gender roles. As of 2016, the NGO is facing difficulties due to external financing. At the same time, Edwin Madunagu maintains, mostly at his own personal expense, CIINSTRID's marvellous and, in Nigeria, unique library in Calabar. It is not a lending library but its reading room is open to the general public. It is Madunagu's conviction that only by way of selfless help, education, enlightenment, will Nigeria escape a terrible fate of descent into darkness.

A segment of the Nigerian left after 1989 joined the civil society movement and set up NGOs. Usman Tar's entire oeuvre focuses on civil society and its fate under neoliberal rule. According to more anti-capitalist voices, the civil society movement enveloped the left and suffocated much of its emancipatory energy. Madunagu writes:

Today Nigerian leftism and leftists are not consciously and explicitly anti-capitalist. And yet the globalization we bemoan is capitalist globalization. The neoliberalism we hate is capitalist neoliberalism, and the imperialism we rally against is capitalist imperialism. To put it differently, and perhaps, more strongly: for a leftist, or radical, or socialist, to say that he or she is anti-neoliberal, or anti-globalist, or anti-imperialist, without being fundamentally, consciously and explicitly anti-capitalist is to bark at the moon.[207]

4

International Relations
of the Nigerian Left

Official Nigeria, from colonial times until today, has stayed firmly on the side of the West, especially close to the Anglo-Saxon powers. For two brief moments, first during the civil war when the USSR was the federal government's main arms supplier amid a Western arms embargo,[1] and again in 1975 when Murtala Muhammad recognised a Soviet-backed revolutionary government in Angola (this famous anomaly of Nigerian foreign policy came about when racist South Africa decided to descend upon Angola's government with its usual naked violence), things seemed otherwise.[2] Both these anomalies quickly gave way to the reappearance of the foreign policy status quo. Yakubu Gowon's Nigeria did a *volte-face* in the early 1970s, away from the USSR, and during Obasanjo's first reign, Nigeria again did precious little that would indicate a major shift of the pro-Western line, in relation to the frontline states against apartheid. Kenoye K. Eke wrote a detailed study about the latter *problematique* at a time when Obasanjo tried to adopt the garb of an international progressive, with some moneys spent on liberation movements.[3] However, the Nigerian polity, shaped and moulded by a comprador, non-productive and criminal upper crust, could never abandon its staunchly pro-British, and later pro-American, outlook. In Nigeria, even ascetically fundamentalist, sharia-minded *ogas* are 'viscerally pro-American'. When the emir of Kano escaped an attempt on his life in 2013, he ran to London.[4] These rugged, boisterous and elephantine men are rarely touted in the media as the darlings of Washington and London. But there they are, President Obasanjo with President Clinton, as Azikiwe had been with the Queen.

From the 1970s onwards, the Nigerian sense of direction, and also its sense of fashion, prompted a turn to the United States, away from England, in the cultural sense. The Nigerian South, and Southerners in the North, turned to the most bigoted US versions of charismatic Christianity, away from indigenous religions, and also away from the Anglican or Catholic faiths of their fathers and mothers. In the 1990s, with MTV and emigration, a tremendous sympathy developed in West Africa – and especially in Nigeria – towards US rap and hip hop. Still in

2015, these are the most popular music styles among Nigerian youth, especially their commercialised variety. Lumpenised urban youth soundtrack their sordid means of survival with the lyrical glamour of a US ghetto.[5]

The single most important international relationship for official Nigeria was the Atlantic nexus. Aping Americans even to the point of adopting *faux* US accents in Enugu,[6] the Nigerian elite enjoyed nothing more than the vulgar shopping sprees of the US middle class, and their ambitions centred on conspicuous consumption, preferably abroad.[7] Whether there was ever an alternative to this kind of unilateral cultural and foreign policy orientation, bordering on the absence of foreign policy due to its conspicuous lack of choices, is an interesting question in its own right. However, one must recognise an internal logic that connects a state's foreign policy-making decisions with its domestic political system. One group of scholars emphasises cultural determinants of foreign policy decisions,[8] and these aspects do arguably have a very important imprint on how foreign policy is conducted. Others see security considerations paramount (lately especially Barry Buzan). However, it is certain that the political economy of a state vitally influences its foreign policy orientation.

In Nigeria's case, professed non-alignment meant the lack of a written defence pact with the Atlantic powers after the 1961 fiasco (see chapter 3), but nothing more. Realist (*à la* Morgenthau) or neo-realist considerations could have pushed Nigeria into the Soviet orbit in the late 1960s (after all, that is from whom they bought their arms). The famous distrust of Russians,[9] socialism and Marxism in Nigeria does not adequately explain the deep-seated animosity that successive Nigerian governments have manifested towards progressive causes – the Russians, the Maoist Chinese, and even to some extent against communist black anti-apartheid fighters in South Africa.

Nigerian elites saw that their entire way of life depended on the literal lack of light. The kind of racket that the Nigerian elite have been running since 1960 could never function without the absence of planning, and the startling lack of rational organisation, management and investment. In a country where royals actively engage thugs in street fights, hatred for the USSR, with its collectivised agriculture and state-owned firms, was a natural phenomenon for the elite – and, by extension, given how that elite shaped the hegemonic culture within Nigeria, for most people. Indeed, it was entirely natural in a way, even commonsensical, for the Nigerian feudalists and their friends to keep within the Atlantic fold as much as it was natural for Pakistan's similarly reactionary landed elite. Thus the international relations of the Nigerian state have been defined by the country's links to the Anglo-Saxon powers and, equally so, to foreign corporations, as ultimately the latter provided the funds upon which the elite lived in luxury.

The Nigerian left had the exactly opposite foreign orientation – this was only natural. Their Soviet, Ghanaian or Polish links were dubbed 'high treason' by the ruling classes, but that was an unfair assessment, given how their own international links have contributed to the desperation of their country, during colonialism[10] and since. From very early on, in independent Nigeria, Marxist elements sought Soviet contacts prior to all others. Later those contacts influenced heavily, through channels of financial assistance, Nigerian Marxism and some of its less Trotskyist and more Eastern European-style communist thinkers.

In this chapter, an account is given of the international relations of the Nigerian left, focusing on Soviet, Eastern European, West African progressive and communist South African links. We now have a much enlarged understanding of Soviet foreign policy motivations in Africa, due to Zubok's magnificent *A Failed Empire*,[11] based on newly researchable Soviet archival material. Zubok's book renders obsolete many pre-1991 Western Kremlinologist works.[12] The USSR failed to bring about the earthly workers' paradise that it had promised. But, while it lasted, it gave a lifeline to many workers' movements in the world, including in Nigeria, and invited African progressives from Ngugi wa Thiong'o to Edwin Madunagu to the country on state sponsored visits.

The link to Western communism, especially that of the Atlantic countries, is more unclear. Jack Woddis, the prolific British communist author, especially on neocolonialism, seems to have been better known in Eastern Europe (where they translated his every work) than his own native England, and more in his native England than in the neocolonial countries such as Nigeria (although Bade Onimode did quote him a great deal). Herbert Aptheker, the US communist whose oeuvre seems to have influenced Martin Luther King, and who wrote about the black slave revolts in the United States and the Caribbean in the context of transatlantic slavery, appears to have been less influential in Nigeria. Claude McKay's temporary pro-Soviet stance in his *Negroes in America* went unnoticed in Nigeria in the 1920s and beyond.[13]

Likewise William Z. ('Bill') Foster's rugged American labour Marxism, as it manifested in the Communist Party of the USA (CPUSA), did not seem to have any discernible effect on West Africa. Not even the party's W.E.B. Du Bois Clubs of America (technically, the party's youth league), nor the black communist attorney Benjamin J. Davis Jr (who represented Harlem on the city council of New York City), seem to have had any influence. But some American communists are referenced more often in Nigerian Marxist works. Angela Davis was the most important author among US communists who made an impact on Nigerian Marxists (especially on Marxist feminists). Davis was a prominent Marxist, a beacon of African-American Studies, an exponent of critical theory, a leading figure in the CPUSA, a fighter against the prison-industrial complex and a civil rights activist. She was acting Assistant Professor at UCLA from 1969 to 1970 when she was dismissed on political grounds under the California governorship of Ronald Reagan. A celebrity in the socialist camp, Angela Davis was quoted in Bene and Edwin Madunagu's 'Conceptual Framework and Methodology: Marxism and the Question of Women's Liberation', in *Women in Nigeria Today,* and also extensively by Ogundipe-Leslie and others.[14]

It seems likely that communist currents in the UK and the US, even when these related to the Nigerian condition in some way, were largely overshadowed in Nigerian eyes by the hegemonic Anglo-Saxon brand of culture. Continental European ('Western') Marxism has been a more significant inspiration, and of course classical Marxism (especially the works of Marx and Engels, but also Rosa Luxemburg and Lenin) made the most important imprint on the Nigerian Marxists. One continental European Marxist intellectual heavyweight with a clear influence on Nigerian thinkers was Antonio Gramsci (especially in Northern Nigeria). Lukacs, the Frankfurt School, Adorno and Althusser also influenced Nigerian Marxism in a palpable way.[15] Naturally, Herbert Marcuse and others were known to Edwin Madunagu, who organised a rural commune in post-1968 Nigeria. Especially also Frantz Fanon's oeuvre had a serious impact on their intellectual outlook. Continental Europe, or the European Communities (later, Community, later still, Union) and its major powers had less immediate presence in Nigeria, except for German company Julius Berger (which makes those few roads that are built), and the French state, which rules the bigger portion of West Africa on not-so-subtle neocolonial terms to this day. Predictably, for most labour organisers on the street, Marxian literary criticism, Lukacs or Althusser were perhaps not so obviously relevant. At the same time, academically inclined Nigerian Marxists often lamented the anti-intellectualism of some of their movements' rank and file, as well as their leadership. Tunji Otegbeye's tirades about Michael Imoudu's lack of English and formal education was often complemented by Eskor Toyo and Madunagu on the lack of meaningful discourse and theoretical acumen in the movement (the latter often blamed especially Otegbeye for this). Specifically, the Trotskyist group of thinkers, especially Toyo and Madunagu, were influenced by a wider range of sources however, with Toyo quoting Mao in earnest, and Madunagu fondly revisiting

Trotskyist US thinker George Novack's essays,[16] or Paul Sweezy's version of Marxist critique.[17]

Nigerian Marxists knew exactly what was relevant for them as thinkers and also as men of action who knew the inside of jails. South African, Ghanaian, Guinean, Malian, Somali, Angolan, Mozambican, Cape Verdean and Congolese Marxism were very important inspirations for Nigerian radical left-wing intellectuals. African Marxist thinkers and organisers – from Joe Slovo of South Africa to Amilcar Cabral of Cape Verde – had a marked influence on them, and here we will also analyse the major ways in which African Marxisms influenced and shaped Nigerian Marxism. The chapter concludes with a discussion of a Nigerian Marxist emigrant thinker Igho Natufe's assessment of Soviet policy in Africa, a work of Marxist theory of relevance in this context.

Soviet and Eastern European Moves and African Marxism

The Soviet Union's foreign policy decisions oscillated between long-term, value-system driven revolutionary goals, and considerations of *Realpolitik*. Much has been written about the weight of ideology, or lack thereof, in Soviet foreign policy-making. One of Matusevich's major themes in his *No Easy Row* is demonstrating how ideology carried no weight whatsoever for the USSR in its foreign policy-making vis-à-vis Nigeria. In general, a peculiar version of paranoid realism seems to have defined Stalin's foreign policy steps since the early 1920s. His penchant for bankrolling foreign revolutions, in particular, was legendarily low, almost nil. Stalin could be startlingly, indeed shockingly stingy with his comrades. Vladislav M. Zubok notes that, during the Korean war (1950–53), Mao's Chinese communists bizarrely had to pay in US dollars for Soviet war materiel to combat Americans in Korea.[18] Stalin wanted a protectorate and naval bases in Libya in 1946, but he was rebuffed by the Western powers.[19] After that, he did not follow an expansionist foreign policy in the Afro-Asian world. He did not even receive Vijayalakshmi Pandit, Nehru's sister and ambassador to Moscow, and he absolutely ignored Africa. Khrushchev (at the helm from 1954 to 1964) was very different: open, optimistic, ideologically driven.[20] Khrushchev reduced the size of the Soviet Army in 1960 by 1.2 million – the single biggest reduction of a standing armed force in modern history.[21] The USSR, after the forced isolation and xenophobia of the Stalin years (especially from around 1930 until Stalin's death in 1953), was eager for international contacts. The Youth Festival of 1957 brought the world to the Soviet capital,[22] with a special emphasis on the Third World. (It was the site of fabled romances, and was soon followed by the birth of a number of mixed race children in the Soviet capital and beyond.)

The laboratory of Soviet Third World policy was in South Asia, with vital relevance for West Africa and beyond. Nehru's India chose non-alignment and accepted a Russian helping hand after the Sino-Soviet rift (1958) in the case of the Sino-Indian border war of 1962. Nehru became a hero in the Soviet press within a single year, 1955. As Legvold notes, 'Soviet attitudes were now obviously a replica of the prevailing view toward the national bourgeoisie in more important regions.'[23] The expression 'national bourgeoisie' demands an explanation: it is the segment of the colonial bourgeoisie that does not derive its existence from comprador relations with the colonial power (gatekeeping) in Soviet and also in Chinese Maoist parlance. For Khrushchev, an independent national bourgeoisie in a newly decolonised country could be a promising ally of the USSR against global corporate interests, former colonial masters and the United States. This view concurred with Mao's in the 1950s, who, after the Hungarian revolution of 1956 wrote his *Contradictions within the People*,[24] in which he extolled the virtues of the Chinese national bourgeoisie as one of the building blocks of communist China – a tenet he would come to revise with the Great Leap Forward and, especially, during the Cultural Revolution. Naturally, the distinction between a national bourgeoisie and a comprador bourgeoisie is sometimes blurred, but it is notable that, in 2013, the Nigerian Marxist thinker Usman Tar still maintained the distinction and classified the Nigerian ruling elite as a comprador (and, in his assessment, petty) bourgeoisie.[25]

The USSR, especially after the Cuban Revolution (1959), was enthusiastic about the prospects of communism in the Third World once again. Importantly, however, contrary to Zbigniew Brzezinski's assertions, the USSR never had a master plan to conduct its own Africa policy. As Sergey Mazov shows in his thoroughly researched essay on Soviet foreign policy in West Africa in the late 1950s to early 1960s, there was a complete lack of such a scheme on the part of Soviet authorities.[26] Mazov, in a masterly contribution to our knowledge about the Cold War in West Africa, proves that Soviet involvement started not with Guinea in October 1958, but earlier, in January 1956, when a Soviet delegation showed up at William Tubman's presidential inauguration in Liberia.[27] A joint communiqué was signed in Monrovia on the establishment of diplomatic relations. Tubman, as declassified US documents show, used that episode of diplomatic dallying with the USSR to exact a higher price for his anti-Soviet stance from the Americans.[28]

After Liberia, there came the well-known cases of Guinea (Conakry), Mali (the former Soudan) and Ghana (the former Gold Coast) as experiments in West African pro-Soviet foreign policies and in building regimes that aimed, at least professedly, at building socialism in the future. Robert Legvold's 1970 *Soviet Policy in West Africa* is still the most important source on the subject of early Soviet engagements in the region. Not at all sympathetic to Marxism, communism or Soviet foreign policy objectives, this book is a serious achievement, with its meticulous detail and honest observations on its subject matter. Written without the benefit of declassified Soviet, or American archival material, Legvold still amazes with the depth and breadth of his knowledge and attention.

Nkrumah's Ghana first kept equidistant from the West and the USSR; in fact, it regarded the USSR as a new imperialist power.[29] Nkrumah's foreign policy adviser was George Padmore,[30] former communist turned pan-Africanist and a *ci-devant* by then, of the international communist elite. Modibo Keita, the new president of Mali came from the *milieu* of a French communist study group.[31] However, in the case of Guinea, this was not the defining factor: Sékou Touré, an aristocrat by birth, campaigned successfully in 1958, for full independence from France. France withdrew so abruptly and took away with it such vital professional expertise that Touré had little choice other than to turn to the Soviets.[32] These friendships cost the USSR a great deal of money. The early 1960s, especially until Touré's *volte-face*, was spent in euphoria over the possibilities for the Soviet Union in West Africa. An entirely new addition to Leninist doctrine was developed, the concept of 'the non-capitalist path to development', which applied to the newly emergent, pro-Soviet countries that evidently could not build scientific socialism because of the state of their economies and their level of education, but that were 'on the right path' in the view of optimistic Soviet analysts and their patron Khrushchev.[33] The USSR was not doctrinaire in its West African alliances, as the case of Senegal showed. Senegal under Senghor was independent only in name and clearly under French tutelage (as it has remained ever since),[34] but the Soviets developed a working relationship with the country, and even gave development aid.[35] For instance, they opened a tuna factory there.[36] Soviet animosity focused more on Félix Houphouët-Boigny of Ivory Coast. The region's USSR-friendly states gathered in the Casablanca group of progressive states in 1961. Touré was awarded the Lenin Prize,[37] Ghana employed a Hungarian economist[38] and Soviet aid entailed the sending of teachers.[39]

Already in 1962 there was a discussion in the USSR as to whether Guinea, Ghana and Mali were socialist (which was also reflected in the British communist press and elsewhere).[40] The Institute of World Economics and International Relations in Moscow opined that those respective ideologies (of the leaders of Guinea, Mali and Ghana) facilitated the transition to higher forms of political and economic organisation. In 1963, Khrushchev endorsed 'socialisms of the national type' in Africa.[41] He endorsed 'revolutionary democratic statesmen' who 'sincerely advocate non-capitalist methods for the solution of national problems and declare their determination to build socialism', effectively labelling the West African socialists authentic socialists in the Soviet, orthodox, Marxist-Leninist, 'scientific socialist' sense. Khrushchev went this far because of high hopes fanned by Castro's communist turn, and also because of Zhou En-lai's attempts to woo West African socialists into the Chinese orbit, boosted by China's natural appeal as a non-aligned power.[42] Sékou Touré made an *étatist*, state (command economy) U-turn once again in 1963 (he hoped that the Soviets would build for him his white elephant project, the Konkouré Dam).[43] Khrushchev was ousted in 1964, and the lack of knowledge of foreign policy of his successor, Brezhnev, was truly startling.[44] He relied on foreign policy advisers such as Arbatov,[45] but his own capacity was very limited and, from 1968 onwards, he was also operating under the influence of tranquillisers.[46] Touré switched sides in 1962, while Modibo Keita was removed by a coup in 1968, just two years after Kwame Nkrumah lost Ghana the same way. The loss of Ghana and Guinea was painful for the USSR, a blow that was reinforced by the ensuing shock from Egypt.[47] It was a major disappointment when Sadat changed allegiance to the West (1971), after costing the USSR 15 billion roubles.[48] Even before that, however, a revision of the 'socialist credentials' of West African states was under way. Although Nkrumah's journal *Spark* sang the praise of scientific socialism,[49] Soviet apparatchiks such as Suslov, Rumyantsev and Ponomarev corrected Khrushchev's enthusiastic assessment of the 'progressives'.[50] Mali took a pro-Chinese course in 1965.[51] Soviet leaders talked of non-capitalist path, but no longer socialism, in the case of the West African states.[52] By this time the Soviets were somewhat cynical about their African proxies. When Nkrumah tried to convince them to train revolutionaries on Ghanaian soil, for the dissolution of Nigeria, the Soviets angrily refused.[53]

One might ask why, after so many disappointments, the USSR still maintained its high profile in Africa, and agreed to establish client states there in the form of people's democracies. Zubok reminds us that Soviet production of crude oil grew from 8 million barrels a day (1973) to 11 million barrels a day (1980), making the USSR the biggest producer of crude oil in the world for a time. Soviet hard currency revenues from oil and gas increased by 2250 per cent in the 1970s, reaching US$20 billion at the end of the decade. Beyond geopolitical considerations, Moscow simply had enough cash to pursue an expansionist foreign policy in

Africa in the 1970s. Imperial bureaucracies (be they Assyrian, British or Soviet) have a general tendency to favour expansion. Brezhnev's permissive attitude towards monetary rewards to his elite included a reliance on 'proconsuls', former ministers and party *nomenklatura*, who swarmed to the swollen African embassies of friendly African states. Development advisers, from engineers and doctors to spies and counter-intelligence agents, received their salaries in 'foreign currency cheques' for diplomats and development workers (to use the Western expression). These cheques could be used in Beryozka shops, where goodies generally unobtainable in the USSR could be found in abundance. With the help of a little barter on the side when back in Russia, these people effectively received ten, fifteen or twenty times the average salary.[54] They bought dachas, private Stalinist-Baroque apartments, pre-revolutionary antiques and gold, and smoked Western cigarettes in the drab capital city of world communism.

New people's democracies (states that professed Marxism-Leninism and scientific socialism as their official ideology) sprang up like mushrooms in the 1970s. The People's Republic of Congo (Brazzaville) was established in 1969. In the same year, Mohamed Siad Barre set up a military dictatorship in Somalia, with a pro-Soviet foreign policy orientation that would eventually change its course when the Soviets chose to back the Somalis' military adversary, Ethiopia, after the latter underwent its Derg-induced revolution in 1974. In 1971, Sudan under Nimeri (Nimeiri) became an African socialist country in all but name. In 1974, the People's Republic of Benin was declared in the former French Dahomey.[55] In 1975 the Democratic Republic of Madagascar was established under Didier Ratsiraka (later Ratsiraka, the Red General, chose the IMF over socialist policies). The USSR was still somewhat sceptical about the 'socialist content' of these revolutions. Cynically, one might point out that Soviet credulity towards African 'scientific socialisms' increased exactly at the point when oil incomes started to fill Soviet coffers. The USSR was, in a way, a victim of the resource curse, using its petro resources in an inefficient manner – from a Marxist point of view, propping up imperial proxies instead of furthering the cause of genuine revolution. In any case, when Ethiopia had an anti-monarchical revolution in 1974, then gradually turned Marxist and finally became the People's Democratic Republic of Ethiopia in 1987 (complete with Lenin statues), it received tremendous Soviet support, both military and civilian. People's republics were set up in the frontline states against apartheid (in both Angola and Mozambique) in 1977, and the USSR was indeed very much involved in the latter. Cubans were already active in Guinea-Bissau before they also appeared in the frontline states.[56] Soviet and Czech aircraft appeared, and the AK-47 became the weapon of choice for freedom fighters, and terrorists, as the USSR initiated an active push forward.[57] This was the very edge of the periphery of the world system. Military activity in such peripheral locations, victories even, are not necessarily indications of strength, but in some ways, because of the emphasis on peripheral regions rather than central ones, might indicate the exact opposite. Mozambican pro-Soviet Frelimo received its first MiG in March 1977 and, by 1984, it had six squadrons, including 44 MiG-21s.[58] Their enemy, racist and white settler-run Rhodesia, and later Rhodesian supported Renamo, kept their air bases in apartheid South Africa. In Angola, the MPLA (People's Movement for the Liberation of Angola) was the primary Soviet proxy. Set up by Portuguese and *mestiço* radicals like Agostinho Neto, the MPLA fought against the Portuguese colonial occupation, and later the South African bully state. As far as Afro-Marxist regimes themselves went, the most well articulated were Angola, Mozambique and Ethiopia, while Benin, Congo and Madagascar were, according to Edmond J. Keller, 'marginals'. The early Robert Mugabe also stated the intention of building an Afro-Marxist regime, but this went wrong due to local dynamics and to Mugabe's own mistakes.[59]

Important researchers of Afro-Marxism, including the Ottaways and Keller, all stressed how those were regimes that appeared, without exception, with the crucial support of superpower backing. None of them were African Cubas, where an indigenous revolution brought about a home-grown and successful socialist political and economic system. They make a fundamental mistake though, by lumping together these states with African Marxisms. Aside from the question of whether or not state socialism as such was ever genuinely Marxist, African Marxism made an important contribution to social revolutions other than in these so-called Afro-Marxist states. Indeed, in Cape Verde Amilcar Cabral, in South Africa Joe Slovo, in Nigeria Edwin Madunagu appeared, all mindful of the USSR's power-projecting capabilities but none forgetting to build systems of thought based on the conditions of their own societies, rather than the availability of Soviet AK-47s or medical aid. There were a few exceptions, cases when genuine and subtle Marxist theoretical works appeared in connection with the appearance of Afro-Marxist states, as in the case of Burkina Faso (with Thomas Sankara) and in Angola, with its Commander Jika, aka Gilberto Teixeira da Silva (*Reflections on the Struggle for National Liberation*), another very important African Marxist text. One solution to this analytical difficulty was proposed by B.D.G. Folson, who made a distinction between Afro-Marxism (the heterodox Marxisms of professedly Marxist African states) and African Marxism as such.[60] Jowitt argued that those regimes were not Leninist, due to some criteria (constructed so as to demonstrate a formal sociological dichotomy and extreme divergence, between Afro-Marxist regimes and Eastern European ones).[61] Such dichotomies might have proven useful for purposes of security analysis (from a US point of view, of course) but say very little about Africa's Marxisms. To understand African Marxisms, it is obviously not satisfactory to discuss these differences (on such a basis, anything may be termed heterodox); a genuine interest in actual Marxian theory is also needed. A general reference volume, or even a general reader, on African Marxism has yet to be written, and the current book is a partial attempt at uncovering some of this rich intellectual tradition.

By the 1970s, *detente* was in full swing, and the Helsinki Conference in 1975 codified the demarcation lines between the superpowers on the European continent. It was not possible for the USSR to challenge the West in Europe. The People's Republic of China took an anti-Soviet turn in the 1970s, so much so that, after Mao's death, it acted virtually as a NATO ally in the international arena. This was already the beginning of gerontocracy in the USSR. Brezhnev in the late 1970s was a sick old man who lingered on. Soviet Africa policy was completely independent of his influence. Foreign minister Gromyko, KGB head Andropov, and General Grechko (and after 1976, Ustinov) were in charge of the USSR's Africa policy according to archival evidence.[62] The USSR was very far from the expansionist monster that US hawks such as Zbigniew Brzezinski portrayed it as being. Its 1977 security doctrine was entirely defensive.[63]

The USSR's leaders realised early on that in Nigeria they had relatively few policy options. It was not for nothing that one of the two Nigerians awarded the Lenin Peace Prize was a man engaged in two activities: the dissemination of Marxist classics and campaigning for trade with the USSR (Peter Ayodele Curtis Joseph; the other recipient was the socialist feminist Olufunmilayo Ransome-Kuti). Nigeria's elite before and after independence was unified in its disgust of anything emanating from the USSR, to the extent that they managed to prevent for a time the opening of a Soviet embassy in the country.[64] The embassy, when it finally opened, was restricted to ten car plates.[65] Embassy personnel spent their first year in a hotel, because the authorities blocked Soviet attempts to buy a plot of land. Dr Nnamdi Azikiwe was invited to the American Frank Buchman's Moral Re-Armament headquarters (an anti-communist global crusader force) at Caux, Lake Geneva, in Switzerland, repeatedly, from 1949 onwards. Azikiwe distanced himself from Zikism and found Moral Re-Armament a most useful way of approaching the leftist challenge: prop up Christian values in emerging nations.[66] Chief Awolowo, the Yoruba Action Group's leader, seemed even more vehemently anti-Soviet on the eve of independence.[67] By 1962, things changed. Action Group was an opposition party, maligned and marginalised by the ruling coalition dominated by Northerners (Northern People's Congress [NPC]) and supplanted by Igbos (National Convention of Nigerian Citizens [NCNC]). Within Action Group itself, this resulted in a power struggle between Awolowo and Samuel Akintola. The only way Awolowo could find to combat Akintola's ideological challenge and his own party's radical marginalisation was by turning around and assuming a pro-Soviet, pro-Ghanaian radical persona.[68] Awolowo touted his defiance against especially the Northern feudalist domination of the first republic. He also aired some radical ideas, especially when it came to his views on universal free education and free health care as desirable goals for the country. However, the entire situation surrounding how Awolowo became a self-confessed socialist actually points to the conclusion that his socialism was lukewarm at best. Never, throughout his entire oeuvre, did Awolowo express a determination to change the relations of production within Nigeria; indeed, he never proposed a radical restructuring of the capitalist and feudal ownership structure. In this he was similar to 'African socialists' like Senghor – a very sympathetic figure as poet-president of Senegal, but someone who represented the near-complete continuation of French colonial rule via the advocacy of his brand of 'socialism'.

Some students studied on generous Soviet scholarships, even prior to independence. From the Nigerian point of view, this was illegal. One of them, Chukwuemeka Okonkwo, later complained of racial oppression, brainwashing, a drab lifestyle, bad facilities, and generally intended to unveil the USSR's academe as a bad bargain for Nigerian students. His case was strengthened when there was an exodus of African students from Bulgaria in 1963.[69] A Ghanaian student was murdered in Moscow in 1963 November, allegedly for dating a Russian girl. Nigerians organised a protest march on the Kremlin: the first unauthorised demonstration in Russia since the fall of Trotsky in 1927.[70] It was only in 1973 that Soviet university diplomas were recognised officially in Nigeria.[71] Some student accounts, especially regarding the boredom of the Soviet capital compared with Nigerian nightlife, were obviously very accurate, while others were clearly motivated by political interests. Some Nigerian student accounts, as quoted by Matusevich, were bizarre and their validity is questionable. For example, one Anthony Okotcha recounts his spy training at Moscow's Lumumba University thus:

Professor Sofronchuk (a Russian spy trainer) proceeded to demonstrate his art. He placed a skull on the table. And from it came a voice, apparently produced electronically: 'I am your ancestor speaking. I command you to go tonight, kill the British Governor, and bring his head and hands to me … I am the spirit of god. I command you to burn that Englishman's house and rape his wife and daughter … I am Shango from the deep waters. I will fetch you if you refuse to join the Communist Party and do whatever its leader tells you.[72]

In the latter days of the Balewa administration however, a new realism came to characterise Soviet–Nigerian relations. Khrushchev was ousted in 1964. Nkrumah and Modibo Keita were overthrown. In 1966, a rapprochement was under way between official Nigeria and the USSR, growing out of Soviet 'ideological laxity and a profound disillusionment in Africa's revolutionary potential'.[73] After Gowon's counter-coup, this rapprochement became more marked, especially when Awolowo was released from prison.[74] Gowon spent a special envoy, Victor Adegoroye, to Moscow. There was talk of development assistance from the USSR, at a time when federal Nigeria was in turmoil and Igbos were being massacred in the North. After 30 May 1967, when Colonel Ojukwu declared Biafran independence for the Igbo heartland, Gowon's federal government was quick to realise that neither the US nor the UK was ready to supply arms to the federal side in the civil war that was brewing, while France and Portugal actively supplied Biafra with weapons. Chief Anthony Enahoro, Awolowo's main aide and commissioner for the Ministries of Information and Labour, was promptly dispatched to Moscow to buy arms and ammunition. The reinvigorated Tunji Otegbeye of the Socialist Workers' and Farmers' Party (SWAFP), was quick to call for total war against the 'vandal Ojukwu', in *Advance*, the party newspaper.[75] Tunji, Wahab Goodluck and S.O. Martins of the Nigerian–Soviet friendship society travelled together to the 23rd Congress of the Communist Party of the Soviet Union in 1969. At this point, relations between official Nigeria and Moscow warmed up to such an extent that Nigeria agreed to receive a Soviet military attaché – something it would never do again.[76] Aminu Kano, commissioner of communications, started working on proposals together with Soviet partners on Soviet economic aid. In 1969, Soviet–Nigerian trade skyrocketed, because of the obvious importance of military *materiel* and related shipments. It was also in 1969 that the parties signalled a willingness to cooperate on the building of Nigeria's first iron and steel complex – the famed Ajaokuta, a massive white elephant project that was to swallow billions but which was never operational even for a day. Ajaokuta is typical of Nigerian mismanagement of funds, and Soviet secrecy in construction and installations. In November 1970, a contract was signed.[77] It took five years for the parties to designate a site for the massive complex that was to be sub-Saharan Africa's biggest industrial plant. The hostility of local people in the area, the difficulty of the terrain and the general impossibility of logistics in Nigeria thwarted the work even before construction could begin. Foundations were finally laid by President Shagari in 1981. Russians were paid in German Deutschmarks and the lowest salary for a Russian technician at the site was US$19,000 a year, a truly fabulous salary for a Soviet expat at the time. Construction was 53 per cent complete in 1985.[78] By 1989, as a Russian undertaking the project was dead. With the help of Western firms, Nigerian politicians started to loot what was there, Ajaokuta never got built and goats now feast in its grounds.

A Nigerian–Soviet Chamber of Commerce was opened in 1969. Gestures of goodwill were myriad, from clergymen visiting each other's countries to submarines deployed in Lagos bay. However, as we shall see, this was truly an anomaly of the first order. 'The Soviets have yet to plumb the depths of Nigerian ingratitude', said a British diplomat at this point.[79] By 1969, the federal government was worried that arms shipments and foreign policy gestures might unduly embolden the home-grown radical left. In 1969, they incarcerated Tunji Otegbeye as a preventive measure. Nigerian Trade Union Congress representatives were harassed, Wahab Goodluck was prevented from leaving the country. The West reappeared even before the cessation of hostilities. Oil companies returned in 1969, along with the World Bank, which proposed suddenly to build a new dam, the Kainji. When Gowon went overseas after the war, he chose the US and the UK as his destinations, not the USSR. In 1972, 50 students headed for the Soviet Union were prevented from leaving and were detained.[80] The Patrice Lumumba Academy of Labour was closed down, and Eagle Garage, which dealt in Lada automobiles, was also forced to close. Although Murtala Muhammad allowed Wahab Goodluck to lead a unified Nigerian Labour Congress for one day on 18 December 1975, the next day he was jailed. In March–August 1976, the so-called Adebiyi Tribunal (named so after its judge) indicted Michael Imoudu, Samuel Bassey and Wahab Goodluck for acting in the interests of a foreign power. Highly publicised and obviously politically motivated, the famous trial showcased how the Nigerian elite wanted to distance itself from Soviet interests, and to be seen as rooting out domestic rebels and fighters.[81] Gowon belatedly visited the USSR in 1974, but focused on aid, especially for Ajaokuta. To highlight his aloofness, he promptly visited Beijing after the Moscow trip. Some Nigerian backing for the FRELIMO in Mozambique came in 1975 under Murtala Muhammad, and this continued under Obasanjo. It was plain, however, that this did not help to create any common ground in foreign policy between Nigeria and the USSR.[82] In the 1970s and 1980s generally, relations between the two countries deteriorated further. Trade remained at a fairly low level, with cocoa beans and cocoa butter as the most important Nigerian exports to the USSR.[83] The USSR sold mainly cars and trucks, bulldozers and tractors as well as arms,[84] the importation of which shot up again in the early 1980s.[85]

Soviet publications on Nigeria also emphasised the practical and economic nature of Soviet–Nigerian relations. Vladimir Lopatov, in his *The Soviet Union and Africa*, mentions Nigeria only in connection with trade, noting that in 1985 the proportion of machinery and equipment in Soviet exports to individual African countries, was 94.5 per cent in the case of Nigeria,[86] along with the fact the National Institute of Petroleum was built by the USSR in the country[87] by Technoexport in Warri.[88] A.I. Timofeev's *Nigeria: Its Stages of Development*, has a similar focus when it comes to Soviet–Nigerian ties. Akinyemi gives examples of development assistance/installations construction, such as the Soviet construction of an oil pipeline from Warri to Lagos and from Lagos to Ilorin.[89]

The fall of the USSR brought a new Eurocentrism and ugly racism in Russia, and a disappointment of untold proportions for left-wing radicals, now abandoned to their own means, in Nigeria. Soviet economic aid decreased and took on a new multilateral form, especially aid via UN agencies. The new Russia was an international pariah: its sphere of influence dwindling, its way of life in ruin, its achievements in working towards a more equal social system now repudiated and laughed at as a pipe dream. The new Russia withdrew almost entirely from Africa. Its proxies reoriented their foreign policies but they would soon discover that, for them, the New World Order of the 1990s meant total marginalisation, indeed the virtual disappearance of Africa from the map of the powers that be. Russia only partially made a comeback in Nigeria with Gazprom's pledge to help draw liquefied natural gas from the Nigerian oil fields, write off some of Nigeria's external debt and enter into bilateral aid programmes.[90] In the volume *Ten Years of Russia's Foreign Policy*, produced by the Russian International Studies Association (RAMI), Africa is not even mentioned.[91]

The story with the other Eastern European states was also characterised by disengagement. As in Comecon (the Council for Mutual Economic Assistance), where countries were allocated specific industries (for instance, Hungary made commuter buses but East Germany produced cars), in the Warsaw Pact, member states were given priority areas in foreign policy ties. East Germany and Czechoslovakia were especially active in sub-Saharan Africa, whereas Bulgaria focused on Iraq, and Hungary on North African Arab states. It was thus not only the USSR that was involved in the warming of relations between the 'peace camp' (as the Eastern Bloc styled itself) and Nigeria back in 1967. The USSR bought 6 Czechoslovak fighter jets, along with 20 MiGs.[92] Later Poland constructed a washing plant for the mine in Enugu in the late 1970s, and established fisheries in the country. From 1973 onwards, Hungary entered production cooperation with Nigerian firms in the pharmaceuticals business.[93] East Germany exported cement and printing machinery.[94] Poland was active in coal mining and sheet glass production. Bulgaria was more active in construction.[95] All that was in line with the (then) usual Eastern European approach to development: focus on heavy industry first, and all else will follow. Industrialisation would have served Nigeria well. Industrial policy, a dirty word in the United States and according to the current Western consensus, could have helped Nigeria escape the fate that it has endured since the 1980s: active deindustrialisation where even traditional handicrafts are supplied to the African consumer by Chinese industry.

There are still remnants today of Eastern European involvement in the Nigerian scene. For example, the National Theatre in Lagos is a state-of-the art multi-functional entertainment centre built in what is today lovingly called East-modern, retro chic, or simply brutalist concrete architecture, although its central air conditioning system has collapsed and it is used by vendors and sex workers. A more heart-warming specimen of Eastern European involvement (because it functions still) is the very layout of the City of Calabar, designed by the Hungarian architect Karoly Polonyi. He also made plans for entire housing estates, condominiums, and many public buildings in the city that is, to this day, the most liveable in Nigeria.

Ghana and Nigerian Labour

Robert Legvold, Roger Cohen, Wogu Ananaba and Hakeem Tijani – that is, all the important historians of the Nigerian labour movement – delve into the forensic historical *problematique* concerning revolutionary Ghana's role, especially in the early 1960s, in fomenting labour radicalisation within Nigeria. President Kwame Nkrumah (1957–66) did not start off as a pro-Soviet, socialist or communist politician, but his transformation in that direction went a long way. According to Legvold's analysis, Nkrumah's main difficulty was a classical one: how to mobilise people in a traditional subsistence economy, for the sake of modern nation building and the grand projects that such visions bring.[96] The ruling (and only) party in Ghana was a nepotistic, badly organised motley crowd, incapable of enacting the role that Nkrumah envisaged for it: the building of a planned economy. Nkrumah's 'adolescent ambition' notwithstanding,[97] the USSR decided on a number of occasions not to underwrite Nkrumah's grandiose development plans financially or otherwise.[98] Nkrumah saw an opportunity to directly intervene in the mess that was Nigeria in 1964, when he set up a subversion camp in his country at Teshi to train Nigerian refugees and rebels in guerrilla combat techniques.[99] The USSR quietly backed out of its earlier pledge to help Nkrumah in those camps. Hungarian economists and East Germans were enlisted as economic advisers,[100] but the USSR was afraid to appear as a troublemaker in the West African scene, after the first three fiascos.

Whether Nigerian labour leaders were aware of Nkumah's immediate policy goals in their country, especially as violence spread from 1963, is unclear. However, the Ghanaian Trade Union Congress, and especially its famed general-secretary John K. Tettegah, was instrumental in tilting the balance of power towards leftists in the Nigerian labour movement by its own means, even before Nigeria became officially independent.[101] Allegedly moving about with the usual suspects (Hungarian and East German spies according to Ananaba),[102] in 1962 Tettegah allegedly employed 50 Ghanaian hooligans to crush what he saw as a rightist labour union conference.[103] Ananaba fails to supply any sources on the subject, but Robin Cohen claims that this was slander (supposedly also involving a bribe of £1000 pounds).[104] After Nkrumah's ousting, Ghana played no further role in the Nigerian labour movement.

An Obvious Inspiration: South African Anti-apartheid Marxists

The single most important peer-reviewed venue for African and Nigerian Marxists has been, undoubtedly, the *Review of African Political Economy* (*ROAPE*), established by the South African anti-apartheid fighter and Marxist thinker Ruth First in 1974 and still edited according to her vision today in London. A part of chapter 6 will be devoted to works that have appeared in *ROAPE*. Ruth First, who hailed from a Latvian Jewish background, studied together with Nelson Mandela and became the editor-in-chief of South Africa's *Guardian*. She fought for racial emancipation in her home country until she was forced into exile in London. A leading member of the South African Communist Party, she then travelled back to Africa and helped the FRELIMO government in Mozambique, until the South African Police murdered her with a letter bomb. A sensitive thinker, with a sense of justice that transcended even her own global communist commitments (she stood up for the victims of Soviet atrocities),[105] Ruth First's papers are currently being researched by a group of dedicated scholars in London including Leo Zeilig.

First's lifetime partner and comrade, Joe Slovo, was a similarly interesting figure who commanded respect and inspired love in many African communists and anti-apartheid fighters, all over Africa but also specifically in Nigeria. Slovo also came from a Baltic (in this case Lithuanian) Jewish background. He spent his early childhood in a typical Eastern European *shtetl*, where his father Wulfus was a fisherman.[106] He grew up so poor that as a child, he had to relieve himself in the back yard even in winter – and that was even after they immigrated to South Africa.[107] Through sheer brilliance, he became a lawyer, and defended communists and other black radicals in apartheid show trials. Chair of the Communist Party of South Africa, and founder and chief of staff of its armed wing Umkhonto we Sizwe, Slovo was, according to Nelson Mandela, the 'personification of the ANC-led alliance' on a global scale. Slovo was a warm-hearted, life-loving, activist politician who wore trademark red socks, loved whiskey and women, and was as much of a quick-witted extrovert as one might expect from a celebrated lawyer. He spent 27 years in exile, mainly in the UK and in Mozambique. After the fall of apartheid, Slovo became minister of housing in the new, democratic polity, but never for a moment did he repudiate his belief that 'socialism was still the answer'.[108] His critical stance on Leninism and the concept of the vanguard party notwithstanding,[109] Slovo thought socialism was not dead even in the aftermath of the collapse of the USSR and the failure of its social model.[110] Edwin Madunagu would echo this sentiment in Nigeria, with clear reference to Slovo.

Nigerian Marxist Scholarship on the USSR's Role in Africa

Beyond constant references to the USSR and the significance of its fall for Africa by authors such as Yusufu Bala Usman, Bade Onimode, Usman Tar, Edwin Madunagu and many others, there has also appeared a full volume entirely dedicated to the study of the USSR's role in Africa by a Nigerian Marxist author. Igho Natufe – research professor at the Institute for African Studies, Russian Academy of Sciences, and president/CEO at Stratepol Consultants Inc. in Ottawa, Canada, senior policy adviser to the federal government of Canada and president of the National Council of Visible Minorities in the Federal Public Service – is the author of *Soviet Policy in Africa: From Lenin to Brezhnev*. The book focuses especially on the role of ideology in Soviet foreign policy. Challenging mainstream scholarship, for instance that of Maxim Matusevich (who argued that Soviet foreign policy in Africa was guided by imperial considerations of zero-sum foreign policy gains vis-à-vis the West), Igho Natufe stresses the role of ideology in formulating Soviet foreign policy even in the 1960s and 1970s.[111] Natufe takes a Khrushchevian attitude to de-Stalinisation and alleges that crushing the Beriya-faction meant an end to Stalinism,[112] even in foreign policy – a mainstream view in the former Soviet Union but one that does not take into account Beriya's total lack of interest in ideology and in Marxism. Natufe traces the Cold War back to 1918 and Western aggression against the Soviet state.[113] He emphasises how the British practised preventive imperialism in the Nigerian theatre of the Cold War,[114] especially when they banned communist agitation in the country.[115] Interestingly, Natufe argues that the partial expulsion of Marxist elements from Nigerian unions was made easier by the Sino-Soviet rift.[116] A curious aspect to Natufe's work is that he consistently uses the grammatical present tense when discussing the Soviet Union – an indication, perhaps, of strong nostalgia for the country where he received a scholarship that enabled him to study abroad and where his career was launched as a specialist in affairs pertaining to visible minorities.

5

Activists, Historiographers and Political Thinkers: Marxism-Leninism versus Heterodoxies

Niyi Oniororo

The firebrand journalist Niyi Oniororo (d. April 2005), was perhaps the most Nigerian, or surely the least Westernised, author among all Nigerian Marxist thinkers in his intellectual outlook. Ola Oni's brother, he may have studied in North Korea (illegally).[1] His statements were never tempered by expectations of restraint – not even when it came to his own movement, Nigerian Marxism. Oniororo published a great number of speeches and also full volumes, on issues pertaining to Nigeria and possible solutions to its myriad problems. After Murtala Muhammad's death, he set up an NGO with the mission to commemorate the president's violent end, an event that he linked with the latter's backing for Angola's MPLA (People's Movement for the Liberation of Angola).[2] He later went on to set up the Nigerian Council for National Awareness (NCNA),[3] a Marxist-Leninist organisation, in 1977,[4] and toured the country's campuses, university clubs, radio stations and community organisations with his message. His books were numerous: *Lagos is a Wicked Place, Nigeria and Socialism, Letters to Nigerian Society, Nigeria's Future: Revolution Not Reformism, Why the Nigerian Masses Are Poor* and, last but not least, *Who Are the Nigerian Comrades? The Story of Opportunists, Revisionists, Reformists and Careerists in Nigeria.* These books today are, without exception, bibliophiles' rarities, almost impossible to find outside the remotest libraries of Wales and England. They are unavailable in Nigeria in public libraries, even when those are relatively well functioning. Even if Oniororo obviously manipulated the membership data of his NCNA – he claimed membership nearing half a million people,[5] and that some members signed membership sheets with their own blood[6] – his presence in Nigeria was widely felt and he was accused of inciting civil unrest more than once. Oniororo's end in 2005 came after a well-publicised and shady affair, in which his son, Dr

Yomi Oniororo, who worked for the Nigerian intelligence services, was apparently murdered.[7]

Niyi Oniororo possessed a sense of humour that reminds one of Rabelais. His books are not for the faint hearted, and they are conspicuously devoid of politically correctness, by the standards of 21st-century Western sensibilities. Oniororo was a staunch supporter of Eastern European solutions. Even at a time when Eastern European leaders themselves usually spoke of the necessity of a one-party state with diffidence and a certain sense of shame (the Hungarian dictator Kadar often referred to 'historical circumstances'), Oniororo had no qualms about advocating one-party dictatorship in the interest of a developmental state. Speaking in 1979 (when the Soviets seemed to be in the ascendant in Africa), he opined that:

> If we return to multi-party politics, we cannot avoid the fanning of tribalism once again … Therefore, from our past experience on the multi-party system, any sober and honest political analyst will agree that a one-party state is the only political safety device that can keep our nation welded and intact.[8]

As brutal as this sounds, it is essentially the same statement as Lukacs' formulation of the 'un-dialectical concept of the majority', by which he meant the frivolity of who numerically, wins an election in a liberal democratic polity: a statement favouring the one-party state in substance if not in form. The lengths to which Oniororo goes in attacking the Nigerian status quo are remarkable indeed. He bluntly calls Nigeria 'the worst country on earth'.[9] He refutes the Nigerian ruling circle's usual line against genuine democracy, which he identifies as essentially 'Can the rabble govern?' as having been proven the wrong kind of question by the policies of social emancipation in the USSR, Cuba, China and elsewhere.

Oniororo had a love of earthy folk wisdom that is frequently seen in his works. 'Hungry dogs do not want to play with the well-fed ones',[10] 'Nigerians are eaters of other Nigerians',[11] 'Two dogs, one bone'.[12] He exposes the Nigerian condition without shame. 'Bush animals are happier than poor Nigerians', he laments.[13] When he toured university campuses, he was especially outraged by what he saw as the gilded lifestyle and expectations of luxury on the part of the future leaders of Nigeria.

What new knowledge in terms of scientific inventions have our specialists and researchers actually contributed to world knowledge? What we discover is the anxiety and morbid ambition of our intellectuals to be labeled 'professors' and doctors of this or that ... The British molded our educational system to fit their own interest.[14]

While this may be a somewhat unjustified criticism given the vast gap in research opportunities between Westerners and Nigerians, he nevertheless went on to propose ways to tackle the problem at hand, first and foremost by tackling illiteracy, a task at which Marxist-Leninist governments have been famously successful, not only in Russia, China, Eastern Europe and Cuba, but also in West Bengal and Kerala in India, where state governments were communist led. He goes further when he recommends 'that every student should be made a worker, and every worker become a student in this country', reminiscent of ideals promoted during the Cultural Revolution in China.[15]

His description of the conditions in Nigeria goes beyond the university. He claims that everyday criminality is a natural consequence of systemic criminality, of a political economy of 'piracy' as he calls it.[16] The biggest criminals are the *ogas* themselves in the country.[17] Both *juju* men and doctors, according to Oniororo, murder their patients at the behest of wives and children who want to claim their husbands' and fathers' property.[18] People become armed robbers because they have no other options to secure a living, and girls enter into sex work for the same reason.[19] He rejects the idea that Nigeria should be doing fine, as some economists argue, based on GDP growth data but no other indicators: 'Some bourgeois intellectuals who are witch doctors of economic planning will like to argue that our country is not doing badly.'[20] His description of Nigeria's particular kind of peripheral, predatory capitalism is gripping in its forcefulness:

We have witnessed how our people worship money as their gods so much that families of the same blood fight one another for money like wild beasts. We have witnessed how morbid ambition for money has gripped our people. We have seen how our people high and low misuse their positions and abuse the trust which people placed in them because of money. We have seen how the businessmen and businesswomen deliberately create shortages to line their pockets at the expense of the ordinary people. We have seen how bosom friends betray themselves because of money. We have seen how some housewives kill their husbands because of property. And we have watched how girls desert their lovers when the boyfriends can no more supply them with money. We have watched how housewives sell their beautiful bodies to men in order to get money. We have watched how people have to steal or tell lies before they can eat. We have seen how friends make fortune out of the misfortune of their friends because of the power of money. We have also witnessed how fathers and mothers sell their daughters to men in order to get money. We have seen how a few people became rich and powerful at the tremendous cost of groans, sweat, and blood of millions. And we have seen that in this chaotic welter of conflicting interests, only the men and women of 'sterner stuff', the cunning and ruthless ones always succeed, always become the respected and powerful people of this society since they can always use their money to punish the poor without scruples.[21]

In almost biblical tones, Oniororo writes about life and misery in Nigeria in no uncertain terms. Indeed, the themes he mentions are the very ones filling thousands of scripts of Nollywood films, designed to entertain but also serving as safety valves for the Nigerian viewer. Unlike Nollywood, Oniororo does not see poetic justice served in the end: the misery is continuous, and the bad guys win. It is remarkable that Oniororo sees any way out of the Nigerian predicament at all. His suggestions for a new life for Nigeria are clear and straightforward, albeit sometimes shocking. At a time when everyone expected the military to finally give way to a democratically elected civilian government (in 1978), Oniororo expresses doubts whether the civilian government could achieve anything substantially different, given that the change of system, for him, simply meant that the contractors and compradors of earlier times would now capture political power. Surprisingly, Oniororo calls for a new, non-elitist army (a 'people's army') and the inclusion of its members in the new power structures to come.[22] Recalling the role of soldiers in early Soviets, Oniororo also quotes Mao (without citation) when he emphasises how political power originates in the barrel of the gun.[23] He envisages a United Front, complete with unions and women's organisations, soldiers, the unemployed, petty traders and construction brigades,[24] along with agricultural cooperatives,[25] to form the backbone of the new government, instead of bourgeois contractors. He sees, especially given the extremely low level of industrial development in Nigeria, a central role for large farms that would function also as voluntary resettlement centres for the urban unemployed. Generally, he unequivocally embraced scientific socialism,[26] a byword in Africa for an Eastern European political system, as something that could help Nigeria industrialise better, or, indeed, at all, given the economics of oil and its way of crowding out investment in other sectors.[27] He is not repulsed by the way Eastern European schools indoctrinated students, claiming that 'in a sense, every educational system involves indoctrination'[28] – something with which some Eastern Europeans might disagree.

However, his central aim is to industrialise Nigeria, make education compulsory (at the primary and secondary levels) and free at all levels, and provide free medical care, social services and a decent life for all.[29]

His position on Nigerian culture was a remarkable attack on tradition-alism, to an extent that would be viewed by some as racist (not to mention profoundly sexist) in today's multicultural discourse. When delivering a speech on Nigerian culture and what it should be like, he radically distances himself from the understanding of culture as preservation of traditional values and even artistic forms. In his bluntness, he denigrates traditional dance as a practice that 'exposes the beautiful parts of our ladies as part of cultural awareness'.[30]

As far as economic policy and the salary gap between professionals and the average worker goes, he envisages in *Revolution Not Reformism* a fourfold difference between their remunerations – customary in the 'really existing socialisms' of Eastern Europe.[31] After the fall of the USSR, his views on the desirable level of salary differentials changed. In 1993, in his *Why the Nigerian Masses Are Poor,* he advocated a tenfold differential – still a large disparity, of course, from the point of view of equality, but much lower than real differentials in Nigeria at the time.[32] Indeed, even after the fall of the USSR, Oniororo did not become one of those Nigerian revolutionaries who quickly went over to support a particular local communalist stance in the dogfight for resource allocation. Oniororo, when stripped of the USSR as an example, took to quoting the example of the *kibbutzim* in Israel,[33] the Austrian and Norwegian methods of curtailing landlord's rights vis-à-vis tenants,[34] loans for agriculture,[35] re-forestation efforts, and a commitment to make Nigeria self-sufficient in foodstuffs once more.[36] He quoted George Bernard Shaw[37] and not Lenin to explain why the solution would be taxing the rich.[38] Revelations about the Romanian dictator Ceausescu and his golden toilets disgusted him,[39] but he kept on believing that socialism, self-help schemes, farmers' community associations, were the solution, and not neoliberal SAPs. In fact, he chronicles the lamentable effects of SAPs in shocking detail, especially in terms of the rent situation, where SAPs forced Nigerians to live ten people a room,[40] and 100 people per toilet and shower. He also muses on the tricks employed by some Nigerians, who have become beggars in their desperate attempts to get by. 'Big man, live long!', say underpaid policemen and veterans to passers-by, while expecting a coin.[41] People pretend to be deaf and dumb for money. 'The few people who are employed use their wages for hundreds of relations,'[42] a situation that has not changed for the better since then.

Niyi Oniororo did not mince words when it came to Nigerian capitalism. Neither did he shy away from the most vitriolic attack when it came to his own movement, that of Nigerian communists. In his short but aptly titled volume *Who Are the Nigerian Comrades? The Story of Opportunists, Revisionists, Reformists and Careerists in Nigeria*, which appeared in the late 1970s in Ibadan (not dated), Oniororo attacks his comrades as people who cling to the orders of mysterious ambassadors.[43] 'Many Nigerian Comrades are only interested in getting money from the foreign donors for their own purposes. This group of comrades has lost all conscience and sense of patriotism,' writes Oniororo.[44] He describes a subculture of distinctive habits, manias, and even a specific sense of fashion and special dress code. They wear 'long untidy beards'[45] (Otegbeye, Madunagu, Eskor Toyo and Mokwugo Okoye all did or do in fact wear beards) – Okoye had written a book whose title was *The Beard of Prometheus,* featuring on the cover a photograph of the author, bearded and wearing a classical toga, playing at Prometheus *à la Naija.* Comrades, Oniororo goes on, 'are weary in the face'.[46] They wear 'crazy' shabby dresses. 'The word Comrade tickles their fancy. Honestly it sounds romantic.'[47] Indeed, in some cases, one notices that the word 'Comrade' is inserted between people's given name and family name; in Nigeria, everyone seems to love titles and the communist movement has been no exception.

According to Oniororo, comrades argue in such a manner as to indicate that 'the majority are prospective candidates for the asylum'.[48] Their modus operandi involves frequent travels to the USSR and to China. There are, among them, characters identified with fictitious names like Sammy Castro, Lenin of Nigeria, Omo Mao, Dr Fish Monger, Iron Bottom Bass, Comrade Lucky Joe, Barbar, Imo Power and Mao Toyo. In some cases, cracking these codes is easy (Mao Toyo is Eskor Toyo, Barbar is the Trotskyite Edwin Madunagu, Iron Bottom Bass is probably Samuel Ikpeme Bassey, Lenin of Nigeria might be Tunji Otegbeye); in other cases it is more difficult to crack (as in the case of Omo Mao, Dr Fish Monger and Comrade Lucky Joe). He tells a humorous story, in the form of a cabaret drama, featuring the Ambassador (obviously, of the Soviet Union), Lenin of Nigeria, and others. The Nigerians want to gain approval from the Ambassador for their party banners in advance of a strike, and are expecting to be given money in return, for their operational expenses and other purposes.[49] The Ambassador is displeased, as he has heard that Nigerian communists 'sell scholarships that his country offers', an allegation that has been aired against Otegbeye, especially by the general Nigerian press, and by Eskor Toyo and Madunagu within the movement. After much ado, the Ambassador agrees to give them half of the dues 'but when the demonstration is successful, you can come for the balance'.[50] The foreign wine makes them, if at all possible, even more prone to ideological squabbles than before.[51] Lawyer Eddie Cow (perhaps a disguised Gani Fawehinmi) agrees with the other Trotkyists that the Orthodox Marxist-Leninist group 'only steals'.[52] This short booklet is an attack, indeed a rude one, on the shortcomings of Nigerian Marxists and Marxisms.

Despite that, Oniororo remained a committed socialist. A journalist once asked him about the apparent lack of success of the socialist movement in Nigeria. This was his answer:

It is not a thing that you can achieve overnight – I mean socialism. First of all, you have to set the people on proper awareness, that is consciousness, they have to be aware of what is responsible for their problems. For ill health, for the lack of employment, for bad feeding or for bad housing. Make them aware first of all, of the cause of all these problems. There are certain people who are responsible for this … And that is why we are saying even distribution, that is, everyone should take according to his labour and no individual should be able to exploit his fellow human being … Socialism has become a very popular (topic of) discussion in Nigeria today. There was a time, when it was so difficult to bring in socialist pamphlets into Nigeria. But even among the Nigerian top leaders, it is so difficult for them to condemn it today.[53]

That is more than we can say in 2016. Instead of socialism, top leaders advocate ethnicist communalisms, radical Islam and revivalist charismatic Christianity of the most outlandish kind, and they preach a doctrine of privatisation that has not brought any relief to ordinary Nigerians since its inception in the 1990s. Niyi Oniororo died an embittered man, but his work remains of interest today.

Ikenna Nzimiro

Ikenna Nzimiro was a very different character from Oniororo in many ways. He was not the typical left-wing Naija daredevil, but a versatile and subtle man who was first and foremost a talented academic intellectual. Ikenna ('Zeeee') Nzimiro (d. 2006) was politically and academically active from the late 1940s until the turn of the millennium. Nzimiro had two terminal degrees: a Doctor Philosophiae from Cologne, Germany, and a PhD from Cambridge. When his study on the Biafran class conflict appeared, his dedications went to his personal friend Samir Amin, the leading global figure in dependency theory and world systems analysis.[54] He also narrowly escaped death alongside Chinua

Achebe.[55] Ikenna Nzimiro was a Marxist, but a Marxist whose most seminal academic work dealt with the institution of kingship within the riverine subdivisions of the Igbo, an anthropological study that is still used as a reference work today. It seems entirely natural, in his case, that most of the book was based on extensive fieldwork over the course of five years (1960–64), and conducted in the royal palaces of Igboland where he personally knew all the kings. Nigeria's elite 'considered him as one of their own' even as he attacked them.[56] A Zikist fighter in the late 1940s, especially when the movement turned more radical (see chapter 3), Nzimiro repeatedly and publicly attacked President Nnamdi Azikiwe for denouncing the radicals. An Igbo himself by ethnicity, like Mokwugo Okoye and Edwin Ikechukwu Madunagu, Nzimiro opted out of the 'Nigerian Marxist mainstream' in 1967 when he chose to side with Igbo secession and Biafran independence. Although SWAFP's (Socialist Workers' and Farmers' Party of Nigeria) Tunji Otegbeye was incarcerated in connection with the civil war by the federal authorities, that was a plain miscarriage of justice (chapter 4). Mokwugo Okoye's own standing was less than clear, but he never publicly took the Biafran side. Ikenna Nzimiro, however, saw the civil war as a revolution with a clear class content, and took active part in the Biafran mobilisation effort. He survived and was pardoned in Gowon's general amnesty. He then returned mostly to the world of academe, where he kept 'attacking the Eurocentric notion of class' and remained the single most respected academic anthropologist in the country. After his most famous book, *Studies in Ibo Political Systems*, published by University of California Press in 1972, came *Nigerian Civil War: A Study in Class Conflict* (1982), *The Modernization of Hunger* (1985), *My Stand in Oguta Politics* (1992) and *The Babangida Men* (1993). After Nzimiro died, two articles appeared in quick succession in peer-reviewed journals to analyse his intellectual legacy (by Ottenberg and by Uwazurike, respectively).[57]

Studies in Ibo Political Systems was researched at Cambridge and in Igboland, Nigeria, with the financial help of the Federal Ministry of Education, the University of Ibadan, the Eastern Nigerian government, and several Igbo royals. A towering academic achievement that challenged the prevailing view that Igbo societies were historically always acephalous and which proved that in some regions Igbos also had systems of traditional kingship, the tome was nonetheless entirely devoid of Marxist phraseology and content. Judging by this work, Nzimiro would be more aptly described as 'a Marxist and an anthropologist' than as a Marxist anthropologist. Historical materialism, or even broadly materialist interpretations of history, conspicuously do not appear in this volume, so much so that when he describes the resilience of kingship and its associated institutions, he ascribes it to emotional attachment on the part of subjects – a safe and familiar but entirely reactionary line of historical analysis coming from a Marxian author.[58] Interestingly, he seems to have been aware that even in technical terms Western mainstream anthropology was far from value free. Indeed, he describes in minute detail how the British started to employ anthropologists in the aftermath of the 1929 Women's War against the warrant chief system (see chapter 7 for details). Nzimiro reminds us how in the course of the early 1930s, 200 British intelligence reports were written according to specific guidelines developed by government anthropologists in the country,[59] and how the entire late-colonial local government system was based on the findings of those reports. Lest we think Nzimiro, who had spent time in jail for anti-colonial agitation, had any residual naïveté regarding British methods of rule, perhaps this way of introducing his subject matter is indicative of his innermost thoughts on the matter.

Studies in Ibo Political Systems focuses on the Ogbaru people, a subgroup of Igbos, and its six communities, Abo, Onitsha, Osamari, Oguta – leaving out two, Asaba and Aguleri. He finds that in the latter two, titles and age grades combine to form a system of political rule; whereas in other areas such as Nri, title associations and elders combine in a system of acephalous leadership. His own research focuses however on Abo, Onitsha, Osamari and Oguta precisely because they did (and do) have kings, along with titled chiefs, and title associations and age grades. He describes the political organisations of each mini-monarchy, and shows how the king, his officers and office personnel carry out governmental functions in policy-making, adjudication of justice, execution of laws and the defence of the state. In the second part of the volume, he discusses especially the institution of kingship 'as the enduring focus of political values'.[60] He does not discuss the effect of capitalism, and the penetration of modernity into these traditional systems at any point – a great disappointment, as seeds of change might have already been depicted; kings have since mushroomed in Igboland, and this phenomenon cries out for an anthropological study, and perhaps a Marxist one at that. Nzimiro discusses the role of religion, especially the concept of *Chukwu*, or High God, and the traditional economic bases of these societies, especially farming and fishing.[61] Slavery as an institution is dealt with briefly,[62] along with social organisation and especially the role of title societies.[63] Government rituals, regalia and taboos are discussed in minute detail[64] with regard to Onitsha, and mention is made of how women's organisations, powerful in the pre-colonial past to the point of maintaining a quasi-queen parallel to the male-dominated world of government, lost their traditional standing in colonial times. Secret societies and their interrelations with social stratification are also dealt with.[65] With regard to Abo and Oguta, he focuses on local councils and the rules pertaining to war,[66] and he discusses the particular notions of kingship, myths of group origin, praise names, royal insignia, gifts and tributes due to royalty, ritual duties of the kings, festivals, palace organisation, installation rituals,[67] along with seclusion rituals, investiture rituals, oaths,[68] ritual sacrifices and crowning ceremonies,[69] not leaving out the question of what happened to the sacrificed. Indeed, he establishes that, although human sacrifice did occur in the area, cannibalism was unknown and, by the time he visited the region, only 'goats, bullocks and fowl' were sacrificed, along with the generic cola nuts and palm wine. He gives a loving account of leopard-skin royal dresses[70] (magnificent photos are included in the volume), discusses the role of kingmakers and draws from the histories of these dynasties and kingdoms. He painstakingly proves how the principle of primogeniture did not apply in these ancient states.[71]

Nigerian Civil War: A Study in Class Conflict, another work by Nzimiro, paints a very different picture of the author. Published by Frontline Publishing Company in Enugu in 1982, this volume is still available within Nigeria, at the Library of the American University of Nigeria and elsewhere. This tome grew out of the author's personal disappointment with the fall of Biafra. Edited in Nigeria, the volume lacks the meticulous proofreading and the academic arsenal that characterised the *Study in Ibo Political Systems,* but that is partly by design. His work consciously 'avoids textbook quotations, and aims at the common readership'.[72] It is mostly based on Nzimiro's own recollections as a high-ranking Biafran civil servant: he was Chair of the Material Committee in the Directorate for Propaganda, a member of the Political Orientation Committee in the Directorate, a member of Biafra's diplomatic delegation to Eastern European capitals including Moscow, a lecturer at the Propaganda Unit of the Biafran Organisation of Freedom; BOFF).[73] He sums up his role during the civil war: 'I have not denied my role during the war … My ideological persuasions were contradictory to the Biafran ruling class … [My experience] confirmed the Montesquieu dictum that "a regime that is corrupt is always in fear."'[74] He emphasises how his account is not an attempt to incite class antagonisms in any way,[75] but uses class-based analysis as a scientific approach to best understand what happened in and around Biafra. He makes the important claim that Biafran secession was not, as commonly held, an ethnic conflict at its core, but a class conflict within the ruling classes of the first republic (1963–66). Before trying to prove that main thesis, he obviously had to deal with the problem of whether classes, as such, even existed in Africa, Nigeria or Biafra – something that Western liberals and self-styled 'African socialists' questioned at the time. He asserts that classes do exist in Nigeria, appearing as a result of capitalist penetration by multinational corporations (the United Africa Company [UAC], Unilever and so on).[76] He explains in one passage how, before and after independence, multinationals paved the way to a neocolonial class structure:

> Big multinational corporations like the United Africa Company diversified their strong hold on the economy. UAC became an agglomerate of eleven big companies and evolved the following eleven subsidiaries that constitute the UAC group: Kingsway Stores Ltd, department store and supermarket; Kingsway Chemists Ltd, wholesale pharmacy; African Timber and Plywood Production, which deals with exports of logs, saw timber and plywood; UAC Technical Ltd, which deals with agricultural, earthmoving and electrical equipment and construction materials ...[77]

And he gives an account of how UAC, together with Lebanese and Indian capital and a few other firms like Leventis and Gottschalk, essentially ran the entire modern sector of the Nigerian economy according to their own needs and plans. Traditional society was complemented by a new foreign ruling class[78] that in time nurtured its urban African auxiliaries.

Nzimiro especially blames colonialism for preserving and sometimes strengthening the worst, because most inequitable, traditional structures via indirect rule in the North and warrant chiefs in the South. 'The colonial rulers by preserving the traditional structures of these societies, were able to utilise the ethnic nationalities which composed the rural sectors, against each other.'[79] Ethnic groups are obviously never homogeneous, and their imagined homogeneity is at the core a fascist idea. Internal migrations, language swaps and language adoption, intermarriage, make ethnic purity impossible.[80] According to Nzimiro, even the concepts of ethnic majority and minority are nothing but constructs, and dangerous ones.

> The Igbos living along the River Niger and who constitute themselves as the Ogbarus do not share some of the political and social values of some other Igbo groups. The ecological factor of their area has compelled most of them to seek permanent settlement in upland Igbo areas. Among the other Igbos, the Northern Ngwa do not subscribe wholly to the values of the Igbos along the fringes of the Nsukka area, nor do the Igbos found along the Mbaise Owerri complex subscribe wholly to the values of the Igbos found along the Oritsha-Awka axis.

Even the Igbos among the Udi-Enugu-Adani complex do not share wholly the values of the Igbos found among the Umuahia, Uzoakoli complex, so that those who talk of minority in terms of differentiation in language or geographical location do not understand what minority means. For example, a migrant Igbo group in Calabar could be a minority within the Calabar-Efik complex just as a migrant Opobo-Bonny-Azumili-Akwete complex, even though they understand the Ibo language, will constitute minorities within the Aba-Igbo complex. Among the Ibibios, for example, the Efiks who speak the same dialect with the Ibibios could constitute a minority within the Ibibio-Efik complex just as a migrant Ibibio in Calabar town could constitute a minority in the Calabar complex. We can stretch this argument to anywhere in Nigeria. As a further example, in the Ogoja complex where even though the chauvinistic politicians classify them as minorities within the large Nigerian complex, there are also minority groups within this Ogoja complex.[81]

Ethnocentric ideas follow from 'minority chauvinisms' according to Nzimiro, fanned by the colonial administration and by post-independence Nigerian bourgeois politicians. His basic argument is that although genocide was indeed committed against the Igbos in the Hausa ethnic core area, this was not, contrary to established opinion up to this day, an inter-ethnic genocide committed by the Hausa on the Igbos, but a very different phenomenon. He explains the fallacy of the ethnic line of argument thus:

> None of those (university professors and intellectuals) who sat at Enugu (the Igbo heartland) and wrote the volumes explaining the reasons why secession believed that classes exist. They believed that all were one harmonious group; that ethnicity was the dominant factor and not class, and as such they could not understand the inner contradictions of society and the class phenomena underlying them. To them genocide was committed against Easterners by the Hausas, without drawing clearly the class phenomenon underlying the actions of the Hausa-Fulani ruling nobility, the rising bourgeoisie from this nobility, the higher civil servants and petty bourgeois university students at Ahmadu Bello University, all of whom were in control of the urban and rural proletariat in the Northern cities and who used the unemployed lumpen-proletariat that served as thugs for the NPC [Northern People's Congress] bourgeois cum feudal oligarchies to commit murder and arson. Where even they identified this class in the North, they did not believe that it existed in Biafra.[82]

Biafra was thus understood as a revolution – not as a proletarian one, obviously, but a revolution that ultimately served the interests of the Biafran ruling class.[83]

According to Nzimiro, ethnic politics was launched by Egbe Omo Oduduwa in the Yoruba areas and Igbo ethnic communities, but acquired a vicious character, especially following Azikiwe's betrayal of the radicals, and his way of manipulating ethnic allegiances in elections. He finds the British guilty for the compartmentalisation of Nigeria along ethnic majority lines prior to independence, and suggests that a South Asian-style partition could well have happened in the country upon independence.[84] In terms of the overall class structure in Nigeria, Nzimiro's classification differs from subsequent ones (like Usman Tar's) that equate the comprador bourgeoisie with a petty bourgeoisie. Nzimiro's grand bourgeoisie in Nigeria is, simply, comprador in nature, as he finds no local bourgeoisie that is characterised by its place in actual production.[85] The proletariat, he allows, is small. The lumpenproletariat, however, is a class that has a very marked role in Nigeria.

> These youths who leave schools in large numbers, and who cannot advance their education further, nor acquire the necessary skills to be of use to the community, fall prey to ... exploitation in the urban towns and they become drug peddlers, organized into groups engaged in stealing, and all sorts of crimes. The girls become prostitutes. The capitalist mode of production has its own ethical values. Since the acquisition of property for the individuals takes prominence over the acquisition of property for the use of the millions, the propensity to commit crimes in order to own is more intense. Hence corruption becomes an ethical value of the capitalist system ... The mass of urban youths, faced with the difficulties of life, become compelled to commit crimes against the property of the exploiting and parasitic class ... In Nigeria the lumpen-proletariat supplied the thugs for the political rulers of the first republic.[86]

Interestingly, Nzimiro claims that Biafran secession initially had revolutionary potential. He identifies Marxists in Ironsi's group of officers in 1966.[87] He points especially to the Biafran Organisation of Freedom Fighters, the Propaganda Directorate,[88] the Political Enlightenment Committee[89] and the Political Orientation Committee[90] as representatives of Biafran officialdom that resonated with Marxist ideologies. He quotes Mao and refers to Fidel Castro, Ho Chi Minh and Che Guevara as sources of inspiration for Biafran Marxists especially after it became clear that the USSR would back federal forces, a great disappointment.[91]

When the Biafran Organisation of Freedom Fighters was pushed into the regular Biafran army *en masse*, it meant for Nzimiro that the nucleus of a possibly revolutionary fighting force was diluted in a bourgeois army's structures, a tragic phenomenon, especially as that army soon deteriorated into an occupying force preying on ordinary Biafrans.[92] There was initially in Biafra a strong Trade Union Congress.[93] However, Ojukwu soon started placing the entire burden of the war on the poor,[94] confiscated the best villas to house high-ranking civilians and army officers every time the front retreated, and let contractors engage in the worst kind of wartime profiteering instead of a planned war economy based on cooperatives.[95] He employed Marxists to search for 'a Biafran ideology', especially in the Political Orientation Committee,[96] but used them as a propaganda machine, not as advisers who could influence real decisions that affected people's lives in Biafra. Ojukwu's lofty Ahiara Declaration was only the last in the long list of Marxian, socialist-leaning Biafran documents that were full of exhortations about the values of socialism and cooperation, but devoid of any tangible effect.[97] Right before the end, there was even an anti-socialist witch-hunt in Biafra,[98] while common people suffered and dubbed Biafra '*bia afufu*' (literally: to suffer, in Igbo).[99] This is very easy to understand if we remember that between 1 and 2 million people perished in the Biafran war, and many more lost their health, savings and property. Nzimiro attempts to explain Biafra's social failures by tracing them to the weaknesses of Nigerian socialist movements.[100]

Nzimiro's *Nigerian Civil War* is an attempt at soul-searching, and a very honest account of his own personal involvement. Though he thanks Gowon for amnesty,[101] he never repudiates the concept that Biafra had right on its side in the war.[102] Ethnicity is clearly a central issue in Nigeria even today, and anti-Igbo atrocities are again happening in the North on a weekly basis. After 1989, many Marxist thinkers in Nigeria would champion micro-nationalist (ethnic) causes. This had happened in the late 1950s–early 1960s in the case of the Middle Belt Tiv ethnic group that gave many foot soldiers to Marxist causes. However, after 1989, some emblematic figures of Nigerian Marxism became vocal, intolerant ethnic chauvinists. Yusufu Bala Usman, the PRP's (People's Redemption Party) ideologue and Chinua Achebe's erstwhile comrade, became a Hausa-Fulani ethnic chauvinist who aired views that came dangerously close to fascism. Bala Usman's politics might have changed due to advanced age (his worst tirades came in the 2000s), but Otegbeye also joined a feudalist ethnocentric group (the Yoruba Council of Elders), while Ola Oni and others also championed ethnic causes. Exceptions include the PRP itself, Madunagu and his Calabar group, Gramscians

such as Usman Tar and, not surprisingly, some Marxian feminists such
as Amina Mama, Ogundipe-Leslie and Bene Madunagu. Nigerian
radicalism was born with an ethos that transcended ethnic divisions and
that recognised its evils as early as the days of the Zikist movement. In
the late 1960s and 1970s, prominent socialist figures including Otegbeye
believed that ethnicity was a problem that would disappear once the
dictatorship of the proletariat was established. As with women's liberation,
this signalled at best a failure of analysis on the part of SWAFP leaders
and others, and planted the seed of renewed inter-ethnic animosities that
reappeared with a vengeance, much like in Eastern Europe.

Yusufu Bala Usman

Yusufu Bala Usman (1945–2005), or Bala as he was called by friends,[103]
was again a very different sort of man from both Oniororo and Nzimiro.
A professional historian, Bala Usman was a big-boned Northerner,
of Fulani aristocratic stock from Musawa, Katsina; his privileged
background is clear from the fact that his birth date is known (which
was not nearly universal in his time, or even now, in Nigeria). His was
the figure of a public intellectual, activist and political adviser in the case
of Kaduna state, where he helped bring about a change in the feudal
tax system, triggering violent clashes with many deaths (see chapter
4). Bala Usman's works reveal a deeply personal project aimed against
an imperialism that he hated at a visceral, indeed sometimes even
disturbingly personal level in the vein of Edward Said. In Yusufu Bala
Usman, impeccable upper-class British English and a defiantly elegant
prose go hand in hand with an expressed disdain for maintaining the
colonial heritage in any form. Usman wants to purge the Westerner, or
rather, purge the colonial subject from the Nigerian psyche, including
his own, even if it involves a certain sense of self-effacement. He claimed
that the use of English was a source of confusion in the country, and
dismissed curricula as irrelevant to Nigerian needs. English-language
instruction in Nigeria effectively means an immersion in English
values.[104] Language, after all, imposes reality.[105] He says of English
culture: 'What is there to gain from the detailed study of a culture world
famous for insularity, extremely ethno-centric, elitist and narcissistic?'[106]
He goes so far as to attack the educational focus on Shakespeare and
Milton,[107] not because he disagrees with the notion of their greatness
but because learning about them constitutes for him 'immersion' in an
alien culture; something that should happen only after absorbing one's
own. He claims that neocolonial dependency can only be fought by a
thorough change: 'The Nigerianization of the economy [is] impossible

without the Nigerianization of knowledge.'[108] Ironically, Bala Usman, who was educated partly in the UK, wrote and published approximately 90 per cent of his works in English (and some minor articles in Hausa). (The second language of most Nigerians is not English but Yoruba,[109] a language that still carries connotations of elitism.)[110] The crux of his position was that by neocolonial methods, the US and the UK sucked Nigeria dry of resources: indeed, in his words, 'It is our countries that give aid to the West and not vice versa.'[111] He was most unimpressed with Anglo-Saxon liberalism and its intellectual or practical merits:

> It is a repetition of that inane notion of Anglo-Saxon liberalism that arbitrary government only arises where the judiciary is not independent, where there is no habeas corpus and all the elaborate machinery of the English judicial system – the type of machinery Alec Douglas-Home is busy planning to set up in Rhodesia to 'protect' the Africans from Smith and his gang of white settlers! In fact there is arbitrary government, not only in Africa, but even in countries where the habeas corpus and all that jazz exists, where a strong and pervasive system of social and economic repression keeps the masses of the people in their place so well that serious problems of human survival and dignity never even approach the courts or even get articulated by the victims. Arbitrary government has been perfected in the corporate liberal states of the West, like Britain and America, where the real manipulators are hidden, their existence denied but where even the natural sexual needs and desires of people are used to control and repress them. A term 'repressive tolerance' is used by some people, victims of this system, to describe some of its features; it is a system in relation to which old myths like the division of powers, the independence of the judiciary, are completely irrelevant.[112]

Usman was deeply influenced by Frantz Fanon, whom he repeatedly quotes as he extols the virtues of self-reliance at the commanding heights of the Nigerian economy, and advocates for an end to practices that complement Western global economic structures.[113] He also advocated nationalising oil companies and other British and American assets on the basis of those powers siding with the enemy in South Africa – especially when it came to armaments shipments and other concrete forms of help.[114] He wanted Africans to define the African; not Western anthropologists, and not foreign economic structures.[115]

In Balarabe Musa's words: 'Sometimes, [Usman's] tenacity for excellence, hard work and thoroughness made him appear bullish, intolerant and overbearing to many. His frequent clashes with political "enemies" tended to make him easily too suspicious of other people's motives. He was also one who never suffered fools gladly.'[116] Especially after 1999 when Usman left the PRP, his attacks on his perceived political enemies grew more and more brutal, and took a disturbing turn towards ethnicist clichés. There is little indication of this in his earlier writing, where he continuously attacked ethnic chauvinisms and religious separatisms as divisive and reactionary. His late articles show us a man who had lost all hope for decency, emancipation and rational dialogue, instead attacking 'Yoruba conspiracies' and perceived Igbo schemes. He referred to himself as a Marxist in the past tense in a conversation with William Hansen, an expatriate Marxist intellectual in Nigeria, just prior to his death. The kind of Hausa-Fulani supremacist views that appear in his later newspaper articles and speeches read as if his entire personality were shattered by the shock of 1989, and as if his good judgement had left him prior to his untimely passing.

Before he became what he had always loathed, Bala Usman was one of the most prolific authors on the Nigerian intellectual scene. He authored *The Transformation of Katsina 1400-1883: The Emergence and Overthrow of the Sarauta System and the Establishment of the Emirate* (1981) – an enhanced version of his PhD; *For the Liberation of Nigeria* (1979), *The Nigerian Economic Crisis: Causes and Solutions* (1985); *Nigeria Against the IMF: The Home Market Strategy* (1986); *The Manipulation of Religion in Nigeria* (1987); and his essays were posthumously collected in *Corruption in Nigeria* (2008), published by the Centre for Democratic Development and Training. He edited the massive *Studies in the History of the Sokoto Caliphate* (1979), *Cities of the Savannah* (1979), *Studies in the History of Pre-Colonial Borno* (1983), *The Economic and Social Development of Nigeria* (1983), and wrote the Foreword for Alkasum Abba's *The Misrepresentation of Nigeria* (no date, probably post-2000) that was published by Ceddert Publications.

His works are difficult to come by, and this is troubling, as Usman was perhaps the single most important author on the *problematique* of religion in Nigeria, especially as it relates to the North.

In *The Manipulation of Religion in Nigeria*, Bala Usman attacked the view that religious riots, inter-religious atrocities, religious extremism, the sharia issue or the Maitatsine cult (the early 1980s near-equivalent of today's Boko Haram) are rooted in Islam as such. 'To reduce these violent political campaigns built around religious differences to irrational outbursts by irrational forces is to become a victim of the psychological aspect of the campaign, one of whose purposes is to engender and entrench irrational fears and reflexes.'[117] It is easy for some to fall for the reductionist logic of 'Muslim barbarity' while witnessing abductions, church bombings, suicide attacks and the general march of extremism in a country, such as in post-2012 north-eastern Nigeria. Soothing in its simplicity, if one happens to be a Nigerian Christian or a visible expatriate, the reductionist anti-Islamic argument explains nothing substantial about why these problems persist or get worse in the country. Bala Usman stressed that reliable information about the actual life and teachings of Maitatsine had been deliberately suppressed by panels of official inquiry. In Usman's words, 'Reliable information about Maitatsine before 1980 is so sketchy, and where it is specific, so contradictory, that one can legitimately wonder whether he actually existed; and if he existed, whether he had anything to do with the uprising.'[118] Maitatsine's country of origin was debated (Cameroon and Nigeria were the possibilities),[119] his role in the uprising undefined, and even his teachings on the Qur'an. The tribunal investigating his role established that he declared himself a prophet and preached against accepting the central role of Muhammad and the Sunna,[120] hardly something we would expect from a supposedly Sunni Muslim fundamentalist. He appeared to have lived on *almajiri* alms (donations from his students), but beyond his ban on Western clothing, and on riding the bicycle and motorbike, the panel did not even attempt a systematic examination of his thought. Maitatsine apparently stirred up Muslim youth in Kano, Bulunkutu, Yola, Kaduna and elsewhere, and it took more than five years for the authorities to root out his uprising. But where did it come from? What were its aims? It is well known that finding reliable facts on any matter in Nigeria is a very difficult task, sometimes bordering on the impossible. But the lack of significant information in cases like these is troubling in many ways. Goodluck Jonathan admitted to the public in summer 2013 that he had no idea whether Abubakar Shekau, the leader of the Boko Haram insurgency, was dead or alive. The professed aims and goals of the Boko Haram insurgency (turning all of Nigeria into a sharia state) make little sense; its home state, Borno, has been a sharia state for a decade, and Boko Haram has not ventured into Southern Nigeria. Yusufu Bala Usman's point about the Maitatsine is that its real roots lie in political manipulation and that through it, segments of the Northern elite aimed to entrench their own positions. Lines of argument like these are very common in the Nigerian press and public opinion, and it is important to see how Bala Usman's position differs from conspiracy theory. He identifies the Kaduna mafia,[121] the most important grouping behind the push for sharia legislation, and the inclusion of Nigeria in the Organisation of the Islamic Conference, as divisive for the country. Sir Abubakar Gummi, the Grand Kadi of the North, who had received the King Faisal Prize from Saudi Arabia for proselytising the Saudi brand of Islam, is another of Bala Usman's culprits.[122] Feudal circles, so useful to the British but so central in independent Nigeria, are clearly at the heart of the matter for him,[123] along with the gatekeeper-bureaucratic bourgeoisie. Bala Usman explains how manipulation itself is achieved, beyond the hiring of thugs. A 'sordid circle of non-debate' is maintained, of assertions, threats, then pious pleas for understanding, then again assertions, threats and so on[124] through the media.

He is particularly focused on refuting the concept that the core of the problem is 'the ethnic competition for scarce resources by modernizing elites' in multi-ethnic Third World countries such as Nigeria. First of all, resources are not scarce in Nigeria, he reminds us; the country's elites, far from modernising, are predatory, and in general 'private greed is rationalized in smooth American social science jargon'.[125] Nigeria is a petro-state and Usman's point that it is 'not the resource that is scarce but its utilization, cooperation and collusion'[126] rings very true in a country where today four refineries stand idle because re-export allows higher profit margins for a small circle of unscrupulous, anti-social billionaires. He sees, of course, other explanations for inter-religious violence, such as the racist logic that denies full humanity to black people in the first place,[127] or the developmentalist view according to which economic prosperity will, in time, alleviate these conflicts. He does not waste much time refuting the first, but gives free rein to his sarcasm when attacking the second, pointing to Ireland, Belgium, the racial problem in the United States, and other examples that swiftly disprove it.[128] For Usman, at the heart of manipulation lies the main beneficiary of the status quo – the Nigerian comprador bourgeoisie:

This class is created to serve as the link and intermediary between the people and the wealth of Nigeria and the international capitalist system. It is created to serve as the leading agent of the trading post which has been and still is Nigeria. It can only continue to be dominant if Nigeria remains a trading post; that is a trading post, built to export raw materials and import manufactured goods and services; a trading post where ownership and consumption and *not* production are dominant in the whole system. What I want to get across is that an intermediary bourgeois whether a contractor, financier, bureaucrat, academic, landlord, owner of assembly plants, or transporter lives by appropriating goods and values for consumption which he has no role in creating. He is a broker, a middle man, socially, economically and culturally! He embodies the domination of appropriation over creation; consumption over production. Far from contributing to the creation of material goods, services, or even functioning social and political values and structures, he survives on shortages and blockages in production just as in communication and understanding. He is the quintessential gateman! This is true of the sleek fat cats as it is of the lean cat trying to get fat.

Can this sort of person come out and frankly ask the people to follow him for what he is? So that he can take a piece of paper from one bank to another, from one factory to another, and make millions? What I mean is that the intermediary bourgeois will cease to exist once people can see clearly what his true nature is. Can anybody come out and say 'vote for me so that I can get contracts and build foreign bank accounts and houses with my foreign partners'? Or 'follow me and listen to me so that I can get a plot at Ikoyi or Bompai and get a directorship and shares in UAC or Leventis'? Or, 'follow me so that I can get a big job and you can derive the satisfaction that, although you do not have one square meal a day and your daughter is deformed by and dying of chronic malaria, I am eating dinner costing N15.00 at Federal Palace Suites Hotel on your behalf and that of others in our tribe and religion'? Can anybody come out and say that? No! That is why this class has to obscure its true role and function in our political economy. You cannot stand and win election, even if the electoral college is only two dozen councilors, on the platform that you want to own houses in Ikoyi or London.

What I am getting at is that the intermediary bourgeois cannot appear as what he really is in the political economy of Nigeria. He has to find a cover. He cannot claim political leadership openly on the grounds that he is, or wants to be, an exporter-importer, a contractor, commission agent, shareholder, rentier or rich bureaucrat. He has to take cover as a Muslim or Christian. He has to posture as a 'majority' or a 'minority'. The manipulation of religion in Nigeria today is essentially a means of creating the context for this fancy-dress ball, for this charade of disguises. This game of masks![129]

This passage recalls the Lukacsian dictum that Marxism is primarily a method, and here Usman uses that method with exceptional force and convincing power.

For Bala Usman, the same hidden reason is also behind the introduction of a subtle form of ethnocentric racism that came with state indigeneity and the special political and economic rights it brings, as it was introduced by the 1979 constitution.[130] This was the reason why the constitution only forbade the 'adoption of one religion by the federal republic', but not the 'association' with it, as Bala Usman had wished when he was among the reviewers of the draft version.[131] This is why Article

11 provides that 'every citizen should have equality of rights, rights and obligations and opportunities before the law as long as it does not invalidate a rule of Islamic law or customary law' (!),[132] a non-justiciable provision but a provision that had, even then, laid the foundations for what happened after 1999 when almost every Northern state embraced a Saudi-inspired interpretation of sharia in Nigeria. The solution to this conundrum in Nigeria, according to Usman, would be a uniform land tenure system in the countryside on the basis of peasant emancipation (giving the land to those who work it), and an industrialisation drive focusing on production instead of arbitrage.

The most discomforting element in Bala Usman's works, from a Marxian point of view, is his habitual lack of internationalism. This historian who wrote about, and had personal roots in, the exclusivist Fulani aristocratic tradition, could not seem to accept the idea of genuine solidarity and equality that spans across continents. In his later years, this trait worsened considerably, but even in his bona fide Marxist works from the late 1970s and 1980s, we do not find a single utterance underlining the importance of solidarity with, say, striking British workers, the plight of Chinese peasants, or any other non-African social problem. This intellectual and political limitation was incompatible with Marxism's openness and compassion and, together with the shock of 1989, might help to explain Usman's eventual retreat into Hausa-Fulani ethnic communalism, and especially anti-Yoruba agitation. This might have contributed to his popularity in his native region, but at the cost of eventually losing his intellectual coherence.

Bala Usman's normative political thought, including his answers to the classical question of 'What is to be done?' was most clearly elaborated in his *For the Liberation of Nigeria*. The book sold thousands of copies even in the South of the country, and was a very influential text for the PRP's actual policy decisions in Kano and Kaduna. The text is a collection of articles, treatises, speeches, lectures and political pamphlets focusing on five broad themes: the fundamental problems of contemporary Nigeria, the direction of Nigeria, Nigeria's African policy, Nigerian academe, and apartheid plus frontline states in Southern Africa. In his words, the book is 'about the liberation of the people of Nigeria from Western imperialist domination at the national and continental levels'. It attacks neocolonialism with the conviction of someone who spent his life examining primary sources, that is, the professional historian. His treatment of African history is perhaps as sweeping as Marx's or Morgenthau's of Western (and partly Asian) histories. This makes it challenging to read the text without at least a working knowledge of the specifics of Nigerian history. He does not often care to explain to the reader the facts of what Zikism was, or what the Agbekoya revolts were, but jumps to historical analysis.[133] His intended audience is thus the well-read Nigerian intellectual at home and abroad (the book sold in the UK as well as Nigeria). Bala Usman, a fiery man of action, warned in this work against the neglect of theory. In an exceptionally succinct observation striking for its originality, he writes that 'If we sink … into the morass of the cult of the practical … we shall only remain slaves to the ideas and concepts of others.'[134] He explains why the cult of the practical is so widespread in Nigeria:

> In this country the dominant groups, in the civil service, among businessmen and in the armed forces, are disdainful of definitions, concepts and theory. Even in the institutions of learning like the universities, the cult of the routine, and of the 'practical' is widespread, reflecting the role of some of our colleagues as paid spokesmen of bureaucratic and capitalist vested interests.[135]

In short, the practical mindset helps the gatekeeper, the comprador bourgeoisie. As a historian, he sees the value of providing examples to illustrate his point. At a certain juncture in the 1970s, bureaucratic inefficiency (a mild way of stating the fact that bureaucrats rarely bothered to show up at work) was thought to be tackled by increasing the perks of office. The reasoning went that bureaucrats are rational and if they are more generously rewarded, they will have less reason to be corrupt. The so-called 'Udoji awards' in question went to bureaucrats, teachers and doctors. Bala Usman explained in articles how in Nigeria this would not get the intended results, as what is lacking is not practicality but the ethos of public service. 'Reducing somebody who teaches his brothers and sisters, or sees to their health, safety and well-being to the same level as one who sells toothpaste or cigarettes for Unilever and BATs – aligning the public and the private sector, is to subvert the very essence of public service.'[136] (When the army finally had enough of the politicians and launched a *coup d'état*, they revoked the Udoji awards because by then they had recognised their futility.)

'Practical wisdom' is not only faulty from a theoretical point of view, opines Usman, but it does not deliver results either. He also delves into the futility of focusing on the form of government in Nigeria, military or civilian. 'If we look beyond the superficiality of legal form, we can see that the main pillar of state power anywhere in the world is the armed forces,'[137] well illustrated by what had happened to Allende in Chile years before.

Describing the political economy of oil in Nigeria, he follows Schatzl in the argument that the Nigerian oil industry was developed 20 years after oil was found because the global oil companies deliberately kept it as a source in reserve – detrimental to Nigeria but suiting their own purposes well.[138] 'Monkey de work and baboon de chop' he quotes the pidgin saying regarding the domestic and international division – not of labour but of labour and profits! He also attacks the notion that multinational corporations are really multinational, as their ownership structure is obviously Western:

> The transnationals far from increasing or enhancing productivity in the satellite countries limit it seriously through three major ways: a) Use of capital-intensive methods; leaving a larger and larger sector of the population unemployed; b) Creating tastes and attitudes which commit the population to their products, especially wasteful luxury consumer goods; c) By draining away the wealth which would be used for productive investment, in legal and illegal ways. The tastes of the ruling class in European goods, holidays, etc. is one of the major ways of doing this. The transnationals are opposed to democracy. This is clear.[139]

Usman stood for outright confiscation of ill-gotten wealth,[140] something that Murtala Muhammad was murdered for trying to do.[141] Usman felt that Murtala was a martyr, and remembered his execution-style assassination thus:

> It was not madness, as some people say. Murtala's killers, and the forces they represent wanted to totally negate, destroy and eliminate not just his life but his understanding of Nigerian society, his courage, his commitment and his spirit. The forces of imperialism and Nigerian reactionaries, whom these killers represent, expressed their ferocity towards what Murtala represents and stands for in the way they shattered his body with bullets. There is nothing peculiar about this. Patrice Lumumba, another hero and martyr of our people, was also, like Murtala, not just killed. His body was dissolved into a tank of concentrated sulphuric acid. Eduardo Chivambo Mondlane was not just killed; his body was blown to shreds, into tiny fragments of flesh and bone. Che Guevara, on another continent but standing for the same cause of the oppressed and exploited masses, was also not just killed; his body was burnt to ashes in a high intensity furnace and some people say the ashes were burnt into gases. What they have done to Murtala, Lumumba, Mondlane and Che, they have done and are doing to many others, not because of madness but out of ferocious

hatred and basically the fear of a conception, of a commitment and action based on these.[142]

His proposal for a political economy that would suit Nigeria goes thus: cooperatives were to be set up in the rural countryside, along with state-financed urban housing schemes and a tenure law that protected the rights of tenants: these steps were, according to Usman, the first in the line of political change. Importantly, his argument did *not* entail that a one-party political system, 'the dictatorship of the proletariat' or setting up a vanguard party were crucial. Indeed, Bala Usman was anything but subservient to the Soviet understanding of 'scientific socialism' in his works. But he focused on criticising the West and not the Soviet Union or the People's Republic of China:

> In any case if the Soviets and China were to vanish today, it will not change by an iota the educational system of Nigeria or the nature of our economy. They will remain substantially dominated by the Anglo-Americans. So why should I criticize the Russian policy towards the kulaks? Just to get a pat on the back as a neutral?[143]

Bala Usman had no connections to the SWAFP-dominated Soviet continuum in the country. He was active in the PRP and he was also a trustee of the Nigerian Labour Congress,[144] along with his other roles such as on Murtala Muhammad's Committee for Nigeria's Foreign Policy, the Constitution Drafting Committee, the 1976 Nigerian Delegation to the People's Republic of Angola, Special Adviser to the Nigerian Delegation at the UN General Assembly twice, secretary of the Kaduna State Government (PRP) 1979–82, and various other foreign policy and domestic roles.

He constantly advocated for a radical foreign policy orientation, based on the confiscation and nationalisation of Western assets in the country, and solidarity with anti-apartheid and radical causes across Africa. He disdained the so-called 'moderate' foreign policy stance of consecutive Nigerian administrations, with the significant exception of Murtala Muhammad. ('Moderate', of course, often indicating little more than an alliance with the West, even in the case of a religiously extremist regime such as Saudi Arabia.) Usman felt that Nigeria after independence underwent a deeper satellisation than even under formal colonial rule.[145] On the larger African scene, his characterisation of the US stance on apartheid ('The US view is that apartheid is evil because the blacks cannot be made to accept it')[146] reveals a deep concern for the limitations of the US focus on formal democracy. His attacks on the

Nigerian academy also grew out of his desire for genuine independence. Education did not mean only the transfer of technical skills, but also planted in students a particular *Weltanschauung*.[147]

Mokwugo Okoye

Mokwugo Okoye (1926–98) is still a well-known man in Nigeria, and his obituary in *The New York Times* indicated that there was at least some awareness abroad of his role in the Nigerian independence movement (though not his role as a Marxist).[148] Memorial lectures honour his name at home, poems are still written as homage to him, and there is a website and a Facebook page dedicated to him even today. There has been at least one PhD thesis written on his thought.[149] His books, published from the mid 1950s to the 1980s, can still be found second-hand. He is the only Nigerian Marxist thinker included in a compendium on African Philosophy,[150] with his argument that Christian churches spread hypocrisy, 'making rogues of honest men'.

A principal concern for Okoye was to stay honest, as a man and as a thinker, against all odds. A hero of the independence movement in the 1950s who sat in jail for 33 months on charges of sedition, he held posts as a journalist in the broadcasting service in independent Nigeria and was an Officer of the Federal Republic of Nigeria in 1965. That he was honest and took no bribes was evidenced by the fact that he was still driving a Peugeot 403 round Enugu in the 1990s.[151] Edwin Madunagu, in his *For Our Departed Radical Patriots*, recounts how Okoye lived in financial need in the 1990s. He was thrown out of the NCNC (National Convention of Nigerian Citizens) by Azikiwe in 1955 (readmitted in 1957), but he kept his political role to a minimum, addressing the holders of political power instead via his books and pamphlets and journalism. In 1994, he teamed up with fellow independence era fighter Anthony Enahoro to launch the Movement for National Reformation, right after Sani Abacha, the most murderous of all Nigerian dictators, seized power.

Okoye's personal example, warm heart and social conscience were striking. He travelled widely in Western Europe, Eastern Europe and developing countries, but he was never tempted to stay abroad, not even to pursue a scholarship or a full-time education. Remarkably, Okoye did not even have a formal post-secondary education, but he completed a correspondence course with a college in Britain, and later he wrote so many volumes of essays that, in 1986, he received a PhD, *honoris causa*, for his literary endeavours. His wife Ifeoma Okoye is also a well-known intellectual in Nigeria, an emeritus professor of English, and an author of many children's books and novels (most recently *The Fourth World*).

Mokwugo Okoye's many volumes include *Some Facts and Fancies, African Cameos, Fullness of Freedom, Some Men and Women, Vistas of Life: A Survey of Views and Visons, The Rebel Line, Against Tribe, African Responses: A Revaluation of History and Culture, People and Places, Storms on the Niger: A Story of Nigeria's Struggle, The Beard of Prometheus, The Growth of Nations, A Letter to Dr Nnamdi Azikiwe, Points of Discord, Sketches in the Sun* and *Embattled Men*. Most of these are heavy tomes, several surpassing the 400-page mark. Indeed, Edwin Madunagu comments on Okoye's voluminous writing and 'quotism' in *Departed*. In all these works, with the partial exception of *A Letter to Nnamdi Azikiwe* (written as an open letter with a political purpose), the style is free-floating, open-ended prose, more in the tradition of French and Russian essay writing than the British one. He revelled in the riches of book culture; he was the most erudite Nigerian Marxist author, with unparalleled depth and breadth of reading. His style is that of a belletrist, not a professional philosopher, and he was not afraid to use arguments, direct quotes and points taken freely from hundreds, if not thousands, of thinkers. He mentions in one single page of Ghanaian proverbs, Gertrude Stein, the Soviet Africanist Potekhin, his favourite Chinese belletrist Lin Yu-tang, Czechoslovak president Masaryk, Stalin, Dante, Trotsky, Kossuth, and even Hitler, along with Anglo-Saxon liberals, conservatives, and figures in art and culture. He read Sartre, Camus, Jung, Tolstoy, Marx, Lenin, Ho Chi Minh and Machiavelli with equal gusto. A fellow Igbo, he is similar to Edwin Madunagu in his admiration for books.

He lectured briefly at the Lagos School of Political and Social Studies in the early 1960s,[152] and was made governor of the Nigerian Broadcasting Corporation and later the East-Central State Broadcasting Service.[153] Even Azikiwe, who outmanoeuvred him in the 1940s and mid 1950s politically, and to whom Okoye, in return, addressed his scathing *Letter to Dr Nnamdi Azikiwe*, must have retained a measure of respect for him, as he later wrote, as the president of the country, a foreword to Okoye's *African Responses*. The new Nigerian elite paid him homage, but they were annoyed by him in equal measure. He also had an important influence on fighters for ecological rights in the delta. Che Ibama Ibewura, founder of the Aklaka Project, listed Okoye as the single most important living influence on his political agitation for the rights of delta peoples.[154]

It is prudent to start a discussion of Okoye's works with those that expressed a more directly political goal. *A Letter to Dr Nnamdi Azikiwe*, 'a classic of radical thinking' for Madunagu,[155] is a thin book that contains the entire original open letter that was composed in 1955, as a reaction to Okoye's ousting from Azikiwe's NCNC. It also contains a short historical introduction to the Zikist movement, and a poem. The letter was written immediately after Okoye was ejected from the main Nigerian force for national independence, his intellectual and political home. It was written with the determination of a man who, having served a 33-month jail sentence for sedition as the secretary-general of the Zikist movement, had a claim to a leading role in the independence movement. Okoye was already embittered that the independence movement did not make the release of political prisoners a precondition of participating in the new government in 1952, as had happened in India and Ghana.[156] He saw his intra-party trial in 1954 as an anti-leftist purge orchestrated by Azikiwe to please his friends at the Moral Rearmament Movement and in the UK and US governments. The tone of the letter is harsh:

I rarely read your journals these days: hackneyed, long familiar sophistries and rhetorical phrases devoid of positiveness and direction, flat witticisms or calumniations, songs of praise to your genius and of the bureaucracy you head – all this has become too commonplace and boring for one who is desirous of moving forward with the world. You may not realize it, but nationalism is no longer enough in the modern world of independence and social welfare and may in fact be a cover for atavism or swindle. What we want today is a vital social ideal for which to live and labour and a mechanism that will ensure the equitable distribution of the fruits of our labour. The younger generation has long outstripped you by a decade in the understanding of facts and events and has lost faith in you who will go down in history as one who lost his fort to secure his position. Of all Nigerian leaders, you only commanded the necessary loyalty, reputation and admiration to mobilize our people for a wholesale war against the forces that enchain them – the forces of feudalism and capitalist-imperialism – but the young men who over the years rushed to the call of your trumpet came away frustrated because you betrayed them. Instead of honest and capable men you have chosen crooks and genuflecting mediocrities to try to translate our dreams into reality – you have confessed to a parliamentary party meeting that you would rather work with 'sticks' (dullards) who would be loyal to you than with the best brains who would not – and though you sometimes pay lip service to the romanticism of youth, it is the cold realism of demagogues who trade on your name with their flashy cars, cheques, and connections, that count with you now. Clogged by careerists and crooks, is it any wonder that you have trodden the path of cautious mediocrity rather than that of a revolutionary leader?[157]

He would later call Azikiwe a revolutionary playboy in *Sketches in the Sun*.

The *Letter* opens thus:

> Dear Dr Azikiwe, I am obliged to address you openly since you have barred, by your latest Stalinist purge, the conventional channels of communication between us, and I am happy to do so on this first anniversary of my suspension from the party executive. True heresy is not the pride of a saint or superman but a comrade's voice helping others, and in this letter I shall essay to analyse some of the fundamental issues that have divided the reactionary from the radical in our Party [the NCNC] and country.[158]

The *Letter* was a success: Okoye was readmitted into NCNC in its wake.

In *The Beard of Prometheus*, Okoye positions himself as a spent force politically, despite being readmitted. 'How do I know that I have failed? As I know that I am alive.'[159] He tempers this observation by the admission that *equating success with truth* is a 'Nazi' pursuit in essence,[160] and he seems full of melancholy for the lost political momentum for a turn to the left in Nigeria. Okoye understood his own value and strengths: in this semi-autobiographical book his role is presented as that of the Prometheus of Nigeria, one who brought the revolutionary flame to the country. He quotes from Ancient and African mythology and lore, seeming more at home with their polytheistic concepts than with Christianity and Islam, which he considered to be imperialist religions.[161]

As to his beard: it was indeed a hallmark of the Nigerian Marxist subculture. Tunji Otegbeye, Eskor Toyo, Edwin Madunagu and many others have grown well-groomed beards that were medium-long and pointed at the chin, but cut to shape at the sides. Okoye wrote an entire essay playfully explaining the significance of wearing a beard across continents and cultures, with a note on how beards 'cost a man female love'.[162] This short essay is entirely typical of Okoye the essayist: free and uninhibited, not in the least confined to 'elevated topics', Okoye often entertains as well as enlightens. The same may be said about his Marxian credentials as a thinker. For Okoye, although he read Marx, Engels, Lenin and Gramsci voraciously, Marxism was far from an exclusively scholastic exercise (he delights in writing about Marx's affair with his maid).[163]

He declares that 'Caesar, Pericles, Mohammed, Talleyrand, Palmerston and even Nehru … owed their rise to women,'[164] in the last case no doubt giving credence to the widespread speculation that Nehru had had an affair with Lady Mountbatten. Although by no means a Fabian socialist himself,[165] Okoye reserved his greatest respect for Nehru among his contemporaries, seeing his role as that of a voice for uncompromised independence for the Afro-Asian countries, and for a scientifically informed, socially conscious set of policies domestically (though Nehru's legacy has been questioned within India since the early 1990s). Okoye loathed the forces of social reaction, especially when they work in tandem with religious hierarchies. He talks of 'the Church's unflinching support for the fascist dictators of our times: Mussolini, Hitler, Tojo, Salazar, Petain, Franco, Pilsudski, Battista, Peron etc.; the popish blessing of the Italian rapers of Abyssinia and the Japanese rapers of Manchuria; the post-war Arab-Jew, Hindu-Muslim riots and depredations'.[166] His condemnation of faith is unequivocal: 'Faith – firm belief in something for which there is no evidence – is, historically, a harmful quality since it invariably leads to fanaticism, narrow-mindedness and cruelty; failing to convince with reason it has invariably resorted to persecution and violence ...'.[167] He stoically states that politics is for crooks in general,[168] but, specifically, imperialists were for him nothing but rogues.[169] Communism for him 'reflects, however crudely, the basic impulses of broad humanity for equality'.[170] He was convinced of the eventual outcome of the revolutionary struggle: communism will win. Its moral superiority was what made this outcome inevitable for Okoye. A man of very deep emotion, who wrote an entire essay about his unrequited love for a girl named Rose,[171] Okoye did not waver in his conviction that what is just has to be justiciable.

In *African Responses*, his aim was similar to Basil Davidson's in the latter's *African Genius*: a celebration of Africa's contributions to world civilisation. Okoye knew about Davidson's works and had high praise for his *African Awakening*,[172] but *The African Genius* had not yet been written when Okoye completed his work. The foreword, as already mentioned, was written by President Azikiwe himself. This 400-page survey of Africa's history, social traditions and culture was intended as a reference work for Nigerian nationalists seeking roots of African pride. To the detriment of the book's eventual status in the Nigerian historical imagination (which is meagre), Okoye included chapters on African socialism, quoted Plekhanov and Marx on capitalism, and Lenin on imperialism. The work is a testament to the riches of Africa's ancient history. Okoye embraces the contested notion that Ancient Egypt was a Black civilisation. He also attacks racist notions of European superiority from many possible angles. Countering the European concept of African fetishism, Okoye attacks what he perceives as European dog-love. After discussing the history of Ancient Egypt, he focuses on Ethiopia, the West African and East African empires, the Elamites of Persia,[173] the Ethiopian Falashas and other possible Jewish influences (especially the hypothesis that links Igbos with the lost tribes of Israel, to which he would return in *Embattled Men*).[174] In a chapter on 'Adventures of Black Blood', he explores the issue of inter-racial love, reminding us that Louis XIV of France and Pope Clement VII both had biracial children, along with the well-known examples of Thomas Jefferson and Baudelaire, and the escapades of Napoleon's sister Pauline, as well as the fact of Gustavus IV of Sweden's African heritage.[175] On the theme of African liberation, Marx and Frantz Fanon and W.E.B. Du Bois are more relevant to him. But he attacks the snobbish hypocrisy of European elites and their historians with the reminder that El Cid, the Spanish *reconquista* king, himself fell to a Senegalese king,[176] that the Chief Black Eunuchs headed the imperial household in the Ottoman Empire[177] and finally how, in old Ethiopian culture, heroes were black and devils were white.[178]

In *Embattled Men*, Okoye focuses on those who, against the tides of the times, sided with the common people, especially in the field of culture. On the other hand, 'the churches, by destroying the people's cultural artifacts and social mores ... have created tension'.[179] And:

> For instance, why is it that although Nigerians are one of the most outwardly religious people in the world ... many of us lack simple charitableness, honesty, and humility that most religions enjoin on their adherents, and our crime rate is one of the highest in the world?'[180]

He has similarly harsh words for the men who brought foreign religions to Nigeria. The white expatriates of Nigeria, he quotes John Whitford, 'were rude, uneducated men who prided themselves upon coming in at the hawse-hole and going out at the cabin windows'.[181] A son of ordinary people, Okoye discusses his own role as 'a man of two worlds',[182] someone who had once participated in celebrations at the village shrine. While Okoye regarded himself as a thinker, he happily embraced what he saw as the old Igbo worldview, in 'which tradition not knowing, mercifully, does not kill'.[183] In traditional African intellectual life, as well as in traditional African society, 'the emphasis is on mutual cooperation rather than competition'.[184] This notion is different from the widespread 'African socialist' dream of classless modernising African societies, however. For Okoye, the presence of classes in Africa was obvious, even as culture was influenced by ties of family and age groups to a significant measure.

In the book he expounds on the role of the intellectual in classic Leninist fashion (though he is much more open about it than Lenin, in some ways.) In summarising that role, he claims that 'it is not the most wretched and under-privileged who are most concerned about social justice and about the future'.[185] He embraces completely the Leninist concept of professional revolutionaries and the vanguard party.[186] He compares the majority of African intellectuals to the 'superfluous individuals' of 19th-century Russian novels. 'The consequence of all this is that the average African intellectual is forever adjusting his values to the prevailing orthodoxy,'[187] a claim similar to that found in *Africa Works*, but here applies only to the non-Marxist majority. As to the ruling class itself, it partly grows out of this parasitic intellectual class, and produces the monstrosity that he calls 'the bourgeoisie of the civil service'.[188] Addicted to ill-gotten wealth, this bourgeoisie is the class that needs to be overthrown by revolution. Okoye did not denigrate the values of democracy, but believed that democracy meant the rule of the people, and included Maoist China, the Soviet Union, Eastern Europe, and Cuba among the world's democracies, along with Nehruvian India and Tito's Yugoslavia.[189] Okoye evokes Antonio Gramsci to explain why the bulk of the Nigerian intelligentsia is not socialist: the power of the hegemonic culture.[190] All the Nigerian elite in the 1970s are, in effect, status climbers, full of 'pettiness, vulgarity and envy'.[191] This elite is ostentatious and wasteful, addicted to tourist extravaganzas and spending sprees amid the unspeakable suffering of the majority.[192] Its public policy is 'nothing but a patchwork of occasional accommodation'. He goes so far as to compare the Nigerian elite to the French aristocracy before the revolution.[193] Okoye hails Beatniks and student rebellions as giving hope for the future, waxing lyrical about the potentialities of student rebellion in Africa and beyond.[194] At the same time, he does not wish to see philosophers in power, a proposition that he finds ridiculous:

> For there is a case for believing that the cerebral type often sees through the time-wasting futility and moral debasement of political power and is at least as bad as everybody else in forming satisfactory social relationships that are the sina qua non for political success. In forming such relationships, philosophers are not markedly more philosophical than ordinary people.[195]

Okoye did not think that pre-modern relations could be brought back to Nigeria, but he felt a sense of loss over them nonetheless. A man who loved nothing more than voracious reading, and writing collections of extremely witty essays, he recapitulates his sense of nostalgia for the old Africa in *Points of Discord* thus:

> A few years ago, many of us in Africa bathed happily – and nakedly – in streams (if we were fortunate enough to live near one), romped

about in bare feet on open moors for birds' eggs, squirrels and berries; we wrestled in the village agoras and took our turns in the task of keeping clean the village streets and the shrines, in securing its rights and celebrating its time-honoured festivals and rites. But today, we sit in our rooms and watch others shoot or dance on the TV screen, while a few swashbuckling, venal politicians and bureaucrats (sometimes in army uniforms nowadays) manage or mismanage our affairs. Once, we built (with the help of kinsmen and age-sets) our houses to live in, but now we merely build (or rather they are built for us) to look at and hide in; once, we went in for what we wanted, but now we go about it in a circuitous way, probably because of fear that others may be making the same ignoble end as ourselves and in such a context honesty is the worst policy.

But perhaps the greatest failure of our effort at assimilation of Western culture in recent years is our acquisitive instinct, devoid of any aesthetic sense.[196]

He is disturbed especially by Lagos, claiming that 'Only in a city like Lagos will a mother and her grown up son sleep with their paramours in opposite beds in the same room,'[197] but he underscores in no uncertain terms how this is a factor of economic depredations. He sees the urban better-off, the lower middle classes, as guilty of self-deception about their state, or victims of false consciousness, as 'essentially, their lives are failures'.[198] On the role of the writer, his position is that, although they of course have greater (creative) freedoms, they also suffer serious limitations due to the state of affairs generally; this is especially the case with postcolonial writers who write in English, unfit essentially for African storytelling.[199] Okoye himself achieved fame in the 1960s and 1970s, especially within Nigeria and, to some extent, the UK.

Eskor Toyo

Eskor Toyo was a mysterious figure of the Nigerian left: ascetic, incorruptible and a larger-than-life presence within the movement. He wore a Castro-style beard and, in his later years, took to sporting a habitual walking stick. He died in late 2015. Toyo was a professor of economics at the University of Calabar, who had been educated in Poland up to PhD level. It might have followed that Toyo would develop as a regular Eastern European-style 'high priest of socialism', pontificating about the virtues of state planning while enjoying Soviet handouts, *à la* Tunji Otegbeye. In fact, the opposite happened. Although Toyo was a published academic author in the Polish language, he was the very antithesis of a kept intellectual. In fact, Niyi Oniororo nicknamed him Mao Toyo in *The Nigerian Comrades* for a reason: he stood to the left of the USSR, drawing on ideas from Trotsky and Mao as ardently as from Lenin and Marx. He was categorically opposed to entryism as a conscious policy, and scolded Nigerian Marxists for their roles in non-Marxist parties. In 1963 he joined the SWAFP, but within a year he was out and setting up the Nigerian Labour Party together with Michael Imoudu, 'labour leader number one'. Edwin Madunagu looked up to Eskor Toyo as someone who was not afraid to apply Marxist thinking to any given subject, even the subject of Eastern European economies.

Toyo's independence cost him opportunities to publish. Although he is among the best-known of Nigerian Marxists within the country, and even foreign scholarship noticed his central role (Matusevich, *ROAPE* [*Review of African Political Economy*]), Eskor Toyo had to make do with stencil duplicating machines for the reproduction of most of his works. These were distributed as *samizdat* during the years of the country's military regimes. Madunagu's CIINSTRID (Calabar International Institute for Research, Information and Development) library has a marvellous collection of these stencilled works, and it would be a worthwhile exercise to compile a compendium. Here, however, I will concentrate only on those works of his that are available to the non-specialist: his *An Open Letter to the Nigerian Left* (which appeared in *ROAPE*), and a stencilled work, *Primary Accumulation and Development Strategy in a Neo-Colonial Economy: A Critique of Dependence Theory*, which is available today via the British Library.

Toyo's *Critique* is a scathing dismissal of dependency theory as it relates to Third World countries in general and Nigeria in particular. Toyo wrote this work in the early 1980s, when dependency theory was very fashionable in Nigerian academia, even in more mainstream, non-Marxian circles. That was precisely what bothered Toyo – he thought that the Nigerian intelligentsia was enamoured by dependency theory and the work of André Gunder-Frank for the wrong reasons:

> Precisely because dependence theory does not stress the development by indigenous initiative of a capitalist mode of production in the peripheral country, it can be taken over by those who advocate indigenization and self-reliance as means to overcome dependence without getting involved in ideology.[200]

For Toyo, the indigenisation of enterprises was a sham of the Nigerian second republic, stretching over to the 21st century in the form of expatriate quotas that are routinely circumvented and signify nothing.

Also, in Toyo's view, dependency theory is 'based on the theme of contradiction between national economies rather than classes'.[201] And: 'The exploiting bourgeoisie in less developed countries would want us to understand exploitation as a relation between nations, between undifferentiated populations.'[202] Furthermore:

> If the bourgeois economists are silent on the category of primitive accumulation, replacing it simply with saving on the one hand and with an a-historical development theory on the other, it is not an adequate answer to them for Marxists to also ignore this category and replace it with a dependence theory, which sometimes even goes to the ridiculous extreme of denying that any development goes on in the capitalist-oriented third world countries.[203]

It would be wrong to dismiss Toyo's criticisms. These lines were written before Babangida's neoliberal SAP, and before Nigeria started deindustrialising, and, of course, before it became the near-failed state that it is today. Toyo's recommendation for Nigeria here is to embark on the path of a socialist orientation in its economy. He dismissed the New International Economic Order as a sham, and embraced the Eastern European position, which emphasised that the East was not to blame for the effects of neocolonialism (as was commonly done within the rubric of the North). More surprisingly for a professor who was the product of an Eastern European education in economics and political economy, Toyo in his *Critique* subscribed to Ernest Mandel's view on socialist countries, and claimed 'that these economies have registered enormous achievements in a direction away from capitalism and in the direction of socialism and communism'.[204] While it was standard Eastern European thinking to postpone the arrival of communism to the distant future, it was almost shocking to implicitly claim that Eastern European countries had not already attained a socialist mode of production/political system.

In *An Open Letter to the Nigerian Left*, Toyo goes even further in his heterodox approach, and advocates a turn to the peasantry as the main bearer of revolutionary tasks in a distinctly Maoist fashion. Again, he does not openly posit this as a question of international orientation, but the significance was surely not lost on the Soviet ambassador. Quite apart from the question of foreign relations, however, Toyo's *Open Letter* was a realistic assessment of the revolutionary potential of Chinua Achebe's, Balarabe Musa's and Abubakar Rimmi's PRP, a Northern-based party that had won the governorship in two states at the time. The late 1970s and early 1980s were times of revolutionary upheaval in Nigeria, and others also predicted that there seemed to be momentum for the Nigerian left to coalesce around a core, possibly of the PRP. In Toyo's words:

> The Marxists who sit in their armchairs to attack the PRP are not right. Of all the different 'lines' for Marxists in Nigeria, the most correct for the present phase is joining and working in the PRP. There are a number of reasons for this. First, the 'Marxists' are not doing politics at all who are not in the PRP. They are merely criticizing the bourgeoisie, not mobilizing the people against the bourgeois establishment. The time for merely criticizing the bourgeoisie in Nigeria is past. One has to find a platform for going into action.
>
> Second, the programme of the PRP is not merely a democratic one but a revolutionary one. The PRP by its programme seeks the total abolition of imperialism, feudalism and capitalism. It seeks the substitution for the present day neo-colonial state of a new social order. This order is defined as one in which production relations are redefined to abolish all exploitation of man by man. This new order is to be brought about by a people's state, a people's democratic dictatorship. Quite frankly, I do not know what else the 'Marxists' say they want in the name of a revolutionary programme. I have the impression that they want the name 'Marxism' or 'Leninism' and some phrases such as 'class struggle' and proletariat instead of a programme that the masses can understand. They want the verbal forms, not the essence, of a revolutionary programme. The non-PRP 'Marxists' are infantile and subjective …
>
> Fourth, the non-PRP 'Marxists' have a special form in their minds for the growth of a socialist movement. In their undialectical minds there must first be a 'Marxist party' to 'lead' the revolution. If such a party does not exist, one must not fight even where the daily experiences of the masses prepare them for political struggle against feudal rule and the nouveaux riches. To our stereotyped 'Marxists', let it be pointed out that there was no 'Marxist party' for Augustino Neto, Samora Machel, Amilcar Cabral, Mengistu and the Sandinista militants to join. In Cuba there was a Communist party for Fidel Castro and his associates to join, but happily they did not. That party was as dogmatic, sectarian and blind to the revolutionary potentialities of a broad anti-establishment people's movement as Nigeria's 'Marxist' parrots are …
>
> Sixth, the People's Redemption Party is a daily school for the masses and for the Marxists. One learns of the bourgeoisie of one's own country, not in text-books but in combat.[205]

This was a clarion call for Marxists to gather around the PRP, and abandon their armchairs, as a group. Some (like Madunagu, Achebe and others) rallied behind the PRP, others kept their distance. The alternative, according to Madunagu's analysis, was a turn to fascism,[206] which duly came in the form of Buhari's military rule from 1983.

Edwin Madunagu

Dr Edwin Ikechukwu Madunagu, or frequently Eddie Madunagu, is perhaps the most visible Marxist public intellectual in Nigeria today. An ethnic Igbo whose own first language is Yoruba,[207] Madunagu nonetheless renounced his allegiance to any politicised ethnic cause in the country.[208] Madunagu has three gainful professions: he is a professor of mathematics at the University of Calabar, a celebrated columnist at *The Guardian*, and the head of an NGO committed to conscientising male adolescents about gender. His unpaid role, as top organiser of the Nigerian Marxist movement, however, is arguably the most important one. Today he is perhaps the single most revered voice in Nigerian leftist circles due to his organisational capabilities and his intellectual strengths. A three-day session of extended interviews with him was conducted in Calabar for the purposes of research for this book. Madunagu was forthcoming, witty, devastatingly quick, subtle and refined in his conversations and throughout our correspondence. The only time he proved less than forthcoming was when discussing some former comrades who had turned away from Marxism after 1989. I attributed that to his sense of personal loyalty, to his non-judgemental character and to his deeply human approach to political issues. After 1989, together with his mentor Eskor Toyo, Madunagu conspicuously remained a Marxist, but a Marxist who engaged in much soul-searching over what had gone wrong with mainstream Marxism, in Nigeria as well as in Eastern Europe and the wider world.

Generally, it is fair to categorise Madunagu as a Trotskyist, but with interesting caveats. His wife Bene Madunagu, a formidable leftist feminist thinker in her own right, developed a sharp feminist politics against the patriarchal oppression so prevalent in the country. When Sani Abacha shut down *The Guardian*, Madunagu retreated to NGO life. So successful was his anti-patriarchal initiative that *The New York Times* quoted his work as one of the most successful examples of gender education in all sub-Saharan Africa,[209] and gender-related research in the West also picked up on his NGO's achievements.[210] Foreign researchers also noted his role as a leading Nigerian Marxist (Matusevich), while some Nigerian critics unfairly dismissed him as a vulgar Marxist.[211]

Madunagu wrote most of his theoretical works (*The Philosophy of Violence, The Tragedy of the Nigerian Socialist Movement, Human Progress and its Enemies, Problems of Socialism: The Nigerian Challenge, The Political Economy of State Robbery*) in the 1970s and the 1980s,[212] when he was a noted student organiser, who was dismissed from his job and incarcerated under the military regime of Yakubu Gowon in 1975. From June 1976, he organised a village commune built on radical, gender and political equality in the rural countryside (in Ode-Omu in Osun State),[213] away from Obasanjo's police. He served briefly, with other leftists, on President Babangida's Political Bureau, until that body showed complacency towards Babangida's newfound neoliberal agenda. When formal democracy was reinstituted, he re-joined *The Guardian*, where he resumed his Thursday column. He also published the best of his journalism in *The Making and Unmaking of Nigeria, Contradictions of Progress: Critical Essays in Defence of Socialism, Radical Politics* and *Understanding Nigeria and the New Imperialism*. He remains active in labour unionism and is working towards consolidating a socialist centre in Calabar.

Madunagu is a voracious reader. His erudition may only be compared with Mokwugo Okoye's in the Nigerian Marxist context. His commitment to education underpins his every effort, from setting up a free public library using his own resources in Calabar (the best library on history, Marxism, sociology and a host of other subjects in the state), to his conviction about the role of education in emancipation. Indeed, in his *Problems of Socialism*, the main political strategy put forward for the Nigerian socialist cause was the establishment of a research centre. Instead of solutions imported from elsewhere, he is deeply committed to local solutions to local problems. His idealism was such that he openly accused the USSR of destroying Nigeria's revolutionary potential by subsidising a segment of orthodox Nigerian communists (the SWAFP, the NTUC [Nigerian Trade Union Congress] and later illegal groupings): such help, in his view, fostered undue influence.[214] Gorbachev's USSR would nonetheless invite him later on a short state visit, during which he acquired first-hand knowledge about the USSR, its positive and negative sides included. While Madunagu is a true internationalist (he was the first non-Hungarian I met who could pronounce Imre Nagy's name correctly), the focus of his attention is Nigeria and Africa.

Madunagu's writing style is dense. Perhaps this is an influence from his first language, Yoruba; we encounter the same density that Wole Soyinka's sentences exhibit. At the same time, Madunagu's essay prose is stricter. He is a mathematician. His sentences are very far from the Proustian, long and lyrical writing that we see with Mokwugo Okoye.

Madunagu makes frequent allusions, but delivers them usually without express citations (indeed, he talks of Okoye's 'quotism' in *For Our Departed Radical Patriots*), and his style has a staccato feel that follows the rhythm of thought very closely. At the same time, his writings are packed with historical references and information, sometimes making the read difficult, especially if the reader is not well versed in Nigerian history. His attention to that history and the history of the Nigerian socialist movement are so encyclopaedic that one could reconstruct the entire history of the movement drawing solely from his oeuvre.

He never quotes Bernstein, but he seems to operate, and to write, on the principle that the movement is everything. He regularly woos students into radical discussions on campus after class. He helps the widows of departed labour unionists. He organises tirelessly, every force in his state and beyond who is inclined to help, including, sometimes, left-leaning businessmen and entrepreneurs. His articles especially are veritable lectures on history, but he consciously uses history for a political purpose. He teaches and conscientises *The Guardian* readership, the adolescent boys who attend his NGO's popular lectures and his comrades who hear him out in meetings. He was known in the movement as a near-anarchist 'ultra-left' *enfant terrible*, and a born *raconteur* at meetings.

It is sometimes claimed that mathematicians reach the zenith of their intellectual powers earlier than social scientists. While we are unable to discuss Madunagu's merit as a mathematician, either in his youth or in his later years, this seems true when it comes to his works on Marxist theory. According to his own assessment too, he reached the peak of his theoretical prowess in the 1970s–80s.[215] The succession of his major works started with *The Philosophy of Violence* in 1976. (Today, this tome is very hard to come by: there is one single copy on reference in the UK, and none in Nigeria.)[216] In this book, Madunagu reflected on the implications of the death of a student rebel, Kunle Adepeju, who had been shot down by the police in front of Trenchard Hall, University of Ibadan, five years earlier. Violence, according to Madunagu, is a 'force which sometimes conceals its material basis'.[217] He warns that physical violence is only a part of the phenomenon, and that malnutrition (for example) constitutes economic violence on the part of the exploiter.[218] As for the violence of Nigeria's society (which was not then as dangerous as it is today), Madunagu emphasises that 'The man who beats up his wife or houseboy is … responding to a chaotic social arrangement,'[219] as well as the armed robber, who operates within exactly the same framework. Quoting Ben Bella and Amilcar Cabral, Madunagu differentiates between predatory violence, the very mainstay of the status quo, and violence that liberates.[220] He fully endorses the latter on a theoretical basis,[221] quoting the Agbekoya revolt as the most important positive example (see chapter 4). Regarding the appearance of mass scale physical violence in Nigeria, he ridicules the British concept of 'colonial pacification' and emphasises how the real era of violence on a massive scale was in fact ushered in by the colonial power.[222]

His next work, *The Tragedy of the Nigerian Socialist Movement*, appeared in 1980. Again, *Tragedy* is a book that is very hard to find: there is one reference copy in London, and none in Nigeria. Luckily, Madunagu seems to have incorporated some of its material into a subsequent work, *Problems of Socialism: The Nigerian Challenge*, published not in Calabar but in London by Zed Books, and easily found today in libraries and with second-hand book sellers. The earlier work, however, is the more radical of the two. In both, Madunagu quotes Trotsky on the necessity of a vanguard party – 'Without a guiding organization, the energy of the masses would dissipate like steam not enclosed in a piston box'[223] – a quote that also appears very often in his journalism. Regarding the SWAFP, he underlines its 'artificial' nature as a unified Marxist-Leninist force, when he claims that 'The SWFP [SWAFP] came into being to further institutionalize opportunism in the socialist movement.'[224] He quotes Eskor Toyo on the personal flaws that Tunji Otegbeye seemed to show: acting like 'a bourgeois millionaire benefactor, holding the purse strings.'[225] He emphasises, in both works, the erosion that the oil economy, the resource curse, unleashed on Nigeria.[226] He comments on student vanguardism, quoting Gramsci ('intellectuals may exist, non-intellectuals certainly do not exist, since every human labour involves some mental exercise').[227] The volume also contains a separate essay on the philosophy of industrial relations, interesting in its own right, which sheds light on Madunagu's deepest convictions. This exercise might have been prompted by Eskor Toyo, who urged Madunagu to tackle difficult issues of Marxist theory head on. In this essay, Madunagu calls the USSR a degenerate workers' state that breeds a parasitic bureaucracy, closely following Mao's *A Critique of Soviet Economy*. Workers are, according to Mao and Madunagu, given material incentives in the USSR, where their individual material interest is built into the system both theoretically and, even more, in the way the Soviet economy really worked.[228] One is perhaps tempted to dismiss outright this line of argument as sectarian and ultra-leftist, suggesting that the only saving grace of Eastern European economies was the way they tried to raise working-class living standards. This point of view comes so naturally to many of us that we do not notice how capitalist-conservative it actually is. Eszter Bartha, in a ground-breaking new Marxist study *Alienating Labour*[229] uncovers how the use of this carrot simply forced Eastern European governments on a right-wing trajectory, shutting down every real leftist alternative as a consequence of narrow, indeed bourgeois, concepts of efficiency, where it mattered most: in the minds of ordinary working-class people in those countries. The apparent ultra-left bias does not invalidate the veracity of this argument, so splendidly argued by Bartha. According to Madunagu too, a true socialist project has to transform men, not just production.[230]

Having said that, it is not as if Madunagu wanted to discard the USSR and all its historical experience on the garbage heap of history, like the cynical neoliberal oligarchs who brought to the former USSR and its satellites only destruction, impoverishment and the disappearance of self-worth in the 1990s. Madunagu disliked the bureaucracy of the USSR and attacked what he saw as its degeneracy, but he loved it nonetheless as a workers' state, as a state that at least tried, against all odds, to build socialism. Much later, in 2005, he was so enraged about the self-congratulatory Western dignitaries who celebrated the 50th anniversary of the liberation of Auschwitz (without acknowledging that this was actually achieved by the USSR and its war machine), that he devoted his entire op-ed to this conspicuous exercise in the selective amnesia of imperialist powers.[231] In another, in 2001, he looks back at the USSR and poses questions on the dissolution of the USSR, most importantly, the complexity of its state structure and how it contributed to its collapse.[232] With special (implicit) relevance to Nigeria, where Chief Anthony Enahoro of the Marxist movement advocated a federation of federations comprising 70 nationalities with respective 'homelands', Madunagu comments on how detrimental the Soviet method of complex ethnic governance was, designed by none other than Stalin before he became the Soviet dictator. Madunagu had warned Marxists as early as the 1970s that issues such as ethnicity or the women's question were problems in their own right that necessitated serious theoretical consideration and demanded constant attention, even from Marxists in power, but equally from Marxists in a marginalised position, such as in Nigeria. Balarabe Musa, the PRP governor, called him an ethnicist,[233] and the great men of the Nigerian communist movement repeatedly assured him that, once the dictatorship of the proletariat was established, everything else would come to the nation as if by divine intervention. The subsequent inclusion of many leftists in even the most appalling military governments in Nigeria does make one wonder whether some Marxist intellectuals actually expected a Marxist general to emerge and single-handedly deliver them their coveted 'dictatorship of the proletariat'. In any case, the vanity and intellectual complacency of leaders such as Otegbeye, whose greatest pride was his ballroom dancing, reminds one of Brezhnev in the Soviet context, who loved nothing more than fancy cars. At the same time, it was Madunagu and not Otegbeye, and not even orthodox labour leaders, who kept true to Marxism once the USSR fell in 1991 and no further material help was forthcoming from that direction. Madunagu draws on Eurocommunism and the late Lukacs with regard to the centrality of democracy and democratisation to socialism – or, more precisely, the apparent lack of it, in actual Soviet policy-making.[234] In 1991, he felt that the dissolution of the Soviet Union of that year was a genuine loss for the socialist cause however, because it ushered in unadulterated capitalism in Russia and beyond, and even in 2005 he devoted an op-ed to the role of 7 November in history.[235]

Problems of Socialism: The Nigerian Challenge is a compact work that received attention in the international Marxist movement in 1980, especially from those who concerned themselves with the problems of Africa. The author stresses in the Preface that it is a polemical work and that it has a political objective. He makes clear his political standpoint early on, noting that 'the problems of socialist transformation have not been completely transcended anywhere in the world',[236] but recognises the necessity of such a transformation, especially in criminally governed, failing Nigeria. He lists the attempts at unifying the Marxist movement in the country, and contends that the negation of precisely that unification has become a culture in itself in the Nigerian movement, much to the detriment of its efficiency.[237] His aim with this work is to offer a platform for such unification. He examines in detail the record of Nigerian capitalism, focusing on the recurring battle cry of the fight against corruption. 'Some bourgeois fractions joined in these agitations – not because they were opposed to corruption, but because they wanted a more equal access to the opportunities and benefits of corruption.'[238] He then goes on to give an account of the Murtala–Obasanjo regime (note especially the unity he claims exists between these two), and examines Murtala's anti-corruption initiatives, the purging of individually corrupt officials. 'The new regime acted with such rapidity that even a large section of the political left were dazed, carried away, and integrated into what might be called national illusions.'[239] We may recall how this illusion encompassed thinkers such as Niyi Oniororo, who built a campaign based on Murtala's memory. After much empty pseudo-radical rhetoric, Obasanjo went on to pursue a very different agenda.

A wage freeze had been imposed upon the workers; strikes were banned and offenders threatened with execution, imprisonment or proscription of their unions, inflation was rising; student radicals were being rusticated and universities and colleges were being closed down, while the working-class movement (notably the trade unions) was being subjected to state bureaucratization.[240]

Obasanjo's new constitution was 'fascistic in content but liberal in form', having established a money qualification to stand as a candidate in elections,[241] as a result of which, out of 40 new political parties that appeared in 1979, 'thirty-six parties were a priori declared outside the limits of the people's democratic choice not because their programs were bad but because they failed to satisfy conditions ... by the possession of huge sums of money'.[242] Candidates also had to pay money deposits. Regarding the role of money in the 1979 elections, Madunagu contends that: 'First, a group of people literally bought the core of the party. Secondly, ambitious party members bought their nominations as candidates in the various elections. Finally the party candidates bought the voters.'[243] Manipulation of fears, ethnic and religious, also played their part. The new regime went on to proclaim universal free education and free medical care, but did not make even the slightest effort to implement it. Madunagu compares this to the effects of what the Plateau state government did to help the *talakawa* (Hausa for common people). Instead of lowering their feudal tax burden, it simply abolished the usage of the word *'talakawa'* to officially announce that there were, henceforth, no exploited people in the state![244] In the passage 'The bankruptcy of the neo-colonial solution', Madunagu goes further and explains what he means by the overcoming of neocolonialist dependence in a socialist way:

To be self-reliant is not to withdraw completely from the world market, as some utopians from the Right and the Left advocate. To be self-reliant is to create the conditions under which the need and impetus for development comes from within and not from without; to be self-reliant, a country must first maximally exploit, mobilize and deploy its natural and human resources for the realization of its national objectives ... What this immediately implies is that the volume of exports will be determined only when the products meant for export (e.g. crude oil) have been put to maximal use internally or have been planned for such use. It also implies that the character of imports ... must be determined by the maximal use (or projected maximal use) of internal resources to satisfy genuine national needs.

To be self-reliant in the agricultural sector ... is not only to be self-sufficient in food production ... but also to base industrial development (*what* is manufactured and *how* it is manufactured), on agriculture ... This means an increase in the productivity of the human producers – the farmers ... Standards of living, health, education, housing, water and electricity supplies and communication networks must all be radically improved ... Machetes and hoes must be replaced, not necessarily by modern industrial technology based on advanced technology, but at least by machinery based on the so-called intermediate technologies ... The intermediate machines must be based not on imports ... but on local natural and human resources. Thousands of mechanics, blacksmiths, engineers, technicians, and others at present working in isolation, can be mobilized nationally both for designing and producing these machines on a mass scale ... Industrialization and character of imports must serve the mass of the peasantry ... The importing of cars, television sets, carpets and rugs, furniture, etc., must give way to the local production of ploughing, planting, harvesting, processing and storage machines for agricultural products, building materials, and the development of curative and preventive medicine; the building of modern airports and sea ports must give way to the building of hospitals, health centres, roads, schools, and recreational centres ... Crude oil must now be put to maximum use internally: petro-chemical industries producing fertilizers and other synthetic materials can be developed on a mass scale. These industries then must serve agricultural production ... [This would] deal a blow to the entire culture of consumption.[245]

He dismisses the concern that such a change would create problems abroad (in the developed countries), because of the hiatus in oil. 'The question is what the termination of neocolonial status means to the third world. We are not concerned with the interests of the imperialists.'[246]

After briefly examining the ethnic minority question, he goes on to include a modified version of his earlier work, *The Tragedy of the Nigerian Left,* then smashes the purported 'revolutionary' credentials of Awolowo's United Party of Nigeria, and describes what the Nigerian left should do in order to unify. The final recommendations of *The Problems* exhibit a certain vagueness – as if Madunagu himself reached some conclusions of which he was not yet fully conscious at the time of finishing the manuscript. Indeed, his next work, coming within a year, clarified his recommendations to a large extent. In *Nigeria: The Economy and the People – The Political Economy of State Robbery and its Popular Democratic Negation,* published in 1984 in London but written before Buhari's 1983 military coup,[247] Madunagu focuses on the unfolding economic crisis that resulted from the slump in oil prices in the early 1980s. After giving a brief theoretical analysis and well-documented examples of ongoing state robbery amid a contracting economy and widespread popular misery, Madunagu proposes a struggle for popular democracy.[248] Dismissing the reigning order as the dictatorship of the businessman and of the bureaucratic bourgeoisie, he predicts the fascist takeover of the country as something that inevitably follows from the grassroots conditions of people in 1983. Vindicating Madunagu's prediction, General Buhari was in power in months, with his famed campaigns for national discipline and militaristic regimentation across the board.

During and after Madunagu's role in Babangida's Political Bureau, no major theoretical work by him appeared, and he published compendiums of his journalistic articles after democracy was reinstated in 1999. It would be foolish to dismiss Madunagu's journalism though, as a second-rate part of his Marxist oeuvre. Someone who quotes Trotsky, Lukacs and Althusser as a matter of course, and freely references Howard Zinn's *A People's History of the United States* as a source in an editorial, is not a run-of-the-mill dabbler in journalism. His journalistic articles are short and succinct essays, all written in an unmistakable staccato style so characteristic of Madunagu. Madunagu, who was, and still is, a very busy man, made a virtue out of necessity, and perfected the journalistic article as a medium. His articles very often include clear ending notes, or punch lines, and they deal with only a limited number of factors. But the very minutiae of Nigerian history, and the concepts of alienation in Althusser, constitute those few factors in a given article. He tackles a very wide variety of subjects from sharia through JFK and resource control, to the non-dialectical understanding of the dictatorship of the proletariat,[249] from Obasanjo to Margaret Ekpo, from Le Pen to Mugabe, from Chávez to Guantanamo Bay, from Allende to Rosa Luxemburg, from Bade Onimode to a failed communist movement in Burkina Faso,[250] but always against capitalism, against imperialism, against what he calls 'the world dictatorship'. Surprisingly, he also devotes an article to the Apostle Paul's hymn to love, and posits love as a *conditio sine qua non* for a communist.[251]

The emotional burden of being a committed and honest communist in Nigeria is nothing like it is in the West. Madunagu gives away his books free, and tries to live according to his own categorical imperative in a way most Nigerian revolutionaries do not. To give an idea of the complexities involved, in Nigeria it is expected to 'give back to the community' in ways more profound than in the West. Constructing boreholes, settling personal problems and giving personal advice, are understood as an obligation for the great (which means for anyone even remotely middle class by Western standards). Those of a leftist persuasion are very sensitive to those demands, but this can make them vulnerable to abuse by community members who take it as a carte blanche for excessive demands. Under conditions of extreme impoverishment there is often an overwhelming sense of need, and a corresponding level of stress and pressure put on people who are perceived as able to redress those needs. 'More Complex than Politics' is the title of Madunagu's editorial on these mundane but deeply human problems, associated with the day-to-day life of a university professor, who also happens to be a socialist.[252]

His embrace of feminism is also a core part of Madunagu's socialist project. Madunagu recognised the need of gender-related conscientising for male adolescents in his state, and set up an NGO for this purpose. François Girard discusses this aspect of Madunagu's politics:

Back in Calabar, Madunagu could not sit still for long. After some reflection, he decided that it was time for him to get back to the basics of his progressive activism – to educating and to developing the critical thinking and raising the consciousness of young people. As a first step, Madunagu planned to open a public library and documentation center with the many books he and his wife and fellow activist, Bene, had collected over the years.

The Madunagus' political awareness included gender issues. Eddie's consciousness concerning women's rights had originally grown out of discussions with Ingrid Essien-Obot, a German feminist and Marxist who taught at the University of Calabar until her murder in 1981. His commitment to gender equality as a human rights issue, along with Bene's, only increased in subsequent years.

Back in Calabar, Bene had just established Girls' Power Initiative (GPI) … Eddie Madunagu recalls that he walked in, and said, in a light-hearted manner: 'Don't you know that boys also need this kind of program? Boys are not educated.' Thinking back on that comment, Madunagu explains that he felt concern for the GPI girls, who, with all their newly acquired knowledge, would have to face 'uneducated' boys and patriarchal families.[253]

When leftist political action was ruled out by military dictatorships, Madunagu did not become one of those who ended up helping retrograde causes by joining one or another ethnic lobby. Albeit fully conscious that most NGOs perpetuate the political and economic status quo – in fact, so much so that they become part of the very power structure,[254] Madunagu thought that by maintaining a free public library and his NGO, he did what his Marxist conscience dictated. In the 2000s, Madunagu published short booklets on the heroes of the Nigerian socialist movement: *For Our Departed Radical Patriots, Gani Fawehinmi, Peter Ayodele Curtis Joseph,* and his own *Autobiography*, providing a service to new generations who lack the first-hand experience of veterans.

6

Political Economists

Many economists in Africa and elsewhere shy away from critical theory, or even from any heterodox thought, concentrating instead on purely technical matters to make the status quo more efficient in a narrow, technical sense. In Africa, where the status quo for most people, including brilliant economists, means misery, many economists have recognised the imperative to challenge it. In Nigeria, some became Marxists. Ola Oni, Bade Onimode, Adebayo Olukoshi and Okwudiba Nnoli wrote very important works on the Nigerian political economy from a Marxian angle.

Bade Onimode

Professor Bade Onimode (1944–2001) had perhaps the highest international profile, and the most visible intellectual presence, among all Nigerian political economists. Every year, colloquia are held in Lokoja dedicated to his memory. He is quoted copiously in their oeuvre by 21st-century thinkers such as Usman Tar. Onimode studied at University of Ibadan (1963–67), received his second Masters' degree from the University of Chicago in 1970, and earned his PhD from Ohio State University in 1972. His books included highly successful quantitative textbooks such as *Basic Mathematics for Economics* and *Mathematics for Economics and Business* (both with G. I. Osayimwese), and more qualitative ones such as *Imperialism and Underdevelopment in Nigeria: The Dialectics of Mass Poverty, Multinational Corporations in Nigeria* (with J. Ohiorhenuan and T. Adeniran), *A Political Economy of the African Crisis, The IMF, the World Bank and the African Debt* (vol. 1: *Economic Impact*, vol. 2: *Social and Political Impact*), *A Future for Africa: Beyond the Politics of Adjustment, Issues in African Development* (co-edited with R. Synge) and *Africa in the World of the 21st Century*. He was a consultant to several local and international organisations, including the International Labour Organization (ILO), the United Nations Economic Commission on Africa (ECA), the defunct International Confederation of Free Trade Unions (ICFTU), the Organisation of African Trade Union Unity (OATUU), and the Nigeria Labour Congress. He taught economics at the University of Ibadan from the time he returned to Nigeria in 1972 to his death in 2001. Edwin Madunagu once recounted that when he was scheduled to speak after Onimode, he had to switch into 'agitation mode', or Onimode would have stolen the show by sheer intelligence, coherence, clarity and relevance.

A mild-mannered academic, Onimode made a point of rejecting the narrow quantitative approach of orthodox neoliberal and even some Keynesian economists. His first work, co-authored with Ibadan political economy lecturer Ola Oni (a labour leader and organiser in his own right), was *Economic Development of Nigeria: A Socialist Alternative*. Although Onimode had received a scholarship from the Rockefeller Foundation and finished his PhD in the United States, he did not toe the line of multinational corporations in Nigeria. On the contrary, his first major work was a political economy textbook on how to build a national economy on Eastern European lines. Heavily shaped by Ola Oni's Marxist labour orthodoxy, this book does not yet show Onimode in his best light. The book is unimaginatively didactic with an outlook directly out of Nikitin and other standard Eastern European political economy textbooks.[1] Although this work borrows from André Gunder-Frank (especially the idea of the lumpen-bourgeoisie as it relates to Nigeria), it reads like a 'how-to' handbook, written for a not-so-well-read left-leaning army major who just engineered a coup and wants a crash course in how to construct a planned economy. Jack Woddis and other orthodox Eastern European-style Western authors are also quoted and referenced well in the work. It contains interesting passages, as when the authors remind us how Allende's chief preoccupation was with nationalisation of the means of production in Chile,[2] and some shocking facts (such as that in 1979, Nigeria refined almost 30 per cent of its crude oil,[3] as opposed to 2015 when it refines none). It focuses on refusing Nigeria's 'elitist development strategy where industry produces soft drinks, beer, cigarettes, and such frivolous luxuries'.[4] Frivolity does not begin to express what has transpired since then, as industry has retreated further, and imports include what look like Belgian handmade neo-Baroque sofas for Ini Edo to sit on in the best Nollywood films. Ola Oni's (and Onimode's) solution is disengagement from world capitalism and an industrialisation programme that focuses on capital goods (especially machinery). They posit unemployment as easily overcome, once the socialist project is launched.[5] The book stresses how there is no 'racial or cultural copyright' on socialism and that anyway its tenets have been Africanised by Sékou Touré, Frantz Fanon, Nkrumah and others.[6] Some crafty expressions are found, such as '[capitalism] relegate(s) the masses of our people to the background where as peeping zombies, they are supposed to derive vicarious satisfaction from the wasteful pageantry of the mindless life of the corrupt rich.[7] Not unreasonably, Ola Oni and Onimode posit that a low level of development is in itself no obstacle to the launching of a socialist revolution (China and the USSR launched their own versions), but they fail to give specifics as to the possible Nigerian path to socialism.

Bade Onimode's next major work was *Imperialism and Underdevelopment in Nigeria: The Dialectics of Mass Poverty* (1982). Published by Zed Books in London, this is a major work, perhaps *the* major work by Onimode: a magnificent analysis of Nigeria's political economy alongside an analysis of the history of its power relations from pre-colonial times until the time of the book's publication. This work is perhaps the best single volume on the economic history of Nigeria ever written. It rejects as ahistorical ways of looking at Nigeria's underdevelopment as a factor of any combination of deficiencies taken out of their contexts. Onimode was not a trained historian by profession. Remarkably, there are only two instances in the book which betray this fact: when he writes about slave revolts in pre-colonial Nigeria, but does not supply a single one as evidence;[8] and, second, when he repeatedly makes a mistake with regard to the chronology of India's independence (1949 instead of 1947).[9] But these are rather pedantic concerns, especially when weighed against how elegant Onimode's thesis is, as he traces the origins of structural underdevelopment to the earlier histories of pre-colonial slaving, colonial plunder, and neocolonial extortion in the territories that comprise today's Nigeria (with just 'flag independence', his favourite term). Onimode is more meticulous even than Ananaba Wogu when tracing the first strikes (which he dates to 1897 instead of the 1920s).[10] He is more detailed than Toyin Falola's great *History of Nigeria*, when it comes to the origins of the Nigerian elite beyond the feudalists (especially when he discusses the role of repatriated Brazilian Yoruba elements and Sierra Leonean creoles),[11] and his discussion of the Adebiyi Tribunal of 1976.

Beyond such considerations, of interest mostly to the professional historian, Onimode in this work presents an eminently coherent explanation of Nigeria's retarded development and even retrogression. In 1982, he did not have a clear picture of how far the latter would be pushed with Babangida's later orthodox IMF-induced structural adjustment programmes (SAPs). Indeed, he still thought that Nigeria was on the threshold of capital goods manufacturing,[12] as the Ajaokuta steel complex and chemical industries were expected to open in the early 1980s. By 2016, even traditional Nigerian handmade wax cloths are produced almost exclusively in China, and heavy industries not only did not develop but even what little consumer goods manufacturing existed in the 1970s disappeared. Onimode of course could not have foreseen the 'lost decade' of the 1980s that, with its declining terms of trade, created exceptional hardships in Africa. However, in this work Onimode gives a comprehensive picture of Nigeria's systematic and systemic economic abuse by its elites, nurtured in conjunction with representatives of inter-national monopoly capital.

Written on Samir Amin's advice,[13] the book's 'central idea is that it is impossible to understand the character of underdevelopment without understanding its history':[14] 'From the inhumanity of the European slave trade to the brutality of colonization and contemporary neo-colonial domination, this study reveals the central role of imperialism in generating underdevelopment and dependency' in Nigeria. The 'logical conclusion [is] that the liquidation of underdevelopment and dependency must be predicated on an anti-imperialist struggle for the radical structural disengagement of the country from the exploitative orbit of the international capitalist system'.[15] This in no way implies that Onimode is unaware of how imperialist plunder by multinational oil companies, international banks, insurance companies, and others is aided by the prevailing conditions in Nigeria, with its corrupt elite and its startling skills deficit, or its widespread lack of elementary education. He is not only aware of these, but exposes them as developing in tandem, constituting in fact a dialectical relationship with international capital, with its enclaves of opulence, and its capital flight, which feeds Swiss banks and London jewellery shops. He spells out how ignorance and superstition was bred by both the colonial and the neocolonial conditions in the country.[16]

First he identifies the broad phases of imperialism in the Nigerian context: mercantilist imperialism (late 15th century to late 18th century), when slaves constituted the coast's primary export; free trade imperialism, with its 'legitimate trade' (1772–1850), monopolistic or corporate imperialism with its scramble for Africa and the appearance of monocultures to feed British industry; and multilateral imperialism from 1946 onwards.[17] Strikingly, in this periodisation independence constitutes no meaningful caesura of any kind. The mechanisms of imperialism have included violence (from slave raids to gunboat diplomacy), and 'free' trade itself, along with foreign direct investment and portfolio investment. Aid, with its multiple conditionalities, has been no exception.[18] The core of underdevelopment lies in this relationship, and not in 'the dead weight of tradition' or other racist humbugs: 'it would be false to assert that successful development has been a dynamic process while underdevelopment is a static state of being – the same imperialist process produced them both'.[19] Onimode follows Marx very closely in identifying epochs by their prevailing modes of production, distinguishing between the communal, with its emphasis on self-help, gift-giving, sex and age-grade based division of labour and gerontocratic-democratic leadership practices,[20] and then goes on to more exploitative historical forms. His position on the slave mode of production in Kanem-Borno, the Hausa states, Oyo and Benin is contentious, inasmuch as some historians posit that slavery before the late 1400s was a more domestic affair.[21] His exposition of feudalism is more balanced and an excellent synthesis. It is customary of course, to notice the existence of feudalism in Islamic Northern Nigeria, where emirates operated so obviously, in a feudal manner, but less so elsewhere. Onimode reminds us of how feudal structures governed Oyo, where *isakole* or the tribute on land was part of the legal framework even in the 1980s. It is fair to say that what blinds many contemporary commentators with regards to feudalism in Nigeria is precisely its near-omnipresence, even in the sphere of legal recognition (as 'the law of the land') in the constitution. Even Igbos, who historically experienced less of the institution of kingship and relied more on secret societies and tribal democracy, are constructing new kingdoms in the 21st century. Much of Nollywood's output focuses on royalty, where princesses emerge from the back seats of pick-up trucks as if those were traditional palanquins. Extra-economic coercion is well known to accompany this in Nigeria, with royals and feudalists employing literally armies of thugs to engage in land grabs, dispossessions of widows and suchlike. Contrary to the BBC's eulogies, feudal activities are far from the innocent *durbar* with silk canopy: contemporary feudalism is as criminal as the robber barons were. It would also be wrong to imagine the royals as bearers of a traditional culture, when most of their palaces have been built in the last 20 years in a chunky-and-drab, nondescript style, and none of them is known for collecting traditional objets d'art. Perhaps worst of all is that they provide traditional legitimacy to politicians by arranging for the marriages of their daughters to the most promising, most aggressive, and most criminal.

Onimode then goes on to emphasise how, especially in Kano in the early 19th century, the cloth manufacturing process included a putting-out and collection system, indicating a high level of technological prowess. Blacksmiths produced hoes, cutlasses, knives and guns even before European penetration.[22] He describes how mercantilist slaving robbed and under-populated the land. When he delves into the spreading of cash crops, he gives us rare insights into its dynamic relationship with subsistence agriculture:

> insistence on subsistence agriculture often gives the erroneous impression that this sub-sector provided no surplus. On the contrary,

it generated both actual and potential surplus. The most important components of the potential surplus consisted of its under-utilized labour and land, which later were attracted to export-crop production, mining, and in the case of labour, wage employment. Part of the actual surplus was expropriated by landlords as land-rent, by imperialists in the form of taxes without receipts, and in exploitative prices for imported shoddy manufactures. The rest was lavished on rural festivities.[23]

Colonial infrastructure served entirely the purposes of economic extraction from Nigeria.[24] In a picturesque comment on urban growth under British rule, Onimode comments how 'the same British imperialists who planned the physical elegance of London, with its wide paved streets and parks, bequeathed the disgraceful slum Lagos as the capital of Nigeria.'[25] The Church, and education, served to produce a subaltern consciousness. The first college was opened only in 1948, at Ibadan.[26] While exporting monocultural cash crops to feed British industry, they received cheap mass produced British products, first chiefly textiles, in return: 'imported manufactures – in many cases outright trash – soon displaced many traditional products of domestic trade.'[27] While light industries such as soap and cigarettes were introduced, heavy industries were systematically killed off in the colonies that later became Nigeria.[28]

Onimode attacks the concept that colonialism constituted transfers of technology: 'Colonialism was a fundamental process of elimination without substitution.' 'No technology was transferred when Nigerian labourers were exploited on manual labour, or for that matter, when Nigerians were operators of this or that machine.' 'Nigerian workers were never allowed to know how the machines brought by the colonialists were designed – even their children at university did not get that far.' 'Consequently, colonialists technologically uprooted the Nigerian population in a grand process of de-technologising the country; the imported machinery and equipment were simply other people's furniture.'[29] 'The collective consequence of this rendered colonial Nigeria a technologically impotent imperialist estate with a highly illiterate and unskilled labour force.' 'As a result, the colonial moment in Nigeria's history submerged the country in technological underdevelopment, superstition and obscurantism – to the immense advantage of colonial plunder.'[30] It is not unreasonable to see the value of Nigeria as an expatriate job market, even for technicians, especially prior to about 1993 when the country was still liveable for those who did not hire private security. Onimode's thinking is more than just indiscriminate West-bashing. Onimode presents an unsentimental account, reminding us of historical episodes such as the destruction of the weaving looms of Kano, which have largely fallen out of historical consciousness. Anyone familiar with world history knows how British textiles destroyed the Indian traditional cloth industry, but Kano's fate is much less remembered as is the way in which farmers were brought into employment: by forced labour and by money taxes.[31] As a professional economist of global standing, Onimode is expert at analysing how colonial financial infrastructure facilitated plunder by multiple means, such as a 100 per cent external reserve ratio for colonial currency, no banking examiner until 1959, no minimum liquid asset reserve requirement for bank loans until 1958, and no banking ordinance until 1952.[32] Even in years of surplus, Nigeria was forced to borrow from London at exorbitant rates. He analyses the operations of the West African Currency Board, and how it was in effect a 'passive money changer': 'Any balance of trade surplus automatically increased currency supply by the same amount.' The Central Bank was established in 1958, only two years before independence was granted.[33] Many of the commercial banks started out as slave trading companies (Barclay's was one of them). With near lack of any oversight, there were no reports and banking statistics until 1943 and the war economy years. Nnamdi Azikiwe was one of first who established an indigenous bank. Agricultural export and trade took up most of the commercial banking sector's credit activities, with almost no credit to industry, and most investment going abroad in the first place. The 'persistent denial of basic credit' characterised the system.[34]

In a chapter on class and class struggle in the colonial system, Onimode describes the appearance of the Nigerian comprador class: from Brazilian Yoruba and Sierra Leonean creole expatriates to feudalists and an aggressive new intellectual class, 'mimic intellectuals' and culturally rootless entrepreneurs.[35] He gives a detailed account of Zikist activities and labour radicalism, emphasising how Awolowo's Action Group quietly marginalised its own leftists.[36] After describing the high point of labour and nationalist agitation in the 1940s and 1950s, he goes on to analyse the neocolonial mode of production (ushered in with independence in 1960), which he treats as a subcategory of the multilateral imperialist epoch (from 1946 onwards).

He also explains neocolonialism in general terms. Neocolonialism as a concept has been largely out of vogue since the late 1980s. However, this term still has descriptive force. It is useless to bemoan the immorality of international multinational corporations in the oil business without recognising that their governments help them and nourish them, and that they repatriate significant profits to the global metropole, acting as systemic stabilisers of the international capitalist system. Shying away from this word hollows out the wish for a better future for underdeveloped nations, including Nigeria. Neocolonialism exists, and it is arguably stronger than ever, with mobile telephony and IT adding to the equation of massive profit repatriation from sub-Saharan African countries. Onimode defines neocolonialism in the following terms: 'a "contractual relationship", a collaborative arrangement between the imperialist bourgeoisie and the comprador bourgeoisie of the peripheral Third World country for the mutual, though unequal, advantage of both groups of capitalist exploiters'.[37] The indigenisation programmes of 1972 and 1976, and the capitalist Land Use Decree of 1978, altered the terms of the contract a little, but only to a small extent, in favour of the comprador bourgeoisie. Multinational corporations generally 'sponsor political parties, change governments and finance coups d'etat' in Africa. In Nigeria, oil allowed the local bourgeoisie to have a more marked stake in the governing of their own patrimony. This manifested in some cases, such as when BP was briefly nationalised by Nigeria in response to the UK's decision to sell arms again to apartheid South Africa in 1979.[38] However, systemically, indigenisation has remained a sham, in Onimode's view.

> The national attitude to foreign domination and exploitation has been an uninterrupted combination of active collaboration and superficial indigenization. Both responses have been determined by the domestic petty bourgeoisie's rabid interest in establishing an economic base for its class, through primitive accumulation involving collusion with imperialists in the looting of Nigeria.[39]

Since Onimode's days, this has been partly accomplished, as articles in glamour magazines praising Nigerian style testify in the 21st century. Indeed, parts of the Nigerian bourgeoisie go abroad to take care of even minor ailments, the schooling of progeny, partying and shopping, while some family members stay behind in Abuja to accumulate wealth there.

Indigenisation in the 1970s did not alter the country's mode of production (and anyway it was partly suspended during the 1980s SAPs). Some Nigerian figureheads were employed by boards, some visa documents falsified for expatriates. That was all. With near-zero techno-logical transfer and the pumping of oil from rigs directly to tankers, the net outflow of capital via multinational corporations is so obvious that it is almost superfluous to mention of it in the Nigerian case. Nigeria became a rentier state and a monocultural country, contends Onimode, after the oil bonanza.[40] While protein intake was lower than the minimum human requirement according to the World Health Organization,[41]

Nigeria diverted its attention entirely away from agriculture, the sector where most of its labour force still found employment in the 1970s. Peasants lived short and brutish lives, immersed in a culture of silence.[42] Obasanjo's Operation Feed the Nation managed to establish him as the biggest poultry magnate in the country, but achieved nothing in the way of emancipating agriculture.[43] Onimode saw some modest gains by import substitution industrialisation in the 1960s and 1970s[44] – these have since evaporated with deindustrialisation in the late 1980s. Military dictatorship was very successful in taming trade unionism in the country,[45] but less so according to any other criteria. Successive military governments squandered untold billions of dollars in the country. In discussing class struggle, Onimode agrees with Ikenna Nzimiro in seeing the civil war as an intra-class struggle of the emergent bourgeoisie for comprador positions[46] – without apparently having read Nzimiro's work on the civil war, only his works dealing with anthropology.

Imperialism and Underdevelopment in Nigeria is an important work. Onimode's thought is presented throughout the book with convincing clarity, using scores of tables and official data, and a theoretical subtlety that flows out of the multitude of works studied, as well as from Onimode's own analytical prowess as a Marxist thinker. His work is informed by Sweezy, Jack Woddis, Richard Sklar, Ola Oni, Walter Rodney, Marx, Nkrumah, Lenin, *The Monthly Review*, André Gunder-Frank, Frantz Fanon, and many specialised works on Nigerian history. It would be a great service to Nigerian historical consciousness if this volume were once again brought into print. During the late 1980s, Onimode came to chair the Council of the Institute for African Alternatives in London. As his fame grew, he was employed more and more often as a consultant by the OAU, UNDP, the ILO and various INGOs[47] and labour organisations. His thought underwent some change from the late 1980s. In *Coalition for Change: Alternative Strategies for Africa*, edited for the Institute for African Alternatives (1990), he would still advocate for structural disengagement from world capitalism as the sole viable opportunity to overcome dependence,[48] but he juxtaposed this with involuntary delinking (such as in the case of failed states).[49] He co-wrote this book with others, including labour leader Hassan Sunmonu. They still emphasised how Nigeria's structural disengagement, rather than ushering in an era of autarky, should focus on domestically exploiting the country's raw materials. As Onimode puts it:

MNCs [multinational corporations] typically resist local inputs as inferior and unsatisfactory. Such MNCs should be shown the way out of Africa. Thus local sorghum, millet and maize can be used for bread and beer; cassava can be used for starch, clay brick can be substituted for cement etc.[50]

In his 1992 magnum opus, *A Future for Africa: Beyond the Politics of Adjustment,* he dissects the IMF's SAPs as a politically motivated plot to recolonise the continent. He paints a startling picture of SAPs in all their terrible glory as they brutalised the populations of 34 African nations, including Nigeria.[51] He refutes the glorification of the informal sector that we so often encounter in NGO pamphlets, which discuss, for example, how a village was saved by its traditional crafts. Indeed, the rise of the informal sector is a sure sign of the collapse of a given economic and social system – as in derelict former Yugoslavia where they even called it *'afrikanizacija'*. Onimode still recognised that neocolonialism had not disappeared by 1992, and that indeed imperialism was actually on the rise: he gives the obvious example of the recolonising French, who do this openly.[52] He knows that no democracy can be meaningful if the people have empty stomachs.[53] Onimode even implicitly criticises Chinua Achebe's point that Nigeria's failure is a failure in leadership, pure and simple.[54] He knows that the problem is systemic. But on the other hand, he saw two incredible sea changes in the 1980s: the extreme worsening of the terms of trade for Africa's traditional exports, and the fall of Eastern European socialism.[55] Onimode had absolutely no naive hopes that the fall of the USSR would usher in an era of global prosperity and multilateral decision-making. On the contrary. However, the only ally of the Nigerian left, grudging and sclerotic as it was, vanished with the fall of the Soviet Union. Onimode's line changed: in this entire work, he mentions socialism only once, and even then, in a rather shy way: 'delinking argues for a truly democratic socialist transition',[56] and in an even odder statement claims how 'many feel that some form of socialism' should be instituted in spite of Eastern Europe's *volte face*. Little did Onimode know at the time that Eastern Europe, instead of melting away in a newly grandiose West, would become a nightmare of shattered dreams and would make up the new rust belt of a semi-periphery (and in parts even a new periphery) of the international capitalist system. In this work, Onimode employs those well-worn clichés of INGO papers that talk about grassroots without addressing problems of power. 'There must be sustained pressure from below,' says Onimode in this sad book, pathetically avoiding many of the author's own core beliefs. Onimode identified as a Marxist and as a radical economist up to his death, despite the tactical retreat in his later works.

Adebayo O. Olukoshi's Circle

Professor Adebayo Olukoshi is currently Director of the UN African Institute for Economic Development and Planning (IDEP), and interim Director of the Africa Governance Institute (AGI), both in Dakar, Senegal. He holds a PhD in political science from Leeds University. Until March 2009, Professor Olukoshi was executive secretary of the Council for the Development of Social Science Research in Africa (CODESRIA). He has also previously served as director of research at the Nigerian Institute of International Affairs (NIIA), Lagos; senior research fellow/ research programme coordinator at the Nordic Africa Institute (NAI), Uppsala; and senior programme staff at the South Centre in Geneva. Among his publications are: *Africa and the Development Challenges in the New Millennium: The NEPAD Debate*; *The Elusive Prince of Denmark: Structural Adjustment and the Crisis of Governance in Africa*; *Between Liberalisation and Oppression: The Politics of Structural Adjustment in Africa*; and *Africa: Reaffirming Our Commitment*, co-edited with Jean-Bernard Ouédraogo and Ebrima Sall.

Olukoshi probably would not consent today if one called him a Marxist. However, his political economy programme at Ahmadu Bello University, Zaria, was a hotbed of Marxist thought in the late 1980s and early 1990s. Besides Olukoshi, the group included the Soviet-trained Akin Fadahunsi, Yusuf Bangura, Jibrin Ibrahim, Abdul Raufu Mustapha and, by extension, Bjorn Beckmann (a Swedish expatriate scholar), and Attahiru Jega and Shehu Yahaya from Bayero University, Kano. Some of them would also work as overseas editors of the *Review of African Political Economy*. The most interesting collection of texts they produced (from a Marxist point of view) was *The Politics of Structural Adjustment in Nigeria*, edited by Olukoshi (published in 1993). This work commands respect with its all-encompassing, meticulous scholarship on the economic violence that Babangida's SAPs unleashed on Nigeria. 'Per capita income fell as a result of SAPs from US$778 in 1985 to US$108 in 1989,' a slump that shames wartime depressions globally, while the price of construction materials rose 'more than 500% in three years',[57] rice 'rose by 600% and bread made from wheat 900%'.[58]

Shehu Yahaya, in his article on the privatisation drive (part and parcel of SAPs), gives a fantastic account of the competing visions for socialist and market-based developmental frameworks, demonstrating the inevitable futility of the latter in the given African framework:

Most of the discussion and debate within the radical and Marxist tradition has been primarily concerned with developing a clear and coherent theoretical and analytical framework for understanding the state and its intervention, its dimensions, its success or failure; much less attention has been devoted to addressing the contemporary debate of the state and the market in the context of Africa. This is partly because, even when the inefficiency, mismanagement and ineffectiveness of state institutions are discussed, there is a tendency to argue that only a revolutionary transformation of the state can solve the problem (Toyo, 1984), or simply to shrug it off on the grounds that the private sector in these countries is no better ... But the real and immediate alternative facing most of these countries is between various kinds of state intervention and various forms of the market mechanism, rather than between capitalism and socialism ... But ... public enterprises fulfill important functions for capitalism ... which cannot be performed by private capital ... The criteria ... for an empirical assessment of the performance of state enterprises using both the neoclassical and the radical frameworks are similar.[59]

Except, of course, when the unstated aim of a given elite is not the building of an efficient, productive capitalism even, but the perpetuation of a criminal racket.

The Nigeria Labour Congress prepared its own alternative to orthodox neoliberal adjustment in 1985, but it was ignored.[60] Professionals were crushed along with the middle strata that were thrust into poverty.[61]

Okwudiba Nnoli and His Circle

Professor Okwudiba Nnoli is usually mentioned as a savant of ethnicity's influence on development, especially with reference to his work *Ethnicity and Development in Nigeria* (1994), out of print for many years. Here it is more important to discuss Nnoli's *Dead-end to Nigerian Development: An Analysis of the Political Economy of Nigeria 1979–1989*, edited while he was already at CODESRIA in Dakar, but which he wrote together with his colleagues from the University of Nigeria, Nsukka (H. Assisi Asobie, Chuku A. Umezurike, Ugochukwu B. Uba, Okechukwu Ibeanu), and Abdul Raufu Mustapha from Zaria (the latter would become an overseas editor with the *Review of African Political Economy*).

This work is different from the compendium edited by Olukoshi. Olukoshi's work was symptomatic of economists growing into UN-affiliated, INGO-consulting thinkers, who, under the pressures of the 1990s, turned from champions of liberation to champions of charity. Okwudiba Nnoli's circle did not embark on this trajectory and, perhaps as a result, his subsequent biography appears less impressive than Olukoshi's. Nnoli et al.'s work on the Nigerian SAPs is a terrifying account of the damage that SAPs did, on a par with Olukoshi's, and more firm in its Marxist condemnation of the underlying structures.

The ruling class is simply not active in production, says Nnoli.[62] In the late 1980s, GDP declined on an average 6.3 per cent a year[63] while profits were spent abroad.[64] Violence spread in society, houses were now built like fortresses, and armed robbery became rampant,[65] while most Nigerians started to live (with their families) in one-room 'apartments'.[66] According to Nnoli, even Maitatsine sprang up because of the immense misery ushered in by SAPs:[67] 'The distorted and externally-oriented character of the economy encourages locally generated surplus to be transferred to foreign centers of production. The present crisis can be traced to the cumulative effect of the long-term transfer of such surplus.'[68]

Samuel G. Egwu gives a Marxist assessment of the ethnic question in the country. While the Academic Staff Union was being crushed, and the land decree of 1978 took away land from farmers, to give it to absentee landlords, developers and slumlords,[69] the Naija worker, far from the privileged urban labour aristocracy of academic folklore, looked like this:

> Nigerian workers always lived under very harsh conditions. They cannot afford three meals a day, and in any case, the nutritional content of their meals is very low. They eat meat, fish, or any other animal protein source very rarely. The caloric content of the meals is usually below the minimum recommended by the United Nations. In addition, they cannot afford a reasonable shelter for self and family and usually live in very unsanitary environments. At the same time they cannot afford the cost of education and health care for their families whose members, consequently, suffer from ignorance and endemic diseases. Similarly, they lack access to credit facilities and elementary social amenities as well as basic needs such as adequate transport facilities, pipe-borne water, social security insurance, consumer goods, adequate provision for old age, any help whatever for house work, child care or simple recreational facilities for their children. The Nigerian worker never has reserves. He lives from hand to mouth. Each difficulty or accident compels him to sell his belongings at a trifling price. And once he falls into the clutches of the money-lender … he can rarely escape utter ruin.[70]

Today Usman Tar follows Bade Onimode very closely in identifying the Nigerian ruling class as not only comprador, but a petty bourgeoisie, citing Gramsci in the argument. This of course underlines how the Nigerian bourgeoisie differs from its Western counterparts, who engage (or engaged prior to the 1980s anyway), in production. Still, we might find this classification counterintuitive. To take an example, Atiku Abubakar, former vice-president of Nigeria under Obasanjo, an international billionaire, is obviously a member of the Nigerian ruling class. As a man who had made his first millions as a customs officer, he is perhaps symptomatic of the colossal corruption prevalent in the Nigerian uniformed services, but he is no petty bourgeois. A billionaire who travels in convoys and private jets, he owns houses in most parts of the world, and owns a university, the American University of Nigeria, in his hometown Yola. He belongs to the *haute bourgeoisie* even if he never reads the *New York Times,* does not collect contemporary art, and has no idea about opera. However, exactly to the extent that he is haute bourgeois (married into local royalty, too), Abubakar's life is internationalised. The *hoi oligoi* have to keep their operations of extraction in the country, but spend most of their days abroad, blurring the distinction between imperialists and their compradors.

Review of African Political Economy

The *Review of African Political Economy* is a London-based international peer-reviewed journal. According to its own self-definition:

> Since 1974 ROAPE has provided radical analysis of trends, issues and social processes in Africa, adopting a broadly materialist interpretation of change. It pays particular attention to the political economy of inequality, exploitation and oppression, and to organized struggles against them, whether these inequities are driven by global forces or local ones such as class, race, ethnicity and gender. It sustains a critical analysis of the nature of power and the state in Africa in the context of capitalist globalization.[71]

Known as *RoAPE,* or *ROAPE* (in the 1970s, the journal referred to itself as *RAPE,* to denote 'the rape of Africa,' but later the practice was dropped), the journal was set up largely due to the efforts of Ruth First, but also Chris Allen, Basil Davidson and other Marxist giants. It has consistently provided an intellectual outlet to African authors, including of course, Nigerian authors. It helps its African contributors and readership in new and innovative ways: it allows for free subscriptions from the continent, it provides additional help to contributors whose mother tongue or second language is other than English, and it publishes the best of its archives on the internet for free (articles older than seven years).

Especially from the mid 1980s to 1999, when it became impossible in Nigeria to publish leftist pamphlets or Marxist works of theory, *ROAPE* became the most important single outlet for left-leaning Nigerian intellectuals to publish their work. The journal has had many overseas editors from Nigeria, most notably Abdul Raufu Mustapha, Yusuf Bangura and Bjorn Beckmann (a Swedish expatriate who was at Ahmadu Bello University at the time). Today, *ROAPE*'s contributing editor from Nigeria is Usman A. Tar. Many of *ROAPE*'s Nigerian authors ended up leaving Nigeria as a result of Babangida's military dictatorship, and especially Sani Abacha's reign of terror. Olajide Oyolede ended up in Dakar with CODESRIA and then at the University of the Western Cape, Arthur C. Okolie at Teachers College, Columbia University, New York, Tajudeen Abdul-Raheem in Kenya, Abdul Raufu Mustapha is at the University of Oxford, and Usman Tar even taught in post-occupation Iraq.

The *Review of African Political Economy* has predictably focused mostly on political economy, as its name suggests. Marxist historiography, or Marxian analyses of religion did not feature prominently (although Segun Osoba did expose Yusufu Bala Usman's take on the manipulation of religion in an article). Labour struggle, especially the 1981 general strike, was covered in the periodical (Dafe Otobo), along with a uniquely self-reflective article on the world of the Nigerian Left (Tajudeen Abdul-Raheem, Adebayo Olukoshi). Other articles targeted corruption (especially Osoba's excellent analysis) and political turbulence. *ROAPE* was also acting as an 'official organ' for Bene Madunagu's and Molara Ogundipe-Leslie's Marxian-feminist *Women in Nigeria* organisation. Eskor Toyo published in *ROAPE* his general call for Marxists to join the People's Redemption Party in 1980 (discussed in detail and cited in chapter 5). Student revolts have also figured quite prominently in the journal.

Professor Dafe Otobo of the University of Lagos, today President of the Nigerian Industrial Relations Association, consultant to the ILO[72] and the Nigeria Labour Congress, published on the 1981 general strike and its aftermath, when, in the run-up to the Buhari coup, a devastating economic slump engulfed Nigeria.

Professor Segun Osoba of Obafemi Awolowo University, Ife (not to be confused with Governor Segun Osoba, a mainstream politician), who had in 1978 published a radical minority report together with Yusufu Bala Usman on the draft proposal for the Nigerian constitution,[73] was a well-known Marxist intellectual in Nigeria in the 1970s. Historian Toyin Falola, at the beginning of his career, edited Segun Osoba's articles. Osoba went beyond briefings and short notes in the articles that he contributed to the journal. His 'Corruption in Nigeria: Historical Perspectives'[74] shows him as a sharp-eyed examiner of his subject, who offers no platitudes and is concrete in his examples. After stating how his own article is an outgrowth of his political choices and is not 'value free', he goes on to define corruption; he does not stop at legalities, however, but underlines how corruption 'subverts or diminishes the capacity of the legitimate authorities to provide fully for the material and spiritual wellbeing of all members of society in a just and equitable manner', a radical definition.[75] Also, its 'peculiar form, dynamics and degree of social and cultural acceptability or tolerance being critically related to the dominant mode of capital accumulation; income, wealth and poverty distribution; power configuration', Osoba posits that flag independence was tainted with serious corruption even at the outset, quoting how Azikiwe:

> even before independence ... as premier of Eastern Nigeria had been exposed by the Foster Sutton Tribunal of Enquiry of 1956 into the African Continental Bank (ACB) to have abused his position as head of government to divert huge sums of Eastern Nigerian government funds into his own bank.[76]

After independence, this became a generalised modus operandi for the political elite as a group. Even the devastating civil war of Biafra:

> provided sensational opportunities for unlawful enrichment: for example, the misappropriation of salaries and allowances of soldiers killed in action for several months by their commanders; the gross inflation of military procurement contracts ... the looting of public and private properties in occupied territories by both the Nigerian and the Biafran armies.[77]

Oil in the 1970s increased opportunities for loot. The Gowon era already brought in what may be termed as a kleptocracy, Obasanjo's 'noisy war against corruption' was a farce; and even Murtala Muhammad built rows of tenant housing in Kano that blot his image as a clean leader.[78] The second republic saw generals retreat to business as upstart tycoons. Osoba underlines how the constitutional requirements on registering new parties in the 1979 constitution, actually provided the framework for the corruption to spread. Babangida added to this package 'the culture of impunity' when the Central Bank of Nigeria was subjected to the president's authority in 1988.[79] After 1986, even for middle-class people, it became impossible to live on their lawful salaries and that is how a 'trickle down' effect came into play, when society at large was affected by the kind of predator values that hitherto had characterised only the elite. Osoba's only proposed way out is popular democracy in the vein of Madunagu.[80]

In his article on 'The Deepening Crisis of the Nigerian National Bourgeoisie',[81] Osoba deals with Nigeria's neocolonial economic dependency. His major argument is that in the 1980s the level of Nigerian unilateral dependency on multinational corporations did not decrease: indeed, they were still by far the stronger party when compared with the national (comprador) bourgeoisie.[82] Technological transfer is a mirage,[83] the bourgeoisie are commission agents,[84] and in fact 'nothing, literally nothing, really works in the country'.[85] Osoba's understanding of the petty bourgeoisie differs from Bade Onimode's when he claims that the national bourgeoisie is in itself comprador in nature.[86]

Further important contributors were Abdul Raufu Mustapha and Tajudeen Abdul-Raheem. Abdul Raufu Mustapha is a professor at Oxford, who specialises in development-related issues in Africa, and Tajudeen Abdul-Raheem was the general-secretary of the Pan-African Movement, and deputy director for the UN's Millennium Campaign for Africa, when he died in a car accident in Kenya in 2009. Abdul-Raheem's most interesting contribution to *ROAPE* discusses the 'global pornography of poverty' by way of Bono-style celebrity acts of charity.[87] Shehu Othman too wrote with Abdul Raufu Mustapha on police killings on Nigerian campuses. Tajudeen Abdul-Raheem's most interesting contribution from the point of view of this study was an article he co-wrote with Adebayo Olukoshi on 'The Left in Nigerian Politics and the Struggle for Socialism: 1945–1985',[88] a relatively short but still very perceptive exposition of the role that Marxists have played in Nigeria. After discussing Zikism and early Marxists, they go on to discuss Ikenna Nzimiro's take on communism in Biafra. They challenge Nzimiro and cite the case of other Igbos, such as Ikoku, Eskor Toyo and Mokwugo Okoye, who stayed on the federal side during the conflict – attributing this to genuine political convictions and not expediency.[89] Abdul-Raheem and Olukoshi also discuss the role of the clandestine Biafran Communist Party, an organisation that Nzimiro never once mentions in his version of events.[90] Later they go on to present the flowering of the Nigerian Marxist movement in its institutional contexts, linking it to the oil boom and the financial polarisation that it brought for the country.[91] They concur with this author's assessment (see chapter 5) that the space that Nigerian Marxism opened up for itself was significantly enhanced by Eastern European links, adding Cuba as an important contributor in the form of the Nigeria–Cuba Friendship Association.[92] The authors were critical of Eskor Toyo and especially Madunagu when they associated themselves with the People's Redemption Party around 1982.[93] More interesting though, is their take on entryism as a conscious political strategy, when Nigerian Marxist academics ended up joining mainstream parties and even the administrations of military heads of state:

> From this premise, some Leftists addressed secret memos to state officials, served on government commissions, took up secret and open advisory jobs, and sought to build influence with the powers that be, proffering advice on how the system could be made to work better, in a bid to be seen to be relevant and not just 'armchair theoreticians'. In this way, reformism became a way of life among many and 'pragmatism' became an alibi for opportunism, anti-theory and anti-organisation.[94]

This is a central point and it would be cheap to dismiss it on grounds of Olukoshi's later straying from Marxism, or any such mundane argument. The phenomenon did much to discredit Nigerian leftists. At the same time, one need not dwell for too long on the question of why a Marxist thinker would advise an obviously right-wing government: in Nigeria, such moves have saved lives and provided livelihoods under terrible dictatorships. What is more interesting is why those governments felt the need to ostentatiously woo Nigerian Marxists into their political bureaus and cabinets. This is where the abyss in the popular legitimacy of the Nigerian state plays out in front of our eyes. The representatives of the leftist counterculture were needed even by Abacha, who otherwise preferred to rely on multi-faith prayer sessions to boost the image of his rule.

7

Marxian Feminisms

Feminism as a political viewpoint, as an ethical system or as a research agenda may encompass radically different interpretations and attitudes. For some, the word 'feminism' itself has come to denote mainstream Western liberal versions of the women's movement to such an extent that alternative formulations were offered instead, such as 'womanism'.[1] As with Marxisms, feminisms are indeed many. While the now classical counterculture feminism of the 1970s, especially that of thinkers such as Andrea Dworkin,[2] aimed to fight against pornography as the most grievous form of violence against women, today Mireille Miller-Young, in her *A Taste for Brown Sugar: Confessions of a Black Feminist Academic Pornographer*,[3] offers one example of 'sex-positive feminism' that sees some forms of pornography as empowering. Likewise, it seems obvious that Jean Bethke Elshtain's liberal-conservative views[4] have little in common with Clara Zetkin's wayward feminist Leninism. What appears, however, as a unifying factor between 18th-century forerunners of the movement – the first, the second and even the current third waves of feminism in the West – is that they have mostly been defined by Western women thinkers – even when they came from such Western peripheries as Tsarist Poland (as in the case of Zetkin), or when they hailed from perhaps the single most disadvantaged victim group of US capitalism, Black women (as in the case of Angela Davis). Gwendolyn Mikell's *African Feminism: The Politics of Survival in Sub-Saharan Africa*,[5] which appeared in 1997, although not radical in its political opinions, was a welcome and comprehensive exception to this gap in the global discourse. Mikell and her contributors' case studies focused on empirical research in what she called 'societies in crisis',[6] little anticipating how the 1990s African crisis would become, in our millennium, the new normal.

Marxist analysis, ever more in tune to anticipate structural crises, has had a troubled relationship with many schools of feminism, including Marxian ones. Engels' findings about how the nuclear family was a historical product in *The Origin of the Family, Private Property, and the State* (1845)[7] started a conservative furore, and raised feminist suspicions about the long-term aims of Marxist liberation when it came to the family and women. Did Communists want to deprive children of loving, traditional, nuclear families, and did they envisage a future where they were more or less raised by day-care providers, while their biological parents worked and engaged in promiscuous sexual activity, without any reference to children's emotional needs?

Some would say the very opposite was true, certainly when it came to 'really existing socialist societies' such as the USSR, where Stalin's prudish ethics put Victorian England to shame.[8] Indeed Marxism in general, since perhaps Marx himself, who was rather conservative in his private life, and especially in the workers' movement, came to develop a masculine, ostentatiously heteronormative ethos that seemed to celebrate intellectual austerity and a certain lack of imagination and refinement. As much as one might find questions of the social order paramount, it seems to have been a major weakness of both revolutionary Marxisms and especially orthodox Marxism-Leninism of the Eastern European or the Chinese variety not to allow for the whimsical, and to fight against even the very concept of luxury. Instead of proposing a grand alternative, this rather macho face of Marxism seems to have played into the capitalist narrative that linked the erotic, the feminine, the rare, the exotic, the luxurious, and the refined with the ruling classes, instead of appropriating them for a revolutionary purpose.

Masculine obsessions, and perhaps male narrow-mindedness, come to mind when we read of Clara Zetkin's clash with Lenin:

> The record of your sins, Clara, is even worse. I have been told that at the evenings arranged for reading and discussion with working women, sex and marriage problems come first. They are said to be the main objects of interest in your political instruction and educational work. I could not believe my ears when I heard that. The first state of proletarian dictatorship is battling with the counterrevolutionaries of the whole world ... But active communist women are busy discussing sex problems and forms of marriage – 'past, present, and future'. They consider it their most important task to enlighten working women on these questions.[9]

(Ironically, the po-faced Lenin secretly had an artistic and superbly intellectual French mistress, Inessa Armand, with whom he had the most delectable and open-minded conversations about precisely the same matters. Armand was later buried at the Kremlin Wall Necropolis, but their liaison was kept secret until the fall of the USSR, both within Russia, and in all other countries of the self-styled 'peace camp'.)[10]

Debates on what Marxist feminism should mean beyond the obvious emphasis on class did not stop at Lenin's divan. Alexandra Kollontai, the grande dame of the Russian Bolshevik old guard, who joined ranks with Lenin's party in 1915, was said to have quipped that 'The satisfaction of sexual desires should be as simple as drinking a glass of water.' This story is apocryphal and its probable origin is one of the points of her *Theses on Communist Morality in the Sphere of Marital Relations*, where she states that 'sexuality is a human instinct as natural as hunger or thirst'.[11] Although even Wikipedia busts the 'glass of water' myth,[12] it resurfaces in unexpected places even today (most recently a 2015 article in *The New York Review of Books*).[13] Kollontai was convinced that the nuclear family was destined to disappear under the dictatorship of the proletariat, viewing it as breeding ground for selfish behaviour that would weaken the collective and, as such, something positively dangerous for the revolutionary state (a minority view within Marxist feminism).

The crux of Marxist feminist arguments generally has had less to do with the exact methodologies of day care or possible family structures in the new socialist or communist society than with analysing the complex interplay between gender and class. For traditional old left thinkers, including Marxist-Leninist feminists, the central claim was that discrimination against women affected different classes of women differently; indeed, that alienation, poverty and abuse had a much more brutal effect on proletarian women than on women of the bourgeoisie. In the Marxist-Leninist framework, although bourgeois women were reified in bourgeois marriage, they also had avenues to tackle the patriarchal system that were, by and large, unavailable to their proletarian sisters in a capitalist society. Unpaid work at home, abuse by lovers and husbands, unfair wage differentials that favoured men, the unavailability of free day care or health facilities have had an incomparably more devastating effect on impoverished women in a capitalist society than on the daughters and wives of the haute bourgeoisie. Especially after 1968 and in feminist schools of thought associated with Western Marxism, this entire logic came to be challenged and indeed the most sophisticated Marxist feminist theories today argue for a 'single system' understanding of capitalism, of which gender oppression is an inseparable part.

Women in Eastern Europe under really existing socialism have now received much scholarly attention in gender studies departments in the region and beyond; indeed, today there is even a fairly comprehensive bibliography published on the subject.[14] It is a cliché that Eastern European women entered the workforce but kept their 19th-century domestic responsibilities, and that places like the USSR, socialist Yugoslavia or Romania were macho patriarchies in more ways than one. What is less well known and less studied within the liberal mainstream of gender studies within and without the region, is that general hidden underemployment allowed women to leave their workplaces early, have multiple sick leaves, relax in suburban or rural allotments (as in the dacha cultures of the USSR, Czechoslovakia or Hungary), visit sandy sea beaches for free (as in Bulgaria), or visit ubiquitous nudist establishments (as in East Germany). Super-cheap communal eateries (as in Poland), free nurseries, kindergartens, schools and universities helped women, along with (usually rural) grandmothers who often moved in with young urban families, and represented a traditionalist, communitarian ethos within the urban housing projects of industrial socialism. What women in these countries yearned for, and what these economies frequently could not provide, were consumer goods in sufficient number, and they especially lacked any kind of ability to cater for personal artistic tastes or niche markets. Subsidised children's clothing and similarly subsidised uniform boots for the young could not offer a viable psychological compensation for many women, especially in countries where consumer choices before state socialism had already been fairly wide. Obviously, job security helped women as much as men – perhaps more, as children's survival and life's basic necessities were guaranteed. The legally enshrined nature of job security (Eastern Europe's version of Mao's *iron rice bowl*), did allow for cavalier attitudes when it came to performance on the job (after 1953, when Stalin died and repressive methods lost their teeth), but also helped to reduce stress, contributing to health and security, and a liveable world for families. Needless to say, women *qua* women had more rights than women as individuals: individual human rights (especially political rights) could not be exercised in Marxist-Leninist systems.

Women were represented in most national parliaments in socialist Eastern Europe but they rarely rose to the very top, with some notable exceptions. Jovanka Tito, Elena Ceausescu, or Lyudmila Zhivkova earned their second places in their respective countries due to the men in their lives. The Soviet Ambassador Kollontai, or Ana Pauker, who was Romania's first communist foreign minister and was forced out by Stalin's anti-Semitic campaign, or Yekaterina Furtseva (USSR minister of culture 1960–74), a glamorous and somewhat improbable Soviet grande dame, who habitually flew to Yugoslavia for weekends to meet up with her beau and had a defining influence on Soviet culture in her years in office: these were self-made women of communist politics. In the People's Republic of China, as the unquestioned leader of the Gang of Four, Mao's last wife Jiang Qing seemed, for a brief moment, the most powerful leader of the country, but was quickly deposed and in 1980 tried and sentenced to life imprisonment. Women also rose to prominence in some left communist organisations such as the Red Army Faction in West Germany: Ulrike Meinhof was so important in the organisation that it was known as the

Baader-Meinhof group. In Britain, Sylvia Pankhurst, the suffragette and anti-fascist hero represented the anti-Leninist, left communist ideology of pure revolution (also within the embryonic Communist Workers Party once she was forced out of the Communist Part of Great Britain). It is heart-warming to read Pankhurst's scholarship on Ethiopia[15] – she became in her later life a close associate of the Emperor Haile Selassie.

When it comes to the women's question in sub-Saharan Africa and specifically in Nigeria, one must keep in mind historical realities lest our understanding succumbs to Western clichés. Walter Rodney reminds us that economic and political development (in the sense of Marxian formations following each other in the course of a multifaceted developmental process) does not result in greater and greater freedom for most people, but the contrary.[16] The fact that the acephalous Igbo communities of south-Eastern Nigeria were, before British colonisation, practitioners of a form of communalism (that is, not 'developed') does not translate in any way into a greater oppression of women in those lands. Perhaps surprisingly, the very opposite was true. Ifi Amadiume's entire oeuvre is dedicated to these questions, and Marc Matera, Misty L. Bastian and Susan Kingsley Kent in their excellent *The Women's War of 1929: Gender and Violence in Colonial Nigeria*, remind us about the historical position of women in Nigeria:

> Not thinking of themselves as oppressed or kept in what used to be called 'the domestic sphere' – like their female counterparts in western societies even in quite recent history – these women could be secure enough in their own sense of importance and worth to take an active part in social transformation, to try to effect change, and even to see advantages to themselves in change that was properly regulated (by them). We are not trying here to argue that African women enjoyed 'liberation' before western women even dreamed of such a state. Rather we assert that early colonial Igbo and other southeastern women's lives were more complex and interesting than western notions of gender allow.[17]

This conclusion, albeit elegant, seems timid. To state the authors' core message even more forcefully, these women, who ran the marketplace and had obvious public functions and responsibilities in the land, were not more liberated (as in: liberated from a patriarchal system), but were definitely *freer* than their Western sisters. The assertive qualities so often attributed to African women may well find their roots in this historical reality, and may still influence African women's successes from Liberia to Kenya, including, of course, successes in Nigeria.

The Ogu Umunwaanyi *(Women's War/Aba Riots)*

The single best-known example of women in Nigeria standing up for their rights *qua* women was the Women's War of 1929/30 in Igbo and Ibibio areas, in Owerri and Calabar provinces of the south-eastern regions of amalgamated colonial Nigeria. The Women's War shocked colonial interpreters because, although it displayed no ideological links to modern Western feminist trends of the day, it was an uprising of women for specific political and economic objectives. Degraded as a 'return to savagery' by colonial officers, who themselves turned it into a one-sided bloodbath against the women rebels, this uprising was 'women's last effort to salvage their autonomy'[18] in the politico-economic sphere. The Women's War made use of conservative ideologies and expressed women's aims within the framework of a traditional (Igbo) world view. None of its participants were members of the minuscule English-educated elites of the day. Unlike in Yoruba areas of the south-west, in the East it was women themselves who ran the marketplace (the *Afia*), which was open, transparent, heterarchical, extremely competitive and 'democratic', and where the shrines were kept and maintained by women themselves. They also ran specific women's associations. *Umuada* (lineage daughters) were responsible for peace-making, and *Inyemedi* (lineage wives) ran local markets together and cared for market shrines[19] (women lived in their husbands' polygamous compounds). Traditionally, women could not only approach local elders (*ezeala*)[20] but had their own (parallel) ranks that carried economic, political and ritual power. As the uprising took place before the British finally decided to dispatch qualified anthropologists to study the people that they had subjugated, the colonisers seem to have had absolutely no capacity to understand the nature of the uprising, especially as it appeared in reaction to the loss of very real and meaningful freedoms. In the British narrative, until the 1970s the Women's War was seen as either a misguided revolt against the taxation of women only (this was, undoubtedly, part of the problem), or an obscure conservative movement against colonial modernity and rationality.[21]

Ancient ways did influence some of the demands of the women's movement, but not in the way misogynistic colonials thought. The full-body coverage demanded by Christian missions took away older women's role as guardians of young ones' moralities (nudity allowed the former to easily see signs of pregnancy);[22] the banning of polygamous marriages for converts resulted in husbands sending home wives and thereby destroying their emotional and economic well-being;[23] illiterate women were unable to make sense of new legal frameworks; new fines and rules appeared in the marketplace without prior consultation with women;[24] *corvée* labour took away husbands;[25] and, finally, the taxation of women was detrimental to their market role. (The counting of people, in the Igbo world view, could cause death,[26] which also explains the determined opposition to the registration for tax purposes of womenfolk by colonial authorities.) It would be a misrepresentation of historical reality to suggest that patriarchy did not exist in the Igbo context: it did, as compounds belonged to husbands. However, patriarchies and matriarchal institutions seem to have existed in a cooperative, overlapping, complementary fashion even in the strictly economic sphere. Men had the duty to harvest palm fruits, but women and children extracted oil from them, whereupon the oil belonged to the men but the kernels to women.[27]

As Matera, Bastian and Kent convincingly show, women's mobilisation into an *Umunwaanyi* (the collectivity of women) had happened already in 1925.[28] The British had destroyed shrines and the form of this earlier uprising was a traditionalist one: Christian women were attacked;[29] young women were denuded (for reasons outlined above). The women ritually swept chiefs' compounds and danced ritual *Nwaobiala* dances.[30] They also protested perceived injustices in the economic rewards of prostitution,[31] campaigned for the banning of male traders,[32] and demanded the closing of new colonial roads as those were thought to have brought the devastating influenza virus in 1919.[33]

The *Ogu Umunwaanyi* (Women's War) of 1929/30 was less centred on Ala, the market deity, was more inclusive of Christian women, and covered a much larger geographical area. It started on 23 November 1929 in Oloko[34] with a row over the counting of people, sheep and goats by a clerk who worked for a local warrant chief. Hated by women, colonially installed local administrators took wives without paying the customary bride price, confiscated women's produce and animals arbitrarily, manipulated divorce cases to their advantage, and generally ran government business in bewildering secrecy and as a men-only activity.[35] Okugo, the local warrant chief, was defrocked by women (with the district officer's final go-ahead).[36] On 13 December, however, on the road to Aba, a medical doctor ran over women who were blocking the passage of his car; on 15 December, 18 women were murdered[37] and 19 injured[38] by gunfire without warning at Utu Etim Ekpo. On 16 December, at Opobo, 39 women were murdered, again by gunfire without warning, and many more wounded.[39] These women, although they looted European shops and property, and burned warrant chiefs' compounds and ate their yams, nevertheless had not killed anybody.

Matera, Bastian and Kent show that 'Britishers' overreacted as a result of their own ignorance of the meaning in the local context of gestures, ritual dancing and denuding, and probably also because they were (almost without exception) ex-soldiers traumatised by the Great War, scandalised by what they saw as unbearable sexual overtones in the form taken by the women's uprising, sexually frustrated by anti-concubinage ordinances[40] and the system whereby they mostly served in Nigeria without their wives. The soldiers' ignorance was such that they believed that when women demonstrated wearing loincloths only, they could only have been prostitutes, although in the region at the time, prostitutes were precisely the women who were most likely to wear European style clothes.[41] The early 20th-century fixation with sexually transmitted diseases,[42] and a hysterical fear of the native and especially the female native's sexuality, added to the mix.[43] It seems fair when these authors of the best monograph on the subject make a connection between the violence exhibited by veterans who targeted women after the First World War in Britain, and the way that British veterans acted in the face of what they perceived as a violent women's movement, or, as they came to call it, the Aba Riots. In 1930, many houses and villages were burned before the British could 'pacify' the uprising. There was no outcry in Britain, although 58 women died – shocking, especially in comparison with the reaction that followed the Amritsar massacre.[44] The Women's War did however galvanise African American and Black British responses, along with reactions from C.L.R. James, Kenyatta and George Padmore.[45] Perhaps as a result of this the British Colonial Office suspected that there were agents from Moscow behind the uprising – perhaps the first of such misinterpretations in the long list of uprisings in Nigeria.[46] The colonial power reacted in a meaningful way only by dispatching anthropologists and trained spies to the affected regions.[47] Many works have appeared on the Women's War, the first feminist one by Judith Van Allen[48] but later also those by Toyin Falola and Ifi Amadiume.[49]

Olufunmilayo Ransome-Kuti

Frances Abigail Olufunmilayo Thomas before her marriage, afterward Olufunmilayo Ransome-Kuti, Funmilayo Ransome-Kuti, Funmilayo Anikulapo-Kuti, Iyaegbe, Iyalode, Beree, Funmi, FRK (each name denoting the same person),[50] was a Yoruba democratic socialist and feminist from the south-west of Nigeria who came to prominence in the independence movement and also as a democratic fighter against military rule. A female Che Guevara of sorts, she hailed from the elite (and studied in the UK at a time when this was the ultimate privilege for a Yoruba woman), joined ranks with the downtrodden, and fought bravely for women's rights and interests along with her wider political ideals in a very trying environment. (She was the mother of the global

Afrobeat star Fela Kuti; she died as a result of the injuries she suffered when soldiers acting on the orders of military head of state Obasanjo threw her out of a window before burning her son's compound, the Kalakuta Republic.) Ransome-Kuti was the recipient of the Lenin Peace Prize in 1970.[51] She did not produce theory herself, but her praxis was the catalyst for much of Nigerian feminism ever since her political debut in the 1940s; and socialist feminists such as Gambo Sawaba and Amina Mama have emphasised how FRK's efforts had fermented their respective ways of thinking. She was also much praised by Zikists, pro-democracy and student rebels of the 1970s, and her legacy is not forgotten in today's Nigerian labour and socialist circles either.

Earlier I emphasised how Nigerian socialisms appeared within the modernised sectors of the Nigerian economy (contrary to Fanon, who argues that Africa's urban classes are pampered and unworthy of socialist attention).[52] Ransome-Kuti's experiences in the UK, the USSR, China, socialist Hungary or Nkrumah-led Ghana were an asset when she articulated modern ways of resistance to modern problems. *Nwaobiala* dances and the coming together of marketplace women, although a fascinating subject for the historian, were doomed to fail as perhaps the African counterparts of Europe's peasant revolts: they were the expressions of bygone communal economic and political systems – the quaint and enchanting past. FRK, who was most likely a bully when it came to day-to-day politics, a forceful orator and a woman who understood the importance of public relations (as when she opted to wear Yoruba dress instead of her girlhood's habitual European attire), also genuinely represented the interests of Nigeria's non-elite womanhood: the class interests of market women, peasant women, itinerant petty traders and labourers. This issue cuts to the heart of problems of representation, as Ransome-Kuti certainly was among the colony's most privileged especially in terms of cultural capital.

The formidable FRK fought thousands of day-to-day battles over the water rate, taxation levels, temporarily deposed a king and finally became the international face of the specific class struggles for empowering Nigeria's female masses. The Soviets recognised her usefulness and made her one of the vice presidents of their Women's International Democratic Federation in 1953.[53] She outwitted them in her usual formidable style when she also sat on Women's International League for Peace and Freedom (a pro-Western front set up to counterbalance the former).[54] FRK was not a communist in her own understanding[55] but was 'not frightened or repelled by communism either'.[56] A scrupulously clean politician, she did a lot to expose the corruption of colonialism (she even wrote a telegram to Queen Elizabeth in 1960 about the Sharpeville massacre in South Africa),[57] the corruption of flag independence, and the corruption of male chauvinism with all its multifaceted infrastructure.

Markers of her elite standing were multiple, beginning with the fact that her great-grandmother was already a liberated Egba Saro 'recaptive' (that is, a former slave freed by British anti-slavery patrol ships) in Freetown, Sierra Leone[58] – a former slave who returned to Yorubaland from the place of her exile. FRK's mother already received a British-style education.[59] Wole Soyinka, who was the grand-nephew of FRK's husband,[60] included vivid descriptions of FRK's political agitation in *Ake: The Years of Childhood*. She and her husband owned a car in 1936[61] – at a time when a car was a luxury not only in Nigeria but almost everywhere except in the United States. Her first two ladies' clubs in Abeokuta, in the late 1920s[62] and after 1932,[63] had no specific inclination towards the poor – they started off as social clubs for elite women. However, by 1944, FRK's views had changed enough that uneducated market women were allowed to join the latter organisation.[64] She also started holding literacy classes for market women – a very practical and much needed approach at the time when most were illiterate;[65] and soon she learned of the myriad problems that rice sellers faced, including taxation levels and the water rate.[66] In 1946 the Abeokuta Ladies Club became the Abeokuta Women's Union, a veritable anti-colonialist force that fought for the elimination of the entire Sole Native Authority System, battled the *Alake* (the king) and demanded the abolition of the flat rate tax.[67] The organisation had 20,000 registered members.[68] Ransome-Kuti faced numerous court cases because she constantly and pointedly refused to pay her own taxes.[69] Her organisation's massive demonstrations succeeded in forcing the local king to abdicate his throne in 1949, for almost a year (Awolowo's Action Group would reinstate him later).[70]

Abeokuta Women's Union became the Nigerian Women's Union in 1949, a democratic federation of autonomous branches that stood for decolonisation, proportional representation for women and universal franchise in all of Nigeria (the latter was especially important in Northern Nigeria, where women gained the right to vote only in 1977).[71] FRK was so fearless that in fact she wrote to the military government after 1966 urging it to enfranchise Northern Nigerian women.[72]

She recognised her own alienation from impoverished women when she wrote that 'the true position of Nigerian women had to be judged from the women who carried babies on their backs and farmed from sunrise to sunset … not women who used tea, sugar, and flour for breakfast'.[73] It would be erroneous to use the same markers for elite standing today, as in early 21st-century Nigeria sugar or tea are no longer luxuries, and it has become decidedly less common to farm from sunrise to sunset (although babies are still carried on women's backs even in towns). However, the same divide remains between women who are chauffeur-driven to exclusive restaurants in Abuja's Silverbird Mall and those who are periodically evicted from Abuja's shanties with their children; the latter are often forced to spend half of their income on their commute because of the anti-poor policies of Nigerian municipalities.

In the international sphere, Ransome-Kuti was Nkrumah's friend from as early as 1946,[74] and had enough friends in the Fabian Colonial Bureau[75] and the British Labour Party[76] to be referred to in the Women's International Democratic Federation (WIDF) already in 1945. She visited Paris,[77] Budapest,[78] Helsinki,[79] Beijing,[80] Copenhagen,[81] Moscow, Prague, Warsaw,[82] Algeria, Dahomey, Guinea, Liberia, Togo[83] and, naturally, Nkrumah's Ghana. Molly Mandel, secretary-general of WIDF, paid her a personal visit in Abeokuta.[84] FRK's contributions were included in the organisation's publications.[85]

As a result of her incessant activity, Prime Minister Tafawa Balewa personally refused to renew her passport in June 1957 – and she was only to receive a valid passport again after 1960.[86] Her biography by Cheryl Johnson-Odim and Nina Emma Mba, a somewhat hagiographic monograph that often falls back on phrases such as 'strict but fair',[87] still seems very apt when describing how FRK found herself in a political vacuum after 1966.[88]

Her private school was shut down by the authorities in 1974, and her favourite son Fela was attacked by government forces in a very literal sense. Fela operated the self-declared Kalakuta Republic on FRK's property.[89] He was first charged with drug use and then, on 18 February 1977, Obasanjo sent 1000 soldiers to overrun the compound. Many inhabitants were defenestrated, women's clothes torn off as they were raped; Fela himself was hospitalised as a result of his injuries. The 77-year-old FRK was taken by her hair and thrown out of the window – her leg was broken, and most sources link her subsequent death to this incident:[90] she never recovered and, on 13 April 1978, she died.[91]

It is especially interesting to learn of the Anglican FRK's views on religion:

I believe in my God. You could be a pagan and be godly. As far as I can see, if you don't think of cheating people you are godly and I think if there is any paradise you will get there. Many pastors as I see them will end up in hell. I will see God in the sort of life I lead, not because I go to church every Sunday.[92]

Almost Kabbalistic in its simple affirmation of God as an ethical concept and as a force of, from and within the betterment of this world, FRK's inclusive, humane and loving worldview shines through, even as she was a fierce politician and a tireless practical actor who was not much given to quietist contemplation.

It would be tempting to analyse her favourite son Fela's thought under a Marxian rubric – but, to be fair, this cannot be done without stretching Fela's own ideologies in an unnatural way. Fela was a pan-Africanist who believed in a self-styled spiritual framework which included empathy for the poor, but not exactly Marxism. There are numerous biographies of Fela, and some talk of his socialism, but in its classless universalism we may identify influences of négritude, *Ujamaa*, or traditional African religions more than the works of Marx.

Gambo Sawaba

Hajiya Gambo Sawaba (1933–2001) felt closer to Marx – so much so that she hung his picture on her wall.[93] We should not be glib about this – such actions could be dangerous in Northern Nigeria. Notwithstanding the Marx portrait, Sawaba was even less theoretically inclined than was Ransome-Kuti; but she also lived and worked in a very different environment. Northern Nigeria was a place where modern ideas such as feminism were most difficult to implant among conservative Fulani, Hausa, Kanuri and other Islamic/Islamised/Islamising peoples. Although it would be wrong to equate the Fulani jihad of the early 19th century with the Saudi version of Salafism or the Wahabiyya (as this is frequently done in Nigeria today), it would be equally wrong to suppose that Northern Nigerian women enjoyed the kind of economic or political freedoms that they did in Igbo country or even in Yorubaland in the early 20th century. Probably least of all in the cities and towns, as rural regions were less Islamised.

Sawaba's father was an unusual figure: a Ghanaian with roots in Benin City, he converted to Islam and took his new identity so seriously that his family was considered Hausa by acculturation.[94] He worked for the railways; again we encounter a family with international ties, technical expertise and a wider outlook. The only published biography of Sawaba not only reads like a chapter in *The Lives of the Saints* but, especially given its obvious sympathies towards Sawaba's party, the Marxian anti-feudalist NEPU (Northern Elements Progressive Union), it is surprising how much emphasis is given to the protagonist's supposed supernatural powers and capabilities. She 'could foretell the future'[95] according to the author, and was 'accessible to invisible spirits',[96] but it is also expressly stated that her paranormal abilities were linked to Sawaba's having been born after a set of twins.[97] None of those interpretations are questioned in any way by her biographer Rima Shawulu. One reviewer of this biography could not hold back his disdain for the book and called it 'superficial',[98] partial, and a work of no merit as no dates or exact details are in fact supplied throughout the core chapters. While I agree and regret that this shortcoming makes it nearly impossible to make sense of Sawaba's political work within the NEPU–PRP (People's Redemption Party) continuum, Shawulu's biography was written for a Northern Nigerian *talakawa* audience. It is not coincidental that Boko Haram's Abubakar Shekau could pontificate there successfully on the flatness of the earth: Northern Nigeria's educational levels were frighteningly low in the mid 1900s, and they are scandalously low today. Shawulu's book, with all its spelling mistakes and lack of cohesive grammar, attempts to bring an enlightened left-wing feminist fighter, Sawaba, to Northern Nigerian readers and especially reading women – people who otherwise are increasingly unable to access any other knowledge than that provided by *madrasas*. Gambo Sawaba's NEPU's Women's Wing received active support from Olufunmilayo Ransome-Kuti, especially in support of the struggle for women's franchise, which was won largely thanks to the political efforts of these two women in 1977.[99] Gambo Sawaba was jailed 17 times, was beaten, was charged with prostitution in a show trial, and was banned from the city of Kano by the emir as a result of her political activity.[100]

Bene Madunagu, Molara Ogundipe-Leslie and their Place in Nigerian Feminism

Here I have no choice but to discuss two main protagonists together, as they belonged to the same, institutionalised feminist movement, Women in Nigeria (WIN); in fact, their influence there was definitive.

Nigerian feminism built upon a very strong legacy that started with matriarchal systems in many tribal structures, many having matrilineal inheritance,[101] with children even sometimes bearing their mothers' names.[102] In modern times, the memory of the Women's War and Olufunmilayo Ransome-Kuti's activism until the brutal assault that led to her death, together with Sawaba's colourful political activism in the North, provided starting points for Nigerian feminist organisers and thinkers.

Much of Nigerian feminism, or even women's activism that refused to be classified as 'feminist', was naturally receptive to social and political problems that were not necessarily the most important for

Western feminists. Such generally non-Marxist, some would say even somewhat traditionalist, female thinkers as Mary E. Modupe Kolawole are confronted with the enormity of their sisters' economic suffering, a condition that their oeuvre cannot escape.[103] Kolawole refers to Angela Davis when she emphasises how African and Afro-American women had been strong traditionally, stronger perhaps than their non-African counterparts,[104] and that in light of how imperialism tears apart the traditional African family (as by apartheid laws),[105] she rejects Western feminism as a middle-class pursuit that creates walls between sisters.[106] Even without emphasising Kolawole's multiple references to Molara Ogundipe-Leslie, it is striking how Marxism informs this ostensibly 'traditionalist' thinker. She goes further in her veritable panegyric on Ogundipe-Leslie, when she writes these lines:

> Molara Ogundipe-Leslie is a dynamic ideologue who has combined literary criticism with poetic creativity ... This critic-poet is categorical and definitive about her triple preoccupation as an African, a woman, and a Marxist.[107]

Ogundipe-Leslie in her poems attempts to recapture especially the pre-colonial past, in a defiant and assertive gesture. Her poem to Nefertiti speaks about women and power:

> How long shall we speak to them / Of the goldness of mother, of difference / without bane ... / How long shall we say another world lives / Not spined on the axis of maleness / But rounded and whole, charting through / Its many runnels its justice distributive? / O Nefertiti ...[108]

With other Nigerian feminist thinkers, this openness transfuses into an intellectual struggle with Marxism, much to the benefit of the reader. It is most interesting to follow this in especially Ifi Amadiume's scholarly output. Amadiume drew a lot from Ikenna Nzimiro's work on Igbos (see chapter 5).[109] She was of course fully cognisant of Nzimiro's Marxist credentials, and in *Male Daughters, Female Husbands*, she attacks what she sees as Nzimiro's diehard Marxist concepts on Igbo anthropology.[110] As I have shown in chapter 5, it is difficult to decipher any Marxist element in that work, and Amadiume suggests that Nzimiro only saw classes where they were obvious to the naked eye. Amadiume goes on to directly criticise Marxist feminism as follows:

It seems to me, therefore, that to expect Black women to separate racism from feminism or to minimize racism in favour of class, which is the position of socialist feminists and international socialists (see *Review of African Political Economy* Double Issue No. 27/28, 1984), is adding insult to injury. Socialist and radical feminists argue and theorize about the need for an autonomous women's movement; feminism before socialism; challenging sexism in their mixed socialist organizations; suggesting only an alliance with socialist men. Because they never tackled the question of race, it never occurred to them that their Black sisters would follow the same mode of argument in prioritizing race.[111]

All the more interesting, then, that Amadiume would soften her position on 'class-based interpretations' in her *Reinventing Africa*, which came out six years after the fall of the USSR and at the lowest point for leftist initiatives globally in the last century and a half. In this book, she notices 'a class dimension to the Ebonics debate',[112] and praises Marxist anthropologists in a long passage,[113] while reiterating that Engels was wrong to talk about the defeat of patriarchy as a global phenomenon.[114] At the same time, she thought it necessary to include a semi-sympathetic section on the Working Women Wing of the Nigeria Labour Congress (NLC).

The NLC formed this wing in 1983, following a directive from the Organisation of African Trade Union Unity. The NLC itself has retained oversight of the financing and organisation of its Women's Wing, which has no representation on the central working committee. According to Amadiume's assessment, the Women's Wing was under the control of elite women, and represented little of genuine working-class concerns.[115]

Amadiume also included a scathing assessment of WIN, to which both Ogundipe-Leslie and Bene Madunagu belonged and for which they were the main spokespersons. Amadiume insinuated that WIN was a 'Trojan horse' organisation:

> WIN is officially committed to change and is ideologically oriented, even though the Marxist-Leninist or socialist leanings of some individual members are not explicitly stated. Some members claim this is for strategic reasons. This loophole, I shall argue, has posed a problem for WIN, as it means the organisation is really not self-defined.[116]

Documents of the organisation show no sign of this: there is an unequivocal and indeed, succinctly outlined ideological stand that runs through all their publications, and that is clearly socialist, committed to popular democracy and, indeed, rather Trotskyite in its overall make-up.

WIN issued a major publication in 1985, very difficult to find today.[117] In this work, Ogundipe-Leslie reminds us how the central problems of feminism are class-defined in ways beyond what Western feminists could fathom:

> At a symposium organized by the Nigerian Association of University Women in 1974, with market-women of the city of Ibadan on the panel, the trading women revealed interest in problems patently different from our middle-class ones. They were, in fact, contemptuous of some of these problems, in particular, the resentment of polygyny by middle-class and Westernized women. They mainly felt men could not be expected to be loyal to one woman while some outrightly claim they needed helpmates in the form of co-wives to assist with housework. They needed younger wives to share or preferably take over the chores of kitchen and bed, so they, the older wives, can be freed to concentrate on travel for business reasons. It may be argued that these trading women are victims of false consciousness and social brain-washing, but for them, the old pre-capitalist system exists, works, and is respected by them. We may ask if they have their humanity, their dignity, their human rights and self-fulfilment, guaranteed within this system. Their only objection was to the rupture or distortion of the older system of marriage, where the older wife now is relegated to the background by an uncaring husband or where the younger wife would not keep her lower and deferent place within that system.[118]

Another interesting point concerns the roles of mothers of men, vis-à-vis wives, under a traditional system, again very different from comparable Western situations:

> Men also tend to be less trusting of wives than they are of their own mothers and sisters, a situation that often alienates the wife throughout her marriage and makes her a stranger in enemy territory all her life. In fact, men here lean emotionally more on their mothers, sisters, and aunts – the womenfolk of their own lineage or kin group than on their own wives. This situation gives some emotional power to women. Thus often women 'take consolation from this fact and help to oppress other women' who come into their own lineages as wives. It is generally known that women in their own lineages form the emotional support of the men to the extent that the men cannot function without them. Yet such men will express in acts and words

the most blatant notions of male dominance. Such emotional power often satisfies women to the point of preventing them from wanting to take other more public action or to resist the subordination they suffer within their own marriages. In addition to the power of female relatives within marriage, there exist the pressure and power of peer group values on the husband; values which often confirm male dominance and encourage even recalcitrant and would-be gentle and just husbands in the direction of male supremacy.[119]

Lest we think that these views reflect a radicals-only take on the subject, it must be pointed out that the problems Molara Ogundipe-Leslie exposes here are among the main themes that we see recurring in Nollywood dramas of the 21st century.

Bene Madunagu's work is testimony to her complete familiarity with her husband's theoretical writings, and it seems obvious that Edwin and Bene Madunagu's respective work was mutually informed and cross-pollinated by each other's Marxist theory. Bene Madunagu rejects claims that the dictatorship of the proletariat would automatically bring women's liberation (the orthodox Eastern European line), quotes Trotsky and dares to build on Engels very freely, demonstrating the Lukacsian dictum that Marxism is a method, and not a set of fixed tenets:

The charge of economic determinism cannot be made against Engels for he was talking about the conditions for the liberation of women and not the liberation of women. Only with their full and equal entry into social production, that is, only with the achievement of equal social rights for men and women, will the conditions be created for the liberation of women from 'their status of unpaid servant in the house.'

Let us briefly consider the implications of Engels' formulation. Since, as we have earlier noted, a woman's status of unpaid servant is linked with the discrimination she suffers as regards pay and work opportunities ... and since oppression of women is much older than capitalism ... Engels' thesis can, in fact, be reversed. A new thesis then appears: Women cannot enter fully and equally into social production until they cease to be unpaid servants in the house, that is, until they are liberated.

We do not advance the new thesis to contradict Engels' thesis – which remains true. We merely intend to show that neither the women's question nor its solution can be conceived mechanically: when this is done, that will follow. No! The oppression of women is too profound for a mechanical solution to be prescribed.[120]

Bene Madunagu also discusses the role that radical women play in Nigerian families, an interesting and rarely discussed subject:

A radical woman is regarded as eccentric or she engenders condemnation or murder for being an embarrassment to a bourgeois husband. Where a radical woman is not stoutly opposed, she meets with a mixture of applause and surprise. In the latter case, derogatory explanations are offered for her activities. It is a historical fact that not only bourgeois men but socialists and revolutionaries as well justify and live these sexist stereotypes. This is a sad indicator of the level of consciousness within the revolutionary movement of our time.[121]

Nigerian Feminisms in the 21st Century – Amina Mama

Mainstream Nigerian feminism acquired world renown due to Chimamanda Adichie's TED talk on the subject, her book based on that talk,[122] and Beyoncé's sample of the former in 'Flawless'. But Adichie's unique gift for storytelling does not make her a political radical.

Luckily, many Nigerian feminist intellectuals are not afraid of controversial issues or near-oblivious to the lives of the downtrodden, and there are even sensitive Marxist feminist Nigerian intellectuals abroad, especially in the UK and the US. First among them today is radical socialist feminist Amina Mama. Born in 1958, the half-Nigerian, half-British Mama lived in Kaduna, which their family left in 1966 because of riots and political uncertainty. When at LSE in London, she became a young member of Bene Madunagu's and Molara Ogundipe-Leslie's WIN. Later, at the University of Cape Town in South Africa, she was director of the African Gender Institute, and was instrumental in founding its journal, *Feminist Africa*. Today, Professor Mama is employed at Mills College Oakland in the United States – a reminder, as Gayatri Spivak warns, that these days in academia 'all roads lead to Rome'.[123] Mama's books include *The Hidden Struggle: Statutory and Voluntary Responses to Violence Against Black Women in the Home*, (1989, 1996); *Beyond the Masks: Race, Gender, and Subjectivity* (1995); *Women's Studies and Studies of Women in Africa During the 1990s* (2000); *Engendering African Social Sciences* (co-edited with Ayesha Imam and Fatou Sow, 2000); and a multitude of influential articles. Mama, who describes Funmilayo Ransome-Kuti and Gambo Sawaba as 'her early heroes', takes the view that 'global capitalism can be viewed as an enemy'.[124] Mama's concept of how class and gender interrelate is a nuanced one:

The concept of intersectionality is now widely embraced within gender and women's studies, as a means of addressing the fact that gender works not as an isolatable variable, but through its pervasive interconnectedness with class, ethnicity, clan, religion, race, sexuality, and nation ... class variations affect women and men differently.[125]

Mama claims that the processes that drain government-run universities of funds all over Africa are detrimental not only to academic freedom but to gendered understandings of social science and the humanities. It is easy to support her argument. The unashamed celebration of privilege that pervades Africa's elite private universities goes hand in hand with the celebration of corporate understandings of feminism. (It was not coincidental that my own former workplace, the American University of Nigeria [AUN], devoted resources to invite Adichie to give a celebrated speech there in 2010, and not Mama, Madunagu or Okoye. AUN, very much representing elite aspirations, also invited Yakubu Gowon, the octogenarian former military dictator of Nigeria.) An important aspect of Amina Mama's oeuvre is the exposure of militarist politics in a radical and gendered way. She is especially critical of the United States Africa Command, and provides feminist explanations of the forces behind US imperialism on the continent. Even as mainstream capitalism continues to accommodate military dictators as long as they serve the right kind of interests, radical and socialist thinkers and activists attack exactly those kinds of established structures.

On a happier note, the NLC, always more committed to gender equity than most political organisations in Nigeria, decided in 2003 to adopt a comprehensive Gender Equity Policy.[126] Its national Women Commission chair now has the standing of vice president in NLC. The NLC reserves 30 per cent of all positions for women, and tries to make sure that individual member unions follow the same directive. The NLC also demands the application of the same ratio for women in all sectors of formal employment. Beyond equal rights in the workplace, the NLC makes sure to focus on widows' rights, the right of girls to education, and family law where it stands behind progressive solutions. The organisation also established day-care centres in its secretariats to provide practical help for working families, and it demands comprehensive, state-backed health coverage for everyone. In its striving to improve women's lives in concrete ways and in backing humanist ideologies, the NLC offers hope that a more liveable and inclusive future awaits Nigerian women as well as men.

8

Conclusion

Analysing Nigerian Marxism

A history of ideas, in this case the highly specialised case study of a history of Marxist theory in Nigeria, may be connected to a historical materialist conception of History itself. Georg Lukacs, in his *Ontology of Social Being* (published posthumously in 1971), describes how:

> peoples, economically underdeveloped, that are trying to get rid of colonialism, have not been able to scientifically uncover (in a Marxist way) their own economic development ... and because of that – without proper realisation – they could not enter avenues of development that would be adequate to their specific circumstances.[1]

Perhaps not coincidentally, this was shortly before the appearance of Walter Rodney's seminal, definitive *How Europe Underdeveloped Africa* (1973), and coincided with the first of a series of excellent Nigerian works that focused exactly on 'scientifically uncovering in a Marxist way their own economic development'. Eskor Toyo, Bene and Edwin Madunagu, Bade Onimode and so many others did exactly that, and in such a way that, by the mid 1980s Lukacs's lacuna was filled by meaningful, sophisticated and relevant studies. In the mid 1980s, an even harsher regime made Marxist theorising much harder, culminating in the regression after 1989. However, what is important to understand is that post-2000 Marxist analyses are informed by 20th-century theory in the country. Also, within the labour movement, this theory provides intellectual ammunition much more palpably than in most other parts of the world.

A more specialised question of theory will be the status of feudalism versus the 'Asiatic mode of production', or even a specific 'African mode of production' in Marxist historiography and related theory. In the 1920s and 1930s, there raged a protracted battle in Soviet historiography over whether feudalism existed in Asia (and, by extension, in heavily Asia-influenced Russia). Stalin, perhaps because he felt that the existence of feudalism in Russia could bolster his 'socialism in one country' project and better serve Russian historical pride, decided that orthodox

Marxist-Leninist historiographies should all make use of feudalism as the only permissible theoretical framework for early Russian history, and effectively banned the conceptual frameworks of the Asiatic or the African mode of production. After Stalin's death, the problem resurfaced with force in both Eastern Europe and in the West. In the 1960s and 1970s, most notably Jean Suret-Canale tried to prove that as classical feudalism operated on the basis of private property and the latter did not exist outside Europe, it was not possible to speak of feudalisms in Asia and in Africa. Relevant to Nigerian history, Suret-Canale argued in his 'Traditional Societies in Tropical Africa and the Asiatic Mode of Production' that: 'As far as we know, we do not find examples of a land ownership structure where private property existed and that could thus be called feudalism.'[2] Still, even he added that 'This might not be valid after colonisation, where chief's privileges were kept up but where private property was encouraged to appear.'[3] Since the 1970s, there appeared non-Marxist but obviously relevant theories of the Nigerian political economy such as the prebendalism developed by Richard A. Joseph,[4] and Jürgen Habermas's concept of refeudalisation,[5] referring to the new role of NGOs and other social pressure groups, and how they exercise power in a polity.

Without denying at all that Nigeria is a capitalist country and an integral and very important, even ideal-typical actor of the global economy (see chapter 2), we are confronted with a number of facts. The 'law of the land' in Nigeria is a valid source of law, bolstering structures that look and act like those of feudalism in Northern Nigeria and elsewhere. There is a proliferation of royal and other traditional titles in the country that puts to shame those of 18th-century Naples or Poland and their respective nobilities. This does not alter the factuality of capitalism but it highlights how systemic violence[6] in Nigeria manifests in actual physical violence (in thuggery), and how social aggression receives 'quasi traditional' backing from a modern and unholy version of feudalism (recalling Hobsbawm and Ranger's *The Invention of Tradition*). This may also validate Walter Rodney's thinking in *How Europe Underdeveloped Africa*; Rodney, as is well known, saw feudalism as ubiquitous in African societies.

From a scholarly point of view, this book grew out of my dissatisfaction with Hakeem Tijani's historical interpretation of Nigerian Marxism, in which he treated the subject exclusively through the prism of the 1950s British anti-communist official, internalising *in toto* not only his class bias but also his lack of knowledge regarding later events. I felt that this was a bizarre standpoint, especially *ex post facto*, when we know that the Nigerian Marxism of the 1950s and 1960s did not overthrow the existing colonial and neocolonial arrangements – on the contrary. My research would have been impossible without Maxim Matusevich's work on Soviet–Nigerian relations, as presented both in his monograph on the subject and his *Russia in Africa*. Leo Zeilig's focus on African radical movements gave another scholarly impetus: I saw his works as a sign that African radical movements, after a hiatus of two decades, are now again receiving attention. The fact that compendiums on African political thought and philosophy completely omitted the subject only heightened my curiosity about the material.

At the same time, I intend with this book to go beyond the specific interests of the academic historian. After living and teaching politics for three years in north-eastern Nigeria, a region that now seems to have become a theatre of irregular war, I felt it was imperative to search for answers to crucial causal questions. How could this happen in an OPEC member state, a country blessed with so many natural resources, a country whose daughters become tiger moms in the United States, Black Africa's literary powerhouse? Living in Nigeria was perhaps the most serious personal challenge that I have faced (I moved there from Afghanistan where I had been an NGO worker, so this is not a frivolous statement), and I searched feverishly for answers to the question: why is Nigeria as it is? Generic answers such as tribalism, religious atavism and the like did not satisfy me. It is crucial to understand that religious atavisms have to be recreated every day, and that they do not linger on through generations like some kind of psychic residue. The same is true for tribal identifications, and even values more dubiously said to be essentially Nigerian (such as criminal schemata, hoarding, conspicuous consumption and the like). 'Residue' and 'culture' are empty concepts when it comes to explaining these behaviours; indeed, they often serve as a cover for an author's conscious or unconscious racism.

As I had developed an earlier interest in some Marxist thinkers, especially Lukacs, it was interesting for me to look for Nigerian authors who made use of Marxian methods in their attempts to understand the world around them. I researched Nigerian Marxist thinkers, criss-crossed Nigeria and visited London a number of times, to access as many primary sources as I could. With this book, I wanted to prove that Nigerian Marxism has been a coherent intellectual movement that provided important answers to the existential questions troubling Nigeria and West Africa, from the late 1940s up to now. I also aim to prove that this movement had living, day-to-day connections with unions, and that in fact it largely grew out of a powerful labour movement in the country. Labour unionism has not forgotten its Marxian theoretical underpinnings, even in the 21st century. Marxian critical theory has informed Nigerian feminism, and has provided one of the most important approaches for understanding a Nigerian political economy up to the present. Understanding Nigerian Marxism helps us in a major way to understand the structural problems of Nigeria and Africa.

This book is intended first and foremost as a monograph on the history of ideas, and how those ideas interacted with reality in the form of uprisings, revolts and military dictatorship. The book sometimes resembles a reader, with many long quotations. This is deliberate, as most of Nigerian Marxism's primary texts are virtually inaccessible to the average reader; the hope is that, in future, a more comprehensive reader will be compiled. In this volume I do not engage in starry-eyed prognosis about Nigeria's revolutionary potential. Indeed, as we can see with Boko Haram, the ugliest forms of resistance, full of nihilism and ignorance, are gaining ground in the country at this moment. It would be wrong to rule out completely John Campbell's gloomy prediction of a multiple partition of the Nigerian state. One might even go further: in Nigeria, as elsewhere in Africa, bizarre and murderous sects, witch hunts, Wahhabi Islam and stranger quasi-Islamist prophets may usher in a future where politics is defined by those forces. But we must reject racialist determinism. One has to keep in mind that, according to Lukacs, witch hunts and an orgy of irrationalism accompanied in Europe not the Dark Ages but Kepler's own century, the days of the scientific revolution, when modernity was being born amid a challenge to the high church.[7] Of course, it would be much better for Nigeria to skip those cataclysms. When I first read Campbell's assessment that Nigeria might well produce in future a Fidel Castro, I thought that the former US ambassador had intuited a very important point. I say intuited, because his works did not indicate any familiarity with the history of Nigerian Marxism, theoretical or otherwise. But intuitive as his statement was, it reinforced what scores of Nigerian Marxists had said before him.

Prior to the 1980s, their message was usually that Nigeria should modernise in the Soviet/East European manner (Imoudu, Enahoro, Oni, Nzimiro, Okoye, Otegbeye, Onimode), or its modified version (Trotskyite for Edwin Madunagu, Maoist for Toyo, self-styled for Oniororo). Later, in the early 1980s for Madunagu, and the early 1990s for most others, a new focus developed, that of 'popular democracy'. We now see how this concept is linked with the populism of Hugo Chávez in Venezuela, especially in the context of an oil-dominated economy for Nigeria. With respect to the Eastern European example of a 'really existing socialism', most Nigerian thinkers display a complex attitude. Of course, we know how triumphant capitalism trampled over even the genuine achievements of Eastern Europe from 1989 onwards, totally neglecting the best aspects of those societies – and proving right the socialist castigation of Western democracy as class rule, as bourgeois democracy motivated foremost by the interests of that class. It is not merely *Ostalgie* that makes one think this way, it is the lessons of the historical record. Eastern Europe was a place where the communal ethos of pre-capitalist Europe thrived, with its lenient attitudes and humour. At the same time, it was also the place from which emerged the KGB, Stasi, the Gulags and, in general, a horrendous police state. Hakeem Tijani was right when he called most early Nigerian Marxists Stalinists (albeit ones unaware of the magnitude of Stalin's crimes). For moral reasons (Madunagu, Osoba) or for technical ones (Onimode, Nnoli, Olukoshi), the Stalinist model lost its appeal for Nigerian Marxists by the 1990s. Indeed, orthodox Marxism-Leninism, with its denial of individual human rights, seems to have lost most of its appeal to Nigerian intellectuals who were persecuted on a personal basis under military dictatorship in the 1990s. This opened up a space for Gramscian, Trotskyist and other heterodox ideas to flourish in the context of Nigerian academia, and among small communist parties and the Nigeria Labour Congress.

Marxist thought did not disappear from Nigeria in 1989. It continues to provide the single most important alternative narrative to Nigerian history and (the lack of) development in the country. When I call it a narrative, I mean this quite literally. Marxism has shaped the literary oeuvre of not only Ifeoma Okoye, Olufunmilayo Ransome-Kuti, Gambo Sawamba, and the Marxist feminist poet and writer Ogundipe-Leslie, but also, in a major way, the novels of Festus Iyayi (his *Violence* was hailed as the first proletarian novel in Nigeria) and of authors like Chinua Achebe in a non-doctrinaire way. This book has presented a prosopography of writers and thinkers, first- or second-generation literates who conquered heights of literary and philosophical achievement, some of them themselves middle class but who recognised the traumatic limitations of middle-class existence in a neocolonial society. Their thoughts have shaped the course of Nigerian history, but, equally importantly, they have shaped its potentialities for Nigeria's future.

Neither did Nigerian Marxism lose all relevance even upon deindustrialisation. There are still 5 million workers in the country,[8] and the Nigeria Labour Congress claims there are 1 million unionised workers (Usman Tar puts their number at 4 million). This is only the classical core of the working class, which is subject to constant erosion. Zeilig explains that a lumpenised urban mass in the context of deindustrialisation still does not mark the end of labour resistance in Africa: 'to see ... instances of protest as simply spontaneous explosions of a slum dwelling multitude is nonsense. More often they are organized or semi-organized expressions of political dissidence ...'[9] Zeilig, in dialogue with Mike Davis and his *Planet of Slums*, presents us with a gripping explanation:

> Davis is, we would argue, right about the culprits of the recent devastation of the potential for genuine development on the continent, but wrong about the working class and the significance of popular protest. Actual class reconfiguration, and how it has manifested itself in the 'myriad acts of resistance' in the South, does not, we believe, suggest a working class entirely dislodged from its 'historical agency.' There has, of course, been a long – and often sceptical – academic debate about the nature, and even existence, of an African working class ... Writers doubted whether bonds of solidarity and consciousness were strong enough for a 'real' working class to bring about social transformation, and suggested that the so-called working class was in any case excluded from other groups in society as 'an aristocracy of labour.' It is undoubtedly true that the formation of the working class has been characterized by a complex and often heterogeneous process of 'proletarianization' in most parts of Africa in the nineteenth and twentieth century – from migrant labour in the mines in Southern Africa from the 1900s to labour in oil extraction and processing in the Niger delta from the 1970s. Davis's vision of 'desperate millenarianism' can be situated within the considerable body of literature questioning the capacity of a Third World or African working class to play its 'historical role.' For Davis, if this class existed, it did so in the past, but now, under the impact of neoliberalism, it has again been recast into a hybrid slum dweller, a lumpen proletariat, unable to lead new progressive social movements on the continent. We disagree.[10]

Zeilig then brings into the discussion the concrete example of Soweto in South Africa:

> There seems at this point to be no surprises. The statistics do not challenge the argument that the effects of mass unemployment – typical of the deindustrialised urban life in the South – have created a new class of the wageless poor, excluded from the world of work. The working class seems now, by implication, a tiny and privileged group, many of whom live outside the township slum and have interests separate from the majority of the urban poor. However, a closer look at the statistics reveals something quite different. If we examine the household, we can see extraordinary mixing of the different and seemingly divided groups of the poor ... There is no 'wall of China' between work and unemployment[11] ... This does not imply that the

effects of unemployment have not had a devastating effect on the poor
… But this has important consequences for the character and pattern of
social unrest. If there is no clear divide in the world of unemployment
and formal employment, then the potential for a similar crossover
exists as regards popular protest and social dissidence.[12]

We could extrapolate from Zeilig's important point by bringing to the
table the revolutionary potentialities of, say, Europe's young 'precariat'.
But for Africa and Nigeria, this discussion is relevant in many ways that
would be alien even to the most precarious of Europe's semi-employed.
In a place like Nigeria, literally tens of people may depend on, and
their views may be influenced by, one single worker; a worker in full
employment in Nigeria may contribute to the livelihoods of as many as 20
different people, in part or in full. A domestic worker, whose occupation
is outside the confines of the national minimum wage (many of them
earn a quarter of that minimum wage) support spouses, children, ageing
parents, siblings and friends on their meagre incomes that hover around
US$40 a month. An industrial worker will usually earn the national
minimum wage or more, but she will be expected to share her income
with every hungry elder, woman, man and child in a compound that
may house 40–50 people, among whom, say, two to three have formal
employment. The world views of these semi-dependent unemployed
people will be heavily influenced and often even shaped in a major way,
by their employed brethren in a still semi-traditional society. Five million
workers in formal employment, many of whom are obviously left-wing
when it comes to their political leanings, means 50, or even 100 million
people who will hear of labour unrest, resistance and organised struggle.

What I would thus add to Zeilig's findings, based on the evidence
presented in this book, is this: not only is there an African proletariat or
a Nigerian proletariat, not only is there organised workers' resistance in
the country and the continent, but this African proletariat can represent
itself in articulate ways and is armed with its own African and Marxist
theory. The African subaltern spoke, speaks and will continue to speak.

Western multinational corporations promote incredible barbarity
and brutal oppression not only through their day-to-day operations but
through the Nigerian state that they, and their respective governments,
keep in its place by electoral fraud. We in the West must understand that
the only way for us to support the fight against the rotten Nigerian status
quo and its brutal exploitation is by standing up to our own governments
who underwrite the rule of the Nigerian comprador bourgeoisie. Standing
up against Shell is important, but standing up against a government that
sells arms to a gang of ruthless criminals called the Nigerian government

is more important still. Nigeria's democracy is a sham, and it is a powerful demonstration that a bourgeois democracy that degenerates into a plutocracy can become an empty shell: unliveable even for its creators, a giant slum, a hell for millions. And we only have to wait until oil runs out to expect even worse outcomes, if the Nigerian status quo is otherwise maintained. Brutality cannot be stopped at borders. No police will prevent the repercussions that come to the developed countries. If we do not stand up against those backing its oppressors, we are accessories to Nigeria's fate. But far more important than what their friends in the West can do, what really matters is what the African worker, the African unemployed and the African market woman can do to rise up and put an end to their plight. In the best of all worlds, they might go beyond an Eastern European-style 'dictatorship of the proletariat' to establish a genuine popular participatory democracy, where workers would have a role in governing, not only via some 'vanguard bureaucracy' but through control of their workplaces and meaningful political participation.

Today, many of the original preconditions for the appearance of Nigerian Marxism are gone, most especially the USSR and its camp. Irrespective of this, some findings remain relevant: first, the centrality of class in social, political and economic enquiry. The centrality of the international nexus and embedded nature of Nigeria's political economy is the second lasting discovery. Eskor Toyo has been proven blatantly wrong when he asserted that dependency theory overemphasised this nexus. It still defines and underdevelops Nigeria today, to an extent that would have been unimaginable to Toyo. Another lasting feature is the obvious interconnectedness of patriarchal domination with colonial and neocolonial forms of exploitation: a point that Bene Madunagu and Ogundipe-Leslie emphasised, but that self-declared non-Marxists and even more traditional feminist thinkers could not escape in their analysis. Yet another core finding relates to the respective roles of the industrial proletariat, the peasantry and the students. Unionised workers are still at the heart of the resistance (as Zeilig proves), but misgivings (especially Madunagu's) about the students' role also proved too pessimistic, as students have consistently been at the forefront of class struggle in the country, along with the anti-feudal Northern peasantry that gives Nigeria its oldest existing political party, the People's Redemption Party (as Toyo and Madunagu predicted). Marxism had its own subculture with its distinct accoutrements like walking sticks, working men's khaftans and shabby Lenin-beards. But it has also been a major analytical framework and an instrument of African self-assertion vis-à-vis the metropole and internationally. It has been the very antithesis of the bourgeoisie under primary accumulation – the latter a class in the making (Sklar), vulgar and increasingly absentee, as extended families move to London to enjoy better the fruits of the loot in the home country. Diametrically different, Nigerian Marxists often consciously chose to remain in their country of birth out of a sense of duty, cultural relevance and a sense of mission. The members of this counterculture cross-referenced and cross-pollinated each other's thinking, not only in the obvious cases, as when the Madunagus both emphasised Trotskyist concepts in their separate intellectual pursuits, but how they themselves – or Eskor Toyo, or Bade Onimode, or Mokwugo Okoye – figure in every other leftist author's oeuvre, displaying a kaleidoscopic richness of ideas. Their scholarship has not only been noticed by non-Marxian scholars (as when Amadiume quotes Nzimiro on anthropology), but also by the people at large.

In this work, I did not engage in independent Marxian theorisation or theorising over the historical material, because the primary objective was the unearthing and analysis of the ideas that Nigerian Marxists themselves have put forth. The most I hope for is that this volume has proven Nigerian Marxists to be qualitatively different from the ridiculous, esoteric dead men that they are sometimes portrayed to be, and that their work is as dazzling and relevant as ever.

Notes

1 Introduction

1. Sarah Riva: 'Desegregating Downtown Little Rock: The Field Reports of SNCC's Bill Hansen, October 23 to December 3, 1962', *Arkansas Historical Quarterly*, 71(3), available at: www.questia.com/library/journal/1P3-2821262761/desegregating-downtown-little-rock-the-field-reports (accessed 12 Sept. 2014).
2. *Workers' Alternative – For the Unity of the Working Class, a Labour Party and Socialism* (based in Lagos, not dated, no details given [perhaps due to semi-legal status]), available at: www.workersalternative.com/ (accessed 12 Jan. 2014).
3. Democratic Socialist Movement (based in Lagos, Trotskyite political party; leader in 2014: Segun Sango), available at: www.socialistnigeria.org/ (accessed 12 Jan. 2014).
4. Samir Amin: *Beyond US Hegemony? Assessing the Prospects for a Multipolar World*, Zed Books, London, 2006, pp. 46–47.
5. Richard McGregor: *The Party: The Secret World of China's Communist Rulers*, rev. edn, Penguin Books, London, 2012.
6. Roderick MacFarquhar: 'China: The Superpower of Mr. Xi', *New York Review of Books*, 62(13), 13 Aug.–23 Sept. 2015, p. 33.
7. John Campbell: *Nigeria Dancing on the Brink*, Bookcraft, Council on Foreign Relations, Ibadan, 2010, p. 142.
8. Toyin Falola and J. Ihonvbere: *The Rise and Fall of Nigeria's Second Republic 1979–1984*, Zed Books, London, 1985.
9. Amy Chua and Jed Rubenfeld: *The Triple Package: What Really Determines Success*, Bloomsbury Publishing, London, 2014.
10. Yusufu Bala Usman: *The Manipulation of Religion in Nigeria, 1977–1987*, Vanguard Printers and Publishers, Kaduna, 1987.
11. *Workers' Alternative*: 'Will Goodluck Jonathan's Emergency Succeed?', 23 May 2013, available at: www.workersalternative.com/national-issues/171-as (accessed 27 Jan. 2014).
12. For more about Nollywood 'home videos', see Toyin Falola and Matthew M. Heaton: *A History of Nigeria*, Cambridge University Press, Cambridge, 2008, p. 269.
13. *Waterfalls*, directed by Lancelot Oduwa Imasuen, produced by Nneka Onyekuru, approx. 2010.
14. Biodun Jeyifo (ed.): *Oxford Encyclopaedia of African Thought*, Oxford University Press, New York, 2010.
15. Edwin Madunagu: *Understanding Nigeria and the New Imperialism (Essays 2002–2006)*, Clear Lines Publications, Calabar, 2006, p. 248.

16. Guy Martin: *African Political Thought*, Palgrave Macmillan, New York, 2012.

17. Patrick Chabal and Jean-Pascal Daloz: *Africa Works: Disorder as Political Instrument*, International African Institute in association with James Currey, Oxford, 1999, esp. pp. 110–63.

18. Chinua Achebe: *The Trouble with Nigeria*, Heinemann Educational Books, London, 1984, p. 9.

19. Hakeem Ibikunle Tijani: *Britain, Leftist Nationalists and the Transfer of Power in Nigeria, 1945–1965*, Routledge, London, 2006.

20. Falola and Heaton: *A History of Nigeria*, p. 255.

21. Darren Kew and Peter Lewis: 'Nigeria'. In: Mark Kesselman, Joel Krieger and William A. Joseph (eds): *Introduction to Comparative Politics*, Wadsworth, Boston, 2010, p. 378.

22. David Harvey: *The Enigma of Capital and the Crises of Capitalism*, Profile Books, London, 2010, p. 44.

23. Eskor Toyo: *Marks i Keynes: Analiza porównawcza metodologii makroekonomicznej* (Marx and Keynes: Analysing their Macroeconomic Thought; in Polish), Tlumaczyl Bartlomiej Kaminski, Warsaw, 1977.

24. Harvey: *The Enigma of Capital*, pp. 63, 10.

25. M.S.C. Okolo: 'Re-establishing the Basis of Social Order in Africa: A Reflection on Achebe's Reformist Agenda and Ngugi's Marxist Aesthetics'. In: Bjorn Beckman and Gbemisola Adeoti (eds): *Intellectuals and African Development: Pretension and Resistance in African Politics*, CODESRIA, Dakar; Zed Books, London; UNISA Press, Pretoria, 2006, pp. 31–49.

26. Molara Ogundipe-Leslie called Festus Iyayi's novel *Violence* the first proletarian novel in Nigeria. Molara (Omolara) Ogundipe-Leslie: 'Violence by Festus Iyayi' (Review), *Review of African Political Economy*, 8(22), Winter 1981, pp. 108–15, available at: www.roape.org/022/17.html (accessed 12 Jan. 2014).

27. Orike Ben Didi (ed.): *Comrade Che at 80: Tributes*, Aklaka Heritage Books, Charleston, 2012.

28. Abayomi Ferreira: *Savagery in Politics: The Hindrance to National Development*, AuthorHouse, Bloomington, 2006.

29. O. Igho Natufe: *Soviet Policy in Africa: From Lenin to Brezhnev*, iUniverse, Bloomington, 2011.

30. Leo Zeilig (ed.): *Class Struggle and Resistance in Africa*, Haymarket Books, Chicago, 2009.

31. Leo Zeilig: *Revolt and Protest: Student Politics and Activism in Sub-Saharan Africa*, I.B. Tauris, London, 2013.

32. Ibid., p. 25.

33. Falola and Heaton: *A History of Nigeria*.

34. Campbell: *Nigeria Dancing on the Brink*.

35. Karl Maier: *This House Has Fallen: Nigeria in Crisis*, Penguin Books, London, 2000.

36. Robin Cohen: *Labour and Politics in Nigeria, 1945–1971*, Heinemann, New York, 1974.

37. Wogu Ananaba: *The Trade Union Movement in Nigeria*, Ethiope Publishing, London, 1969.

38. Richard L. Sklar: *Nigerian Political Parties: Power in an Emergent African Nation*, Africa World Press, Trenton/Asmara, 2004.

39. Ehiedu E.G. Iweriebor: *Radical Politics in Nigeria, 1945–1950: The Significance of the Zikist Movement*, Ahmadu Bello University Press, Zaria, 1996.

40. Tijani: *Britain, Leftist Nationalists and the Transfer of Power in Nigeria.*

41. Tijani's *Britain, Leftist Nationalists, and the Transfer of Power*, is a towering achievement in classical history writing that relies meticulously on a vast array of primary archival sources. Tijani drew from an incredibly rich and varied collection that included every conceivable archive in Nigeria, the UK and the US. He went through tens of thousands of documents, many of them declassified reports by colonial British authorities. The weaker part of Tijani's work is his apparent lack of willingness to understand Nigerian Marxists on their own terms. Tijani narrates on, analyses and presents Nigerian Marxism as a dangerous ideological aberration, its exponents as ne'er-do-wells, if not potential murderers.

42. Tunji Otegbeye: *The Turbulent Decade*, VisionLink Nigeria, Lagos, 1999.

43. Niyi Onororo: *Who are the Nigerian Comrades? The Story of the Opportunists, Revisionists, Reformists and Careerists in Nigeria*, Sketch, Ibadan, n.d.

44. Edwin Madunagu: *The Tragedy of the Nigerian Socialist Movement*, Centaur Press, Calabar, 1980.

45. Bade Onimode: *Imperialism and Underdevelopment in Nigeria: The Dialectics of Mass Poverty*, Zed Press, London, 1982.

46. Usman A. Tar: *The Politics of Neoliberal Democracy in Africa: State and Civil Society in Nigeria*, Tauris Academic Studies, London, 2009.

47. Joe Slovo: *Slovo: The Unfinished Autobiography*, Ocean Press, Melbourne, 1997.

48. Andras Simor (ed.): *Neger kialtas – Fekete-Afrika* (Black Howl – Black Africa), Kozmosz, Budapest, 1972.

49. David Ottaway and Marina Ottaway: *Afrocommunism*, Africana Publishing Company, New York/London, 1981.

50. Ibid., p. 200.

51. Ibid., p. 24.

52. Giovanni Arrighi: *Adam Smith in Beijing: Lineages of the 21st Century*, Verso Books, London, 2009.

2   The Descent

1. 'We Happy Few – Nigeria's Population has been Systematically Exaggerated', Special Report Nigeria, *The Economist*, 415(8943), 20 June 2015, p. 5.

2. Michael Peel: A *Swamp Full of Dollars: Pipelines and Paramilitaries at Nigeria's Oil Frontier*, Laurence Hill Books, Chicago, 2010, p. 128.

3. Darren Kew and Peter Lewis: 'Nigeria'. In: Mark Kesselman, Joel Krieger and William A. Joseph (eds): *Introduction to Comparative Politics*, Wadsworth, Boston, 2010, pp. 377–78.
4. Martin Meredith: *The State of Africa: A History of Fifty Years of Independence*, Free Press, London, 2006.
5. Peel: *A Swamp Full of Dollars*, p. 73.
6. Toyin Falola and Matthew M. Heaton: *A History of Nigeria*, Cambridge University Press, Cambridge, 2008, p. 238.
7. Ibid.
8. Kew and Lewis: 'Nigeria', p. 383.
9. Falola and Heaton: *A History of Nigeria*, p. 238.
10. Ibid., p. 255.
11. Mike Davis: *Planet of Slums*, Verso, London, 2006, p. 193.
12. Peel: *A Swamp Full of Dollars*, p. 79.
13. Davis: *Planet of Slums*, p. 177.
14. Ibid., p. 13.
15. Ibid., p. 37.
16. Gyorgy Kalmar: *A Niger partjan* (On the Shores of the Niger; in Hungarian) Gondolat, Budapest, 1967, p. 32.
17. Davis: *Planet of Slums*, p. 116.
18. Ibid., p. 157.
19. *Wedded Wonderland*, 'Ten Nigerian Wedding Customs that Prove these Brides Know How to Party', 9 June 2015, available at: http://www.weddedwonderland.com/10-nigerian-wedding-customs-that-prove-these-brides-know-how-to-party/ (accessed 15 Jan. 2016).
20. N.A.A. Hussain and T.M. Akande: 'Sexual Behavior and Condom Use Among Nigerian Soldiers in Ilorin, Kwara State, Nigeria', *African Journal and Clinical and Experimental Microbiology*, 10(2), May 2009, available at: http://www.ajol.info/index.php/ajcem/article/view/7514/29823 (accessed 15 Jan. 2016).
21. Interview with Edwin Madunagu, Calabar, Nigeria, 5 Jan. 2013.
22. Peel: A *Swamp Full of Dollars*, p. 84.
23. Falola and Heaton: *A History of Nigeria*, p. 240.
24. Kew and Lewis: 'Nigeria', p. 376.
25. Ibid., p. 397.
26. Karl Maier: *This House Has Fallen: Nigeria in Crisis*, Penguin Books, London, 2000, p. 43.
27. John Campbell: *Nigeria Dancing on the Brink*, Bookcraft, Council on Foreign Relations, Ibadan, 2010, pp. 30–39.
28. Maier: *This House Has Fallen*, p. xxxiv.
29. Kew and Lewis: 'Nigeria', p. 389.
30. Karl Maier: *This House Has Fallen*, p. 7.
31. Campbell: *Nigeria Dancing on the Brink*, p. 87.
32. Jean-François Bayart, Stephen Ellis and Beatrice Hibou: 'From Kleptocracy to the Felonious State?' In: Jean-François Bayart, Stephen Ellis and Beatrice Hibou (eds): *The Criminalization of the State in Africa*, The International African Institute in association with James Currey, Oxford, 1999, p. 31.

33. Amnesty International: 'Nigeria: Welcome to Hell Fire: Torture and Other Ill-treatment in Nigeria', 18 September 2014, AFR: 44/011/4024, available at: https://www.amnesty.org/en/documents/AFR44/011/2014/en/ (accessed 22 February 2016).

34. Kew and Lewis: 'Nigeria', p. 387.

35. Usman A. Tar: *The Politics of Neoliberal Democracy in Africa: State and Civil Society in Nigeria*, Tauris Academic Studies, London, 2009, p. 3.

36. Comparatively few modern scholarly studies have appeared on such issues. Exceptions include: Jacob K. Olupona: *African Religions: A Very Short Introduction*, Oxford University Press, New York, 2014, p. 54 (on campus cults and their ties to politics). An anthropological work of interest here is: Daniel A. Offiong: *Witchcraft, Sorcery, Magic and Social Order: Among the Ibibio of Nigeria*, Fourth Dimension, Enugu, 2001.

37. Falola and Heaton: *A History of Nigeria*, p. 18.

38. Walter Rodney: *How Europe Underdeveloped Africa*, Bogle-L'Ouverture Publications, London, 1973, pp. 60–64.

39. Ibid., p. 101.

40. Falola and Heaton: *A History of Nigeria*, p. 23.

41. Ibid., p. 25.

42. Ibid., p. 29.

43. Joseph Kenny, O.P.: 'Sharia and Christianity in Nigeria: Islam and a "Secular" State', *Journal of Religion in Africa*, 26(4), p. 340, available at JSTOR: http://www.jstor.org/stable/1581837?seq=1 (accessed 19 Dec. 2012).

44. Falola and Heaton: *A History of Nigeria*, p. 42.

45. Ibid., p. 33.

46. Ibid., p. 41.

47. Ibid., p. 51.

48. Lynn Hunt: *Inventing Human Rights: A History*, W.W. Norton, New York, 2007, p. 165.

49. Falola and Heaton: *A History of Nigeria*, p. 57.

50. Rodney: *How Europe Underdeveloped Africa*, pp. 116, 180.

51. Kenny: 'Sharia and Christianity', p. 360.

52. Falola and Heaton: *A History of Nigeria*, p. 64.

53. John Hunwick: 'An African Case Study of Political Islam: Nigeria', *Annals of the American Academy of Political and Social Science*, 524, Nov. 1992, p. 151, available at JSTOR: http://www.jstor.org/stable/1046712 (accessed 19 Dec. 2012).

54. Falola and Heaton: *A History of Nigeria*, p. 78.

55. Ibid., p. 81.

56. Ibid., p. 91.

57. Immigration and Refugee Board of Canada, *Nigeria: Prevalence of Ritual Murder and Human Sacrifice; Police and State Response (2009–2012)*, 20 November 2012, NGA104218.E, available at: http://www.refworld.org/docid/50c84a6d2.html (accessed 15 January 2016).

58. Falola and Heaton: *A History of Nigeria*, p. 98.

59. Chinua Achebe: *The Trouble with Nigeria*, Heinemann Educational Books, London, 1984, p. 6.
60. Falola and Heaton: *A History of Nigeria*, p. 105.
61. Ibid., p. 116.
62. Ibid., p. 121.
63. Ibid., p. 140.
64. Ibid., p. xxi.
65. Ehiedu E.G. Iweriebor: *Radical Politics in Nigeria, 1945–1950: The Significance of the Zikist Movement*, Ahmadu Bello University Press, Zaria, 1996, p. 28.
66. Achebe: *The Trouble with Nigeria*, p. 11.
67. Richard L. Sklar: *Nigerian Political Parties: Power in an Emergent African Nation*, Africa World Press, Trenton/Asmara, 2004, p. xiii.
68. Ibid.
69. Meredith: *The State of Africa*, pp. 146–48.
70. Kew and Lewis: 'Nigeria', p. 370.
71. Ibid.
72. Falola and Heaton: *A History of Nigeria*, p. xx.
73. Kew and Lewis: 'Nigeria', p. 371.
74. Maxim Matusevich: *No Easy Row for a Russian Hoe: Ideology and Pragmatism in Nigerian–Soviet Relations*, Africa World Press, Trenton/Asmara, 2003, pp. 135–40.
75. Ibid., p. 378.
76. Achebe: *The Trouble with Nigeria*, p. 1.
77. Campbell: *Nigeria Dancing on the Brink*, p. 85.
78. Interview with Edwin Madunagu, Calabar, Nigeria, 5 Jan. 2013.
79. Falola and Heaton: *A History of Nigeria*, p. 217.
80. Campbell: *Nigeria Dancing on the Brink*, pp. 24–28.
81. Kew and Lewis: 'Nigeria', p. 405.
82. Falola and Heaton: *A History of Nigeria*, pp. 218–19.
83. Ibid., p. 222.
84. Ibid., p. 223.
85. Patrick Chabal and Jean-Pascal Daloz: *Africa Works: Disorder as Political Instrument*, International African Institute in association with James Currey, Oxford, 1999, p. 27.
86. Falola and Heaton: *A History of Nigeria*, p. 224.
87. Interview with Ashien Kingsley, 21 May 2007, Minami Uonuma-shi, Japan.
88. Falola and Heaton: *A History of Nigeria*, p. 234.
89. Maier: *This House Has Fallen*; Campbell: *Nigeria Dancing on the Brink*; Falola and Heaton, *A History of Nigeria*.
90. Ibid., p. 241.

3   Leftist Movements in Nigeria

1. Ehiedu E.G. Iweriebor: *Radical Politics in Nigeria, 1945–1950: The Significance of the Zikist Movement*, Ahmadu Bello University Press, Zaria,

1996; Hakeem Ibikunle Tijani: *Britain, Leftist Nationalists and the Transfer of Power in Nigeria, 1945–1965*, Routledge, New York, 2006.

2. Alan Feinstein: *African Revolutionary: The Life and Times of Nigeria's Aminu Kano*, Fourth Dimension Publishers, Enugu, 1987.

3. Wogu Ananaba: *The Trade Union Movement in Nigeria*, Ethiope Publishing, London, 1969; Robin Cohen: *Labour and Politics in Nigeria*, Heinemann, London, 1974; Usman A. Tar: *The Politics of Neoliberal Democracy in Africa: State and Civil Society in Nigeria*, Tauris Academic Studies, London, 2009; Bjorn Beckman, Sakhela Buhlungu and Lloyd Sachikonye (eds): *Trade Unions and Party Politics: Labour Movements in Africa*, HSRC Press, Pretoria, 2010; Leo Zeilig (ed.): *Class Struggle and Resistance in Africa*, Haymarket Books, Chicago, 2002.

4. Fatou Janneh: *Marxist Historiography in West Africa*, typescript, available at www.academia.edu/3551977/Marxist_Historiography_in_West_Africa (accessed 13 Nov. 2013).

5. Richard L. Sklar: *Nigerian Political Parties: Power in an Emergent African Nation*, Africa World Press, Trenton/Asmara, 2004, p. xxi.

6. Basil Davidson: *Modern Africa: A Social and Political History*, Pearson, Edinburgh, 1994, p. 35.

7. Michael Peel: A *Swamp Full of Dollars: Pipelines and Paramilitaries at Nigeria's Oil Frontier*, Laurence Hill Books, Chicago, 2010, p. 70.

8. *Bloomberg*, 'Mastercard Chases Africa's Poorest to Tap Continent's Growth', 21 Aug. 2013, available at www.bloomberg.com/news/2013-08-21/mastercard-chases-africa-s-poorest-to-tap-continent-s-growth.html?cmpid=yhoo (accessed 23 Aug. 2013).

9. Toyin Falola and Matthew M. Heaton: *A History of Nigeria*, Cambridge University Press, Cambridge, 2008, p. 121.

10. Iweriebor: *Radical Politics in Nigeria, 1945–1950*, p. 34.

11. Ibid., p. 66.

12. Ibid., p. 56.

13. Cited in ibid., p. 221.

14. Ibid., p. 225.

15. Wogu Ananaba: *The Trade Union Movement in Nigeria*, Ethiope Publishing, London, 1969, p. 72.

16. Iweriebor: *Radical Politics in Nigeria, 1945–1950*, p. 225.

17. Ibid., p. 226.

18. Ananaba: *The Trade Union Movement in Nigeria*, p. 101.

19. Ibid., p. 110.

20. *Vanguard Nigeria*, 'Sunmonu Revolutionized Labour with Workers' Charter of Demands', Editorial, 14 Aug. 2012, available at www.vanguardngr.com/2012/08/sunmonu-revolutionised-labour-with-workers-charter-of-demands/ (accessed 14 Aug. 2012).

21. Karl Maier: *This House Has Fallen: Nigeria in Crisis*, Penguin Books, London, 2000, p. 76.

22. Peel: A *Swamp Full of Dollars*, p. 17.

23. '2015 General Elections and the Working Masses', socialistworld.net, 12 Sept. 2013, available at www.socialistworld.net/doc/6466 (accessed 27 Jan. 2014).
24. Noah Schachtman: 'Inside the Brave New War', Wired, 16 May 2007, available at www.wired.com/dangerroom/2007/05/q_tell_me_a_lit/ (accessed 27 Jan. 2014).
25. '2015 General Elections and the Working Masses', socialistworld.net, 12 Sept. 2013.
26. Ananaba: The Trade Union Movement in Nigeria, p. 1.
27. Ibid., p. 2.
28. Ibid., p. 5.
29. Ibid., p. 3.
30. William L. Blackwell: The Industrialization of Russia: A Historical Perspective, Harlan Davidson, Arlington Heights, 1994, p. ix.
31. Ananaba: The Trade Union Movement in Nigeria, p. 8.
32. Ibid., p. 16.
33. Bade Onimode disagrees with this accepted chronology in his Dialectics of Mass Poverty, and claims there was a strike in 1897 in Nigeria. Bade Onimode: Imperialism and Underdevelopment in Nigeria: The Dialectics of Mass Poverty, Zed Press, London, 1982.
34. Paul Krugman: End This Depression Now!, W.W. Norton, New York, 2013, pp. 164–65.
35. Ananaba: The Trade Union Movement in Nigeria, p. 17.
36. Davidson: Modern Africa, p. 35.
37. Ibid., p. 36.
38. Ananaba: The Trade Union Movement in Nigeria, p. 15.
39. Ibid., p. 10.
40. Ibid., p. 11.
41. Ibid., p. 13.
42. Ibid., p. 33.
43. Iweriebor: Radical Politics in Nigeria, 1945–1950, p. 25.
44. Ananaba: The Trade Union Movement in Nigeria, p. 54.
45. Tunji Otegbeye: The Turbulent Decade, VisionLink Nigeria, Lagos, 1999, p. 187.
46. Falola and Heaton: A History of Nigeria, p. 141.
47. Davidson: Modern Africa, p. 75.
48. Darren Kew and Peter Lewis: 'Nigeria'. In: Mark Kesselman, Joel Krieger and William A. Joseph (eds): Introduction to Comparative Politics, Wadsworth, Boston, 2010, p. 370.
49. Davidson: Modern Africa, p. 62.
50. Iweriebor: Radical Politics in Nigeria, 1945–1950, p. 24.
51. I follow here an argument as presented in Andras Balogh and Laszlo Salgo: A gyarmati rendszer tortenete (A History of the Colonial System; in Hungarian) Kossuth, Budapest, 1980, pp. 417–31.
52. Feinstein: African Revolutionary, p. 264.
53. Falola and Heaton: A History of Nigeria, p. 140.

54. Hakeem Ibikunle Tijani: *Britain, Leftist Nationalists and the Transfer of Power in Nigeria, 1945–1965*, Routledge, New York, 2006, pp. 47–48.

55. Falola and Heaton: *A History of Nigeria*, p. 197.

56. Ibid., p. 197.

57. Michael Janis: 'Igbo and Fang: Feminism in West African Women's Fiction in the College Classroom', Conference material, available at: www.hofstra.edu/pdf/community/culctr/culctr_guinea040209_viajanis.pdf (accessed 27 Dec. 2014).

58. Gyorgy Kalmar: *A Niger partjan*, (On the Shores of the Niger, in Hungarian) Gondolat, Budapest, 1967, p. 87.

59. Iweriebor: *Radical Politics in Nigeria, 1945–1950*, p. 17.

60. Tijani: *Britain, Leftist Nationalists and the Transfer of Power in Nigeria*, p. 16.

61. Davidson: *Modern Africa*, p. 79.

62. Tijani: *Britain, Leftist Nationalists and the Transfer of Power in Nigeria*, p. 13.

63. Edwin Madunagu: *Peter Ayodele Curtis Joseph*, CIINSTRID, Calabar, 2008, p. 13.

64. Iweriebor: *Radical Politics in Nigeria, 1945–1950*, p. 35.

65. Ibid., p. 67.

66. Cohen: *Labour and Politics in Nigeria*, p. 159.

67. Ibid., p. 160.

68. Ananaba: *The Trade Union Movement in Nigeria*, p. 45.

69. Quoted in ibid., p. 44.

70. Iweriebor: *Radical Politics in Nigeria, 1945–1950*, p. 26.

71. Ananaba: *The Trade Union Movement in Nigeria*, p. 56.

72. Ibid., p. 66.

73. Iweriebor: *Radical Politics in Nigeria, 1945–1950*, p. 29.

74. Ibid., p. 57.

75. Ibid., p. 39.

76. Ibid., p. 45.

77. Ibid., p. 53.

78. Ibid., p. 59.

79. Ibid., p. 235.

80. Ibid., p. 30.

81. Ibid., p. 33.

82. Ibid., p. 66.

83. Ibid., p. 38.

84. Ibid., p. 42.

85. Ibid., p. 45.

86. Ibid., p. 53.

87. Ibid., p. 96.

88. Ibid., p. 120.

89. Ibid., p. 44.

90. Ibid., p. 145.

91. Ibid., p. 153.

92. Ibid., p. 171.
93. Ibid., p. 203.
94. Ibid., p. 213.
95. Ibid., p. 246.
96. Cohen: *Labour and Politics in Nigeria*, p. 60.
97. Ananaba: *The Trade Union Movement in Nigeria*, p. 127.
98. Cohen: *Labour and Politics in Nigeria*, p. 77.
99. *Vanguard Nigeria*, 'Sunmonu Revolutionised Labour with Workers' Charter of Demands'.
100. Cohen: *Labour and Politics in Nigeria*, p. 79.
101. Ibid., p. 81.
102. Ananaba: *The Trade Union Movement in Nigeria*, p. 227.
103. Ibid., p. 186.
104. Tijani: *Britain, Leftist Nationalists and the Transfer of Power in Nigeria*, p. 18.
105. Ibid., p. 13.
106. Ibid., p. 31.
107. Ibid., p. 34.
108. Vladislav M. Zubok: *A Failed Empire: The Soviet Union in the Cold War from Stalin to Gorbachev*, University of North Carolina Press, Chapel Hill, 2007.
109. Tijani: *Britain, Leftist Nationalists and the Transfer of Power in Nigeria*, p. 49.
110. *Vanguard Nigeria*, 'Sunmonu Revolutionised Labour with Workers' Charter of Demands'.
111. Tijani: *Britain, Leftist Nationalists and the Transfer of Power in Nigeria*, p. 93.
112. Ibid., p. 94.
113. Maxim Matusevich: *No Easy Row for a Russian Hoe: Ideology and Pragmatism in Nigerian–Soviet Relations*, Africa World Press, Trenton/ Asmara, 2003, p. 69.
114. Ibid., p. 70.
115. Ananaba: *The Trade Union Movement in Nigeria*, p. 145.
116. Tijani: *Britain, Leftist Nationalists and the Transfer of Power in Nigeria*, p. 20.
117. Quoted in ibid., p. 116.
118. Ibid., pp. 51–66.
119. Ibid., p. 58.
120. Ibid., p. 52.
121. Ibid., p. 75.
122. Ananaba: *The Trade Union Movement in Nigeria*, p. 248.
123. Ibid., p. 232.
124. Ibid., p. 251.
125. Cohen: *Labour and Politics in Nigeria*, p. 95.
126. Ibid., p. 97.

127. *Vanguard Nigeria*, 'Sunmonu Revolutionised Labour with Workers' Charter of Demands'.

128. Tijani: *Britain, Leftist Nationalists and the Transfer of Power in Nigeria*, p. 98.

129. Otegbeye: *The Turbulent Decade*, p. 222.

130. Ibid., p. 1.

131. Ibid., p. 38.

132. Ibid., p. 11.

133. Ibid., p. 35.

134. Ibid., p. 68.

135. Ibid., p. 104.

136. Ibid., p. 110.

137. Ibid., p. 138.

138. Ibid., pp. 160–61.

139. Otegbeye: *The Turbulent Decade*, p. 187.

140. Ibid., p. 219.

141. Ibid., p. 246.

142. Ibid., p. 250.

143. Ibid., p. 258.

144. Feinstein: *African Revolutionary*, p. 264.

145. Edwin Madunagu: *The Tragedy of the Nigerian Socialist Movement*, Centaur Press, Calabar, 1980, p. 4.

146. Ibid., p. 7.

147. Tijani: *Britain, Leftist Nationalists and the Transfer of Power in Nigeria*, p. 99.

148. Matusevich: *No Easy Row for a Russian Hoe*, p. 72.

149. Ibid., p. 71.

150. Ibid., p. 97.

151. Edwin Madunagu: *Understanding Nigeria and the New Imperialism: Essays*, Clear Lines Publications, Calabar, 2006, p. 72.

152. Ibid., p. 72.

153. Ferreira: *Savagery in Politics*, p. 68.

154. Mohammed Abubakar Rimi: *Struggle for Redemption: Selected Speeches of Mohammed Abubakar Rimi*, Northern Nigerian Publishing Company, Zaria, 1981.

155. Feinstein: *African Revolutionary*, p. 326.

156. Ibid., p. 329.

157. Edwin Madunagu: *The Philosophy of Violence*, Basic Truth – Progress Library, Calabar, 1976, p. 28.

158. Tunde Adeniran: 'The Dynamics of Peasant Revolt: A Conceptual Analysis of the Agbekoya Parapo Uprising in the Western State of Nigeria', *Journal of Black Studies*, June 1974.

159. Tar: *The Politics of Neoliberal Democracy in Africa*, p. 133.

160. *Vanguard Nigeria*, 'Sunmonu Revolutionised Labour with Workers' Charter of Demands'.

161. Tar: *The Politics of Neoliberal Democracy in Africa*, p. 133.

162. Zeilig (ed.): *Class Struggle and Resistance in Africa*, p. xix.
163. Bade Onimode: *Alternative Development Strategies for Africa*, vol. 1, Coalition for Change, IFFA, London, 1990, pp. 61–75.
164. Tar: *The Politics of Neoliberal Democracy in Africa*, p. 134.
165. Ibid., p. 134.
166. Ibid., p. 136.
167. Ibid., p. 143.
168. Madunagu: *The Tragedy of the Nigerian Socialist Movement*, p. 18.
169. Tar: *The Politics of Neoliberal Democracy in Africa*, p. 143.
170. Ibid., p. 145.
171. Edwin Madunagu: *For Our Departed Radical Patriots*, Clear Lines Publications, Calabar, 2010, p. 17.
172. Tar: *The Politics of Neoliberal Democracy in Africa*, p. 147.
173. Ibid., p. 138.
174. Ibid., p. 149.
175. Madunagu: *The Tragedy of the Nigerian Socialist Movement*, p. 16.
176. Ibid., p. 25.
177. Ibid., p. 29.
178. Ibid., p. 30.
179. Ibid., p. 29.
180. Ibid., p. 34.
181. Ibid., p. 37.
182. Jacob K. Olupona: *African Religions: A Very Short Introduction*, Oxford University Press USA, New York, 2014, p. 54 (on campus cults and their ties to politics). Also of interest here: Immigration and Refugee Board of Canada, *Nigeria: Prevalence of Ritual Murder and Human Sacrifice; Police and State Response (2009–2012)*, 20 November 2012, NGA104218.E, available at: www.refworld.org/docid/50c84a6d2.html (accessed 15 Jan. 2016).
183. Ferreira: *Savagery in Politics*, p. 28.
184. Ibid., p. 28.
185. Madunagu: *Understanding Nigeria and the New Imperialism*, p. 138.
186. Ferreira: *Savagery in Politics*, p. 29.
187. Toyin Falola and A. Goke-Pariola (eds): *Politics and Economy in Contemporary Nigeria: Selected Works of Segun Osoba*, New Beacon, London, 1984.
188. Madunagu: *Understanding Nigeria and the New Imperialism*, p. 335.
189. Edwin Madunagu: 'Looking Back: 25 Years Ago', *Guardian* (Nigeria), 7 Nov. 2002, p. 5.
190. Onimode: *Alternative Development Strategies for Africa*, p. 211.
191. Ferreira: *Savagery in Politics*, p. 110.
192. Madunagu: *Understanding Nigeria and the New Imperialism*, p. 117.
193. Ibid., p. 72.
194. Madunagu: *For Our Departed Radical Patriots*, pp. 6–12.
195. Edwin Madunagu: 'The Tragedy of 1989', *Guardian* (Nigeria), 3 April 2003, p. 5.
196. Rudolf Bahro: *The Alternative in Eastern Europe*, NLB, London, 1978.

197. Madunagu: *Understanding Nigeria and the New Imperialism*, p. 422.

198. Ibid., p. 127.

199. Ibid., p. 125.

200. Ferreira: *Savagery in Politics*, p. 69.

201. Ibid., p. 114.

202. Baba Aye: *Era of Crisis and Revolts*, 2013, unpublished manuscript, courtesy Drew Povey, available at: www.academia.edu/7947545/Era_of_Crises_and_Revolts (accessed 22 March 2016).

203. Segun Sango: *Nigeria on a Cliff Edge*, DSM Publication, Lagos, 2010, available at: www.socialistnigeria.org/page.php?article=1570 (accessed 27 Jan. 2014).

204. Mike Davis: *Planet of Slums*, Verso, London, New York, 2006, p. 196.

205. Madunagu: *Understanding Nigeria and the New Imperialism*, p. 228.

206. For the Democratic Socialist Movement's Education Rights Campaign, see http://educationrightscampaign.blogspot.hu/ (accessed 27 Jan. 2014).

207. Madunagu: *Understanding Nigeria and the New Imperialism*, p. 408.

4 International Relations of the Nigerian Left

1. Maxim Matusevich: *No Easy Row for a Russian Hoe: Ideology and Pragmatism in Nigerian–Soviet Relations*, Africa World Press, Trenton/Asmara, 2003, pp. 105–28.

2. Edmond J. Keller and Donald Rothchild (eds): *Afro-Marxist Regimes: Ideology and Public Policy*, Lynne Rienner Publishers, Boulder, CO, 1987, p. 67.

3. Kenoye K. Eke: *Nigeria's Foreign Policy under Two Military Governments, 1966–1979: An Analysis of the Gowon and Muhammed/Obasanjo Regimes*, The Edwin Mellen Press, Lampeter, Wales, 1990, p. 39.

4. BBC: 'Nigeria: Gunmen Attack Kano Emir's Convoy', BBC Africa, 19 Jan. 2013, available at: www.bbc.co.uk/news/world-africa-21103322 (accessed 19 Nov. 2013).

5. Afua Hirsch: 'African Hip-hop Is Recreating America', *the Guardian* (UK), 3 Oct. 2012, available at: www.theguardian.com/world/2012/oct/03/african-hip-hop-america (accessed 16 Jan. 2016).

6. Nike (Dee Prodigal Daughter): 'Nigerians and their Foreign Accent Syndrome', NigeriaFilms.com, available at: www.nigeriafilms.com/news/18455/34/nigerians-and-their-foreign-accent-syndrome.html (accessed 16 Jan. 2016).

7. Maggie Fick and David Pilling: 'Capital Controls Curtail Spending of Nigeria's Jet Set', *Financial Times*, 10 Jan. 2016, available at: www.ft.com/cms/s/0/45c77cd2-b601-11e5-8358-9a82b43f6b2f.html#axzz3xOc2Jxaf (accessed 16 Jan. 2016).

8. Lucian W. Pye: *Asian Power and Politics: The Cultural Dimensions of Authority*, Harvard University Press, Cambridge, MA, 1990; Amitav Acharya and Barry Buzan: *Non-Western International Relations Theory: Perspectives on and Beyond Asia*, Routledge, London, 2009; Ian Taylor:

The International Relations of Sub-Saharan Africa, Bloomsbury Academic, London, 2010.

9. Janos Besenyo: 'Az orosz vedelmi ipar es Afrika' (Russia's Security Industry in Africa; in Hungarian)(with Zoltan Bokanyi), *Szakmai Szemle*, 2011/1, pp. 133–45, available at: www.kbh.gov.hu/publ/szakmai_szemle/2011_1_szam.pdf, accessed 24 July 2015.

10. See Walter Rodney: *How Europe Underdeveloped Africa*, Pambazuka Press, Nairobi, 2012.

11. Vladislav M. Zubok: *A Failed Empire: The Soviet Union in the Cold War from Stalin to Gorbachev*, University of North Carolina Press, Chapel Hill, 2007.

12. A particularly 'endearing' exercise in Kremlinologist sophistry regarding our focus here is Andrzej Korbonski and Francis Fukuyama: *The Soviet Union and the Third World: The Last Three Decades*, Cornell University Press, Ithaca, London, 1987.

13. Maxim Matusevich: *Africa in Russia, Russia in Africa: Three Centuries of Encounters*, Africa World Press, Trenton/Asmara, 2007, p. 86.

14. Bene Madunagu and Edwin Madunagu: 'Conceptual Framework and Methodology: Marxism and the Question of Women's Liberation', in *Women in Nigeria Today*, London, Zed Books, 1985, p. 30.

15. Edwin Madunagu: *Understanding Nigeria and the New Imperialism: Essays*, Clear Lines Publications, Calabar, 2006, p. 389.

16. Ibid., p. 542.

17. Ibid., p. 548.

18. Zubok: *A Failed Empire*, p. 84.

19. Ibid., p. 248.

20. Ibid., p. 104.

21. Ibid., p. 135.

22. Ibid., p. 175.

23. Robert Legvold: *Soviet Policy in West Africa*, Harvard University Press, Cambridge, MA, 1970, p. 29.

24. Mao Ce-tung (Zedong): *A nepen beluli ellentmondasok helyzes megoldasarol* (Contradictions within the People) Kossuth, Budapest, 1957 (Hungarian edn).

25. Usman A. Tar: *The Politics of Neoliberal Democracy in Africa: State and Civil Society in Nigeria*, Tauris Academic Studies, London, 2009, pp. 127–28.

26. Sergey Mazov: 'Soviet Policy in West Africa: An Episode of the Cold War, 1956–1964'. In: Matusevich (ed.): *Africa in Russia, Russia in Africa*, p. 295.

27. Ibid., p. 296.

28. Ibid., p. 296.

29. Legvold: *Soviet Policy in West Africa*, p. 55.

30. Ibid, p. 44.

31. Ibid., p. 35.

32. Janos Besenyo: 'A francia Afrika-politika valtozasa' (with Ambrus Hetenyi Soma), *Sereg Szemle* (MH OHP) 9(3–4), Oct./Dec. 2011, pp. 199–208,

available at: www.scribd.com/doc/126276223/Sereg-Szemle-IX-evfolyam-3-4-szam-2011-oktober-december-199-207-oldal (accessed 24 July 2015).

33. Legvold: *Soviet Policy in West Africa*, p. 113.
34. Ibid., p. 105.
35. Ibid., p. 103.
36. Ibid., p. 221.
37. Ibid., p. 119.
38. Ibid., p. 137.
39. Ibid., p. 158.
40. Ibid., p. 175.
41. Ibid., p. 188.
42. Ibid., p. 193.
43. Ibid., p. 238.
44. Zubok: *A Failed Empire*, p. 201.
45. Ibid., p. 205.
46. Ibid., p. 208.
47. Ibid., p. 248.
48. Ibid., p. 200.
49. Legvold: *Soviet Policy in West Africa*, p. 205.
50. Ibid., p. 198.
51. Ibid., p. 211.
52. Ibid., p. 228.
53. Ibid., p. 255.
54. Zubok: *A Failed Empire*, p. 250.
55. Keller and Rothchild (eds): *Afro-Marxist Regimes*, p. 4.
56. Zubok: *A Failed Empire*, p. 251.
57. Legvold: *Soviet Policy in West Africa*, p. 223.
58. Keller and Rothchild (eds): *Afro-Marxist Regimes*, p. 55.
59. Ibid., p. 17.
60. Ibid., p. 7.
61. Ibid., p. 8.
62. Zubok: *A Failed Empire*, p. 251.
63. Ibid., p. 255.
64. Matusevich: *No Easy Row for a Russian Hoe*, p. 75.
65. Ibid., p. 79.
66. Ibid., p. 59.
67. Ibid., p. 62.
68. Ibid., p. 63.
69. Ibid., p. 83.
70. Ibid., p. 83.
71. Ibid., p. 156.
72. Victor Lasky: *The Ugly Russian*, New York, Trident Press, 1965, p. 77, as quoted by Matusevich: *No Easy Row for a Russian Hoe*, p. 101.
73. Matusevich: *No Easy Row for a Russian Hoe*, p. 108.
74. Ibid., p. 110.
75. Ibid., p. 114.

76. Ibid., p. 118.
77. Ibid., p. 194.
78. Ibid., p. 215.
79. Ibid., p. 121.
80. Ibid., p. 142.
81. Ibid., p. 143.
82. Ibid., pp. 147–49.
83. Ibid., p. 167.
84. A.I. Timofeev: *Nigeriya: Etapy razvitiya*, (Nigeria: The Stages of its Development, in Russian), Znanie, Moscow, 1978.
85. Matusevich: *No Easy Row for a Russian Hoe* pp. 168–72.
86. Vladimir Lopatov: *The Soviet Union and Africa*, Progress Publishers, Moscow, 1987, p. 112.
87. Ibid., p. 174.
88. A.B. Akinyemi: *Economic Co-operation between Nigeria and Eastern Europe*, Nigerian Institute of International Affairs, Lagos, 1984, p. 34.
89. Ibid., p. 27.
90. Osita C. Eze and Osita Agbu (eds): *Nigeria–Russia Relations in a Multipolar World*, Nigerian Institute of International Affairs, Lagos, 2010, p. 90.
91. Rossiyskaya assotsiatsiya mezhdunarodnih issledovaniy (RAMI – Russian International Studies Association)/A.V. Torkunov (ed.): *Desyat let vneshney politiki Rossii* (Ten Years of Russia's Foreign Policy; in Russian), ROSPEN, Moscow, 2003.
92. Matusevich: *No Easy Row for a Russian Hoe*, p. 114.
93. Akinyemi: *Economic Co-operation between Nigeria and Eastern Europe*, p. 38.
94. Ibid., p. 61.
95. Ibid., p. 65.
96. Legvold: *Soviet Policy in West Africa*, p. 288.
97. Ibid., p. 278.
98. Ibid., p. 240.
99. Ibid., p. 255.
100. Ibid., p. 138.
101. Wogu Ananaba: *The Trade Union Movement in Nigeria*, Ethiope Publishing, London, 1969, p. 17.
102. Ibid., p. 182.
103. Ibid., p. 220.
104. Robin Cohen: *Labour and Politics in Nigeria*, Heinemann, London, 1974, p. 87.
105. Joe Slovo: *Slovo: The Unfinished Autobiography*, Ocean Press, Melbourne, 1997, p. 132.
106. Ibid., p. 22.
107. Ibid., p. 36.
108. Ibid., p. 223.
109. Ibid., p. 225.
110. Ibid., p. 223.

111. O. Igho Natufe: *Soviet Policy in Africa: From Lenin to Brezhnev*, iUniverse, Bloomington, 2011, p. 3.
112. Ibid., p. 79.
113. Ibid., p. 132.
114. Ibid., p. 135.
115. Ibid., p. 149.
116. Ibid., pp. 156–60.

5   Activists, Historiographers and Political Thinkers: Marxist-Leninism versus Heterodoxies

1. Abiodun Olamosu: *Ola Oni: A Biography*, pp. 1–2, unpublished manuscript, courtesy Drew Povey.
2. Niyi Oniororo: *Nigeria's Future: Revolution Not Reformism*, Oniororo Publications, Ibadan, 1979, p. 12.
3. Sola Shittu: 'Oniororo, Veteran Journalist and Human Rights Activist, Dies', Online Nigeria, 18 April 2005, available at: http://nm.onlinenigeria.com/templates/?a=1048&z=12 (accessed 4 Feb. 2014).
4. Oniororo: *Nigeria's Future*, p. 136.
5. Ibid., p. 58.
6. Ibid., p. 138.
7. Shittu: 'Oniororo, Veteran Journalist and Human Rights Activist, Dies'.
8. Oniororo: *Nigeria's Future*, p. 119.
9. Ibid., p. 6.
10. Ibid., p. 15.
11. Ibid., p. 23.
12. Ibid., p. 31.
13. Ibid., p. 103.
14. Ibid., p. 107.
15. Ibid., p. 81.
16. Ibid., p. 57.
17. Ibid., p. 70.
18. Ibid., p. 71.
19. Ibid., p. 7.
20. Ibid., p. 79.
21. Ibid., pp. 94–95.
22. Ibid., pp. 37, 60.
23. Ibid., p. 65.
24. Ibid., p. 38.
25. Ibid., p. 119.
26. Ibid., p. 142.
27. Ibid., p. 83.
28. Ibid., p. 111.
29. Ibid., p. 75.
30. Ibid., p. 56.

31. Niyi Oniororo: *Revolution Not Reformism*, Oniororo Publications, Ibadan, 1979, p. 24.
32. Niyi Oniororo: *Why the Nigerian Masses are Poor*, Oniororo Publications, Ibadan, 1993, p. 32.
33. Ibid.
34. Ibid., p. 56.
35. Ibid., p. 64.
36. Ibid., p. 72.
37. Ibid., p. 40.
38. Ibid., p. 50.
39. Ibid., p. 48.
40. Ibid., p. 15.
41. Ibid., p. 12.
42. Ibid., p. 19.
43. Niyi Oniororo: *Who are the Nigerian Comrades? The Story of the Opportunists, Revisionists, Reformists and the Careerists in Nigeria,* Sketch, Ibadan, n.d., p. 13.
44. Ibid., p. 3.
45. Ibid., p. 5.
46. Ibid., p. 5.
47. Ibid., p. 7.
48. Ibid., p. 7.
49. Ibid., p. 13.
50. Ibid., p. 18.
51. Ibid., p. 22.
52. Ibid., p. 25.
53. Oniororo: *Nigeria's Future*, pp. 145–46.
54. Ikenna Nzimiro: *Nigerian Civil War: A Study in Class Conflict*, Frontline Publishing, Enugu, 1982, p. 12.
55. Ibid., p. 11.
56. P. Chudi Uwazurike: 'Ikenna Nzimiro: Anthropologist, Sociologist and Iconoclast: On the Intellectual Legacies of a Radical Nationalist', *Dialectical Anthropology*, 31(1–3), 2007, pp. 73–97.
57. Ibid., and Simon Ottenberg: 'Two Renowned Nigerian Scholars: Ikenna Nzimiro and Victor Chikesie Uchendu', *Dialectical Anthropology*, 31(1–3), 2007, pp. 11–43.
58. Ikenna Nzimiro: *Studies in Ibo Political Systems*, University of California Press, 1972, p. xvii.
59. Ibid., p. xiii.
60. Ibid., p. xvi.
61. Ibid., p. 4.
62. Ibid., p. 25.
63. Ibid., p. 36.
64. Ibid., pp. 52–53.
65. Ibid., p. 56.
66. Ibid., p. 96.

67. Ibid., pp. 147–64.
68. Ibid., p. 165.
69. Ibid., p. 173.
70. Ibid., p. 178.
71. Ibid., p. 256.
72. Nzimiro: *Nigerian Civil War*, p. 14.
73. Ibid., p. 16.
74. Ibid., p. 12.
75. Ibid., p. 10.
76. Ibid., p. 15.
77. Ibid., pp. 48–49.
78. Ibid., p. 22.
79. Ibid., p. 25.
80. Ibid., p. 32.
81. Ibid., p. 38.
82. Ibid., p. 78.
83. Ibid., p. 13.
84. Ibid., pp. 43–44.
85. Ibid., pp. 53–54.
86. Ibid., p. 56.
87. Ibid., p. 94.
88. Ibid., pp. 101–03.
89. Ibid., p. 133.
90. Ibid., p. 135.
91. Ibid., p. 73.
92. Ibid., p. 108.
93. Ibid., p. 140.
94. Ibid., p. 113.
95. Ibid., p. 124.
96. Ibid., p. 135.
97. Ibid., p. 147–55.
98. Ibid., p. 177.
99. Ibid., p. 129.
100. Ibid., p. 92.
101. Ibid., p. 11.
102. Ibid., p. 96.
103. Abdulkadir Balarabe Musa: 'Yusufu Bala Usman, A Tribute', available at: http://www.dawodu.com/usman4.htm (accessed 4 Feb. 2014).
104. Yusufu Bala Usman: *For the Liberation of Nigeria*, New Beacon Books, London/Port of Spain, 1979, p. 207.
105. Ibid., p. 213.
106. Ibid., p. 213.
107. Ibid., p. 208.
108. Ibid., p. 210.
109. Ibid., p. 206.
110. Ibid., p. 211.

111. Ibid., p. 215.
112. Ibid., p. 214.
113. Ibid., p. 151.
114. Ibid., p. 142.
115. Ibid., p. 154.
116. Musa: 'Yusufu Bala Usman, A Tribute'.
117. Yusufu Bala Usman: *The Manipulation of Religion in Nigeria*, 1977–1987, Vanguard Printers and Publishers, Kaduna, 1987, p. 9.
118. Ibid., p. 79.
119. Ibid., pp. 71–79.
120. Ibid., p. 74.
121. Ibid., p. 97.
122. Ibid., p. 90.
123. Ibid., p. 117.
124. Ibid., p. 16.
125. Ibid., p. 19.
126. Ibid., p. 20.
127. Ibid., p. 16.
128. Ibid., p. 18.
129. Ibid., pp. 21–23.
130. Ibid., p. 29.
131. Ibid., p. 31.
132. Cited in ibid., p. 32.
133. Usman: *For the Liberation of Nigeria*, p. 14.
134. Ibid., p. 52.
135. Ibid., p. 52.
136. Usman: *The Manipulation of Religion in Nigeria*, p. 41.
137. Ibid., p. 42.
138. Usman: *For the Liberation of Nigeria*, p. 23.
139. Ibid., p. 56.
140. Ibid., p. 50.
141. Ibid., p. 16.
142. Ibid., p. 104.
143. Ibid., pp. 215–16.
144. Usman: *The Manipulation of Religion in Nigeria*, p. 153.
145. Usman: *For the Liberation of Nigeria*, p. 167.
146. Ibid., p. 70.
147. Ibid., p. 201.
148. *New York Times*: 'Mokwugo Okoye, Nigerian Writer and Politician, 72', 26 Sept. 1998, available at www.nytimes.com/1998/09/26/world/mokwugo-okoye-nigerian-writer-and-politician-72.html (accessed 1 Feb. 2014).
149. S. Oyeweso: *The Political Thought of Mokwugo Okoye since 1950s*, PhD History thesis, Obafemi Awolowo University, Ile Ife, 1995, typescript, unavailable.

150. Theophilus Okere: *Identity and Change, Nigerian Philosophical Studies I, Cultural Heritage and Contemporary Change, Series II, Africa*, vol. 3, Council for Research and Values in Philosophy, New York, 1996, pp. 9–12.

151. Sahara Reporters: 'Second Memorial Lecture for Mokwugo Okoye', 28 Feb. 2011, available at: saharareporters.com/news-page/second-memorial-lecture-mokwugo-okoye-march-2 (accessed 1 Feb. 2014).

152. Mokwugo Okoye: *African Responses: A Revaluation of History and Culture*, Arthur H. Stockwell, Ilfracombe, 1964, back flap.

153. Mokwugo Okoye: *Points of Discord: Studies in Tension and Conflict*, Frederick Muller, London, 1973, p. back flap.

154. Orike Ben Didi (ed.): *Comrade Che at 80 – Tributes*, Aklaka Heritage Books, Charleston, 2012, p. 8.

155. Edwin Madunagu: *For Our Departed Radical Patriots*, Clear Lines Publications, Calabar, 2010, p. 16.

156. Mokwugo Okoye: *The Beard of Prometheus*, Arthur H. Stockwell, Ilfracombe, n.d., p. 88.

157. Mokwugo Okoye: *A Letter to Dr Nnamdi Azikiwe*, Fourth Dimension Publishing, Enugu, 1979, p. 92.

158. Ibid., p. 40.

159. Okoye: *The Beard of Prometheus*, p. 101.

160. Ibid., p. 101.

161. Ibid., p. 154.

162. Ibid., p. 53.

163. Okoye: *Points of Discord*, p. 109.

164. Okoye: *The Beard of Prometheus*, pp. 125–26.

165. Ibid., p. 18.

166. Ibid., p. 150.

167. Ibid., p. 150.

168. Ibid., p. 104.

169. Ibid., p. 49.

170. Ibid., p. 43.

171. Ibid., pp. 78–87.

172. Okoye: *African Responses*, p. 95.

173. Ibid., p. 187.

174. Ibid., p. 250 and Mokwugo Okoye: *Embattled Men: Profiles in Social Adjustment*, Fourth Dimension Publishers, Enugu, 1980, p. 4.

175. Okoye: *African Responses*, pp. 189–90.

176. Ibid., p. 61.

177. Ibid., p. 194.

178. Ibid., p. 172.

179. Okoye: *Embattled Men*, p. 2.

180. Ibid., p. 59.

181. Ibid., p. 3.

182. Ibid., p. 9.

183. Ibid., p. 10.

184. Ibid., p. 13.

185. Ibid., p. 68.

186. Ibid., p. 69.
187. Ibid., p. 72.
188. Ibid., p. 75.
189. Ibid., p. 78.
190. Ibid., p. 80.
191. Ibid., p. 82.
192. Ibid., p. 84.
193. Ibid., p. 94.
194. Ibid., p. 87.
195. Ibid., p. 233.
196. Okoye: *Points of Discord*, p. 56.
197. Ibid., p. 77.
198. Ibid., p. 84.
199. Ibid., p. 191.
200. Eskor Toyo: *Primary Accumulation and Development Strategy in a Neo-Colonial Economy (A Critique of Dependence Theory and its Implications)*, unpublished typescript, Calabar, n. d., p. 16.
201. Ibid., p. 17.
202. Ibid., p. 18.
203. Ibid., p. 19.
204. Ibid., pp. 31–32.
205. Ibid., pp. 85–89.
206. Edwin Madunagu: *Nigeria: The Economy and the People – The Political Economy of State Robbery and its Popular Democratic Negation*, New Beacon Books, London/Port of Spain, 1983.
207. Edwin Madunagu: *Understanding Nigeria and the New Imperialism: Essays*, Clear Lines Publications, Calabar, 2006, p. 155.
208. Edwin Madunagu: *In Lieu of Autobiography*, Clear Lines Publications, Calabar, 2010, p. 21.
209. Kati Marton and Adrienne Germain: 'Bush in Africa – Saving Women from AIDS', *The New York Times*, 9 July 2003, available at www.nytimes.com/2003/07/09/opinion/09iht-edmarton_ed3_.html (accessed 4 February 2014).
210. Victor J. Seidler: *Young Men and Masculinities: Global Cultures and Intimate Lives*, Zed Books, London, 2006, p. 174.
211. Charles E. Nolim: *Issues in African Literature*, Malthouse Press, Ipswich, 2013, p. 40.
212. Madunagu: *In Lieu of Autobiography*, p. 8.
213. Ibid., p. 6.
214. Eddie Madunagu: *Problems of Socialism: The Nigerian Challenge*, Zed Books, London, 1982, p. 58.
215. Interview with Edwin Madunagu, Calabar, 5 Jan. 2013.
216. Edwin Madunagu: *The Philosophy of Violence*, Progress Library, Ibadan, 1976.
217. Ibid., p. 15.
218. Ibid., p. 11.
219. Ibid., p. 14.

220. Ibid., p. 22.

221. Ibid., p. 19.

222. Ibid., p. 28.

223. Cited by Edwin Madunagu: *The Tragedy of the Nigerian Socialist Movement*, Centaur Press, Calabar, 1980, p. 1.

224. Ibid., p. 4.

225. Ibid., p. 7.

226. Ibid., p. 17.

227. Ibid., p. 26.

228. Ibid., pp. 99–101.

229. Eszter Bartha: *Alienating Labour: Workers on the Road from Socialism to Capitalism in East Germany and Hungary*, Berghahn Books, New York, 2013.

230. Cited by Madunagu: *The Tragedy of the Nigerian Socialist Movement*, p. 100.

231. Madunagu: *Understanding Nigeria and the New Imperialism*, p. 536.

232. Ibid., p. 321.

233. Interview with Edwin Madunagu, 5 Jan. 2013, Calabar.

234. Madunagu: *Understanding Nigeria and the New Imperialism*, p. 322.

235. Ibid., p. 329.

236. Madunagu: *Problems of Socialism*, p. 1.

237. Ibid., p. 3.

238. Ibid., p. 13.

239. Ibid., p. 14.

240. Ibid., p. 16.

241. Ibid., p. 17.

242. Ibid., p. 19.

243. Ibid., p. 21.

244. Ibid., p. 28.

245. Ibid., pp. 35–37.

246. Ibid., p. 38.

247. Madunagu: *Nigeria: The Economy and the People*.

248. Ibid., p. 26.

249. Madunagu: *Understanding Nigeria and the New Imperialism*, p. 92.

250. Ibid., p. 441.

251. Ibid., p. 512.

252. Ibid., pp. 155–57.

253. Françoise Girard: *My Father did not Think This Way: Nigerian Boys Contemplate Gender Equality*, The Population Council, New York, 2003, p. 529.

254. Madunagu: *Understanding Nigeria and the New Imperialism*, pp. 5–6.

6   Political Economists

1. Pjotr Nyikityin (Petr Nikitin): *A politikai gazdasagtan rovid osszefoglalasa* (Political Economy: A Short Course, translated into Hungarian from the Russian original), Kozgazdasagi es Jogi Konyvkiado, Budapest, 1962.

2. Ola Oni and Bade Onimode: *Economic Development of Nigeria: The Socialist Alternative*, The Nigerian Academy of Arts, Sciences and Technology, 1975, p. 12.

3. Ibid., p. 29.

4. Ibid., p. 48.

5. Ibid., p. 61.

6. Ibid., p. 101.

7. Ibid., p. 117.

8. Bade Onimode: *Imperialism and Underdevelopment in Nigeria: The Dialectics of Mass Poverty*, Zed Press, London, 1982, p. 26.

9. Ibid., p. 116.

10. Ibid., p. 87.

11. Ibid., p. 225.

12. Ibid., p. 184.

13. Ibid., p. ii.

14. Ibid., p. i.

15. Ibid., p. i.

16. Ibid., p. 67.

17. Ibid., pp. 4–5.

18. Ibid., p. 7.

19. Ibid., p. 8.

20. Ibid., p. 11.

21. Ibid., p. 12.

22. Ibid., p. 15.

23. Ibid., p. 52.

24. Ibid., p. 62.

25. Ibid., p. 63.

26. Ibid., p. 64.

27. Ibid., p. 73.

28. Ibid., p. 78.

29. Ibid., p. 82.

30. Ibid., p. 83.

31. Ibid., p. 84.

32. Ibid., p. 92.

33. Ibid., p. 95.

34. Ibid., p. 100.

35. Ibid., p. 126.

36. Ibid., p. 129.

37. Ibid., p. 138.

38. Ibid., p. 142.

39. Ibid., p. 152.

40. Ibid., p. 155.

41. Ibid., p. 161.

42. Ibid., p. 167.

43. Ibid., pp. 171–72.

44. Ibid., pp. 179–84.

45. Ibid., pp. 197–218.
46. Ibid., p. 229.
47. That is, the Organisation of African Unity; the UN Development Programme; the International Labour Organization; and international non-governmental organisations.
48. Bade Onimode (ed.): *Coalition for Change: Alternative Strategies for Africa*, Institute for African Alternatives, London, 1990, p. 25.
49. Ibid., p. 23.
50. Ibid., p. 32.
51. Bade Onimode: *A Future for Africa: Beyond the Politics of Adjustment*, Earthscan Publications, London, 1992, p. 124.
52. Ibid., p. 103.
53. Ibid., p. 106.
54. Ibid., p. 159.
55. Ibid., p. 155.
56. Ibid., p. 134.
57. Adebayo O. Olukoshi (ed.): *The Politics of Structural Adjustment in Nigeria*, James Currey, London / Heinemann, Ibadan, 1993, p. 46.
58. Ibid., p. 47.
59. Ibid., p. 24.
60. Ibid., p. 91.
61. Ibid., p. 101.
62. Okwudiba Nnoli (ed.): *Dead-end to Nigerian Development: An Investigation on the Social, Economic and Political Crisis in Nigeria*, CODESRIA, Dakar, 1993, p. 4.
63. Ibid., p. 6.
64. Ibid., p. 8.
65. Ibid., p. 14.
66. Ibid., p. 12.
67. Ibid., p. 15.
68. Ibid., p. 17.
69. Ibid., p. 131.
70. Ibid., pp. 154–55.
71. *Review of African Political Economy*, available at: www.roape.org/ (accessed 27 Feb. 2014).
72. International Labour Organization, www.ilo.org/public/english/iira/about/officers/otobo.htm.
73 Abdul Mahmud: 'Where Is the Left When Nigeria Needs It?' *Sahara Reporters*, 22 Oct. 2011, available at: http://saharareporters.com/article/where-left-when-nigeria-needs-it-abdul-mahmud (accessed 27 Feb. 2014).
74. Segun O. Osoba: 'Corruption in Nigeria: Historical Perspectives', *Review of African Political Economy*, 23(69), Sept. 1996, pp. 371–86, available at: www.roape.org/pdf/6903.pdf (accessed 27 Feb. 2014).
75. Ibid., p. 372.
76. Ibid., p. 375.
77. Ibid., p. 376.

78. Ibid., p. 378.
79. Ibid., p. 382.
80. Ibid., p. 384.
81. Segun Osoba: 'The Deepening Crisis of the Nigerian National Bourgeoisie', *Review of African Political Economy*, 5(13), Winter 1978, pp. 63–77, available at: www.roape.org/pdf/1306.pdf (accessed 27 Feb. 2014).
82. Ibid., p. 63.
83. Ibid., p. 69.
84. Ibid., p. 71.
85. Ibid., p. 75.
86. Ibid., p. 63.
87. Tajudeen Abdul-Raheem: 'Bye to all the B Stars of Global Pornography of Poverty: Blair, Brown, Bob and Bono', *Review of African Political Economy*, 33(107), March 2006, pp. 156–58, available at: www.roape. org/107/13.html (accessed 27 Feb. 2014).
88. Tajudeen Abdul-Raheem and Adebayo O. Olukoshi: 'The Left in Nigerian Politics and the Struggle for Socialism, 1945–1985', *Review of African Political Economy*, 13(37), Winter 1986, pp. 64–80, available at: www.roape. org/pdf/3709.pdf (accessed 27 Feb. 2014).
89. Ibid., p. 71.
90. Ibid., p. 71.
91. Ibid., p. 72.
92. Ibid., p. 73.
93. Ibid., p. 76.
94. Ibid., p. 73.

7 Marxian Feminisms

1. Layli Phillips (ed.): *The Womanist Reader: The First Quarter Century of Womanist Thought*, Routledge, New York, 2006.
2. Andrea Dworkin: *Pornography: Men Possessing Women*, The Women's Press, London, 1981.
3. Mireille Miller-Young: *A Taste for Brown Sugar: Black Women in Pornography*, Duke University Press, Durham, NC, 2014.
4. Jean Bethke Elshtain: *Public Man, Private Woman*, Princeton University Press, Princeton, NJ, 1981.
5. Gwendolyn Mikell: *African Feminism: The Politics of Survival in Sub-Saharan Africa*, University of Pennsylvania Press, Philadelphia, 1997.
6. Ibid., p. 333.
7. Friedrich Engels: *The Origin of the Family, Private Property, and the State*, Penguin Books, London, 2010 (last legal paperback edition in English).
8. Simon Sebag Montefiore: *Stalin: The Court of the Red Tsar*, First Vintage Books Edition, New York, 2005.
9. Vladimir Ilyich Lenin: *The Emancipation of Women: From the Writings of V.I. Lenin*, International Publishers, New York, 1934, p. 101. In: Rosemarie

Tong: *Feminist Thought: A Comprehensive Introduction*, Westview Press, Boulder, CO, 1989, p. 173.

10. R.C. Elwood: *Inessa Armand: Revolutionary and Feminist*, Cambridge University Press, Cambridge, 1992.

11. Alexandra Kollontai: 'Theses on Communist Morality in the Sphere of Marital Relations', available at: www.marxists.org/archive/kollonta/1921/theses-morality.htm (accessed 26 July 2015).

12. Wikipedia: Alexandra Kollontai, available at: https://en.wikipedia.org/wiki/Alexandra_Kollontai (accessed 26 July 2015).

13. Jonathan Mirsky: 'Fighting False Worlds and Worlds', *New York Review of Books*, 4 June 2015, 62(10), p. 74.

14. Mary Zirin, Irina Livezeanu, Christine D. Worobec and June Pachuta Farris (eds): *Women and Gender in Central and Eastern Europe, Russia, and Eurasia: A Comprehensive Bibliography*, vols I–II, Routledge (for the Association of Women in Slavic Studies), London, 2015.

15. Sylvia Pankhurst: *Ethiopia: A Cultural History*, Lalibela House, Addis Abeba, 1955.

16. Walter Rodney: *How Europe Underdeveloped Africa*, Bogle-L'Ouverture Publications, London, Dar-Es-Salaam, 1973, pp. 10–15, 18–19, 60, 74, 95, 191.

17. Marc Matera, Misty L. Bastian and Susan Kingsley Kent: *The Women's War of 1929: Gender and Colonial Violence in Colonial Nigeria*, Palgrave Macmillan, London, 2013, p. 11.

18. Ibid., p. 235.

19. Ibid., p. 25.

20. Ibid., p. 36.

21. Ibid., p. 5.

22. Ibid., p. 41; p. 123.

23. Ibid., p. 39.

24. Ibid., p. 37.

25. Ibid., p. 30.

26. Ibid., p. 105.

27. Ibid., p. 19.

28. Ibid., p. 27.

29. Ibid., p. 108.

30. Ibid., p. 109.

31. Ibid., p. 118.

32. Ibid., p. 127.

33. Ibid., p. 129.

34. Ibid., p. 136.

35. Ibid., p. 141.

36. Ibid., p. 151.

37. Ibid., p. 155.

38. Ibid., p. 175.

39. Ibid., p. 139.

40. Ibid., p. 68.

41. Ibid., p. 180.
42. Ibid., p. 94.
43. Ibid., p. 70.
44. Ibid., p. 220.
45. Ibid., p. 229.
46. Ibid., p. 230.
47. Ibid., p. 231.
48. Judith Van Allen: 'Aba Riots or Igbo Women's War? Ideology, Stratification, and the Invisibility of Women'. In: Nancy J. Hafkin and Edna G. Bay (eds): *Women in Africa: Studies in Social and Economic Change*, Stanford University Press, Stanford, CA, 1976.
49. Ifi Amadiume: *Daughters of the Goddess, Daughters of Imperialism: African Women, Culture, Power and Democracy*, Zed Books, London, 2000.
50. Cheryl Johnson-Odim and Nina Emma Mba: *For Women and the Nation: Funmilayo Ransome-Kuti of Nigeria*, University of Illinois Press, Urbana, 1997, p. xi.
51. Ibid., p. 173.
52. Frantz Fanon: *The Wretched of the Earth*, Grove Press, New York, 1963, p. 108.
53. Johnson-Odim and Mba: *For Women and the Nation*, p. 140.
54. Ibid., p. 149.
55. Ibid., p. 142.
56. Ibid., p. 143.
57. Ibid., p. 150.
58. Ibid., p. 3.
59. Ibid., p. 24.
60. Ibid., p. x.
61. Ibid., p. 48.
62. Ibid., p. 38.
63. Ibid., p. 64.
64. Ibid., p. 64.
65. Ibid., p. 65.
66. Ibid., pp. 65, 70.
67. Ibid., p. 72.
68. Ibid., p. 75.
69. Ibid., pp. 79, 92.
70. Ibid., p. 90.
71. Ibid., p. 105.
72. Ibid., p. 121.
73. Ibid., p. 136.
74. Ibid., p. 126.
75. Ibid., p. 127.
76. Ibid., p. 137.
77. Ibid., p. 137.
78. Ibid., p. 138.
79. Ibid., p. 145.

80. Ibid., p. 139.
81. Ibid., p. 140.
82. Ibid., p. 148.
83. Ibid., p. 150.
84. Ibid., p. 145.
85. Ibid., p. 137.
86. Ibid., p. 146.
87. Ibid., p. 49.
88. Ibid., p. 155.
89. Ibid., p. 168.
90. Ibid., p. 168.
91. Ibid., p. 189.
92. Ibid., p. 171.
93. John P. Barnard: 'The Story of Gambo Sawaba by Rima Shawulu', *Ufahamu: A Journal of African Studies*, 20(1), 1992, p. 3, available at Permalink: https://escholarship.org/uc/item/4j61p405 (accessed 27 July 2015).
94. Rima Shawulu Kwewum: *The Gambo Sawaba Story*, 2nd edn, Echo Communications, Abuja, 2004, p. 10.
95. Ibid., p. 32.
96. Ibid., p. 33.
97. Ibid., p. 30.
98. Barnard: 'The Story of Gambo Sawaba by Rima Shawulu', p. 2.
99. Johnson-Odim and Mba: *For Women and the Nation*, p. 105.
100. Ronke Iyabowale Ako-Nai: *Gender and Power Relations in Nigeria*, Lexington Books, Plymouth, 2013, p. 260.
101. Ifi Amadiume: *African Matriarchal Foundations: The Case of Igbo Societies*, Karnak House, London, 1987, p. 9.
102. Mary E. Modupe Kolawole: *Womanism and African Consciousness*, Africa World Press, Trenton and Asmara, 1997, p. 60.
103. Ibid., p. 7.
104. Ibid., p. 52.
105. Ibid., pp. 29–30.
106. Ibid., p. 36.
107. Ibid., p. 130.
108. Cited by ibid., p. 132.
109. Amadiume: *African Matriarchal Foundations*, pp. 9, 13, 16.
110. Ifi Amadiume: *Male Daughters, Female Husbands*, Zed Books, London, 1987.
111. Ibid., p. 6.
112. Ifi Amadiume: *Reinventing Africa: Matriarchy, Religion, and Culture*, Zed Books, London, 1997.
113. Ibid., p. 21.
114. Ibid., p. 115.
115. Ibid., p. 175–76.
116. Ibid., p. 173.
117. Bene Madunagu (ed.): *Women in Nigeria Today*, Zed Books, London, 1985.

118. Ibid., p. 123.
119. Ibid., p. 124.
120. Ibid., p. 36.
121. Ibid., p. 135.
122. Chimamanda Ngozi Adichie: *We Should All Be Feminists*, Fourth Estate, London, 2014.
123. Gayatri Chakravorty Spivak: 'The Trajectory of the Subaltern in My Work', University of California Television, YouTube, available at: https://www.youtube.com/watch?v=2ZHH4ALRFHw, at mins 8:17 to 8:30 (accessed 27 July 2015).
124. Amina Mama interviewed by Elaine Salo, 'Talking about Feminism in Africa', reproduced in *Women's World* from *Agenda*, 'African Feminisms I', 50 (2001).
125. Amina Mama: 'The Challenges of Feminism: Gender, Ethics and Responsible Academic Freedom at African Universities', CODESRIA 2012, *JHEA/RESA*, 9(1–2), 2011, p. 3, available at: file:///C:/Documents%20and%20Settings/adam.mayer/My%20Documents/Downloads/1-Amina_JHEA_1_2_11%20(2).pdf (accessed 28 July 2015).
126. NLC Gender Equity Policy, available at: www.nlcng.org/search_details.php?id=11 (accessed 27 July 2015).

8 Conclusion: Analysing Nigerian Marxism

1. Gyorgy (Georg) Lukacs: *A tarsadalmi let ontologiajarol*, III. Kotet (Ontology of Social Being, vol. III; in Hungarian), 'Prolegomena', Magveto, Budapest, 1971, p. 303.
2. Jean Suret-Canale: 'Traditional Societies of Tropical Africa and the Asiatic Mode of Production', 'A tropusi Afrika hagyomanyos tarsadalmai es az azsiai termelesi mod fogalma' (Hungarian translation). In: Tokei Ferenc: *Az azsiai termelesi mod a tortenelemben* (*The Asiatic Mode of Production in History*; in Hungarian), Gondolat, Budapest, 1982, p. 550.
3. Ibid., p. 550.
4. Richard A. Joseph, *Democracy and Prebendal Politics in Nigeria: The Rise and Fall of the Second Republic*, Cambridge University Press, Cambridge, 1987.
5. Jürgen Habermas, *Strukturwandel der Öffentlichkeit*, Suhrkamp, Frankfurt am Main, 1962, p. 292.
6. Slavoj Zizek: *Violence*, New York, Picador, 2009.
7. Gyorgy (Georg) Lukacs: *Az esz tronfosztasa* (The Dethronement of Reason/ The Destruction of Reason, in Hungarian), Magveto, Budapest, 1954, p. 83.
8. Jussi Viinikka: '"There Shall be No Property": Trade Unions, Class, and Politics in Nigeria'. In: Leo Zeilig (ed.): *Class Struggle and Resistance in Africa*, Haymarket Books, Chicago, 2002, p. 122.
9. Ibid., p. 20.
10. Ibid., p. 15.
11. Ibid., p. 15.
12. Ibid., p. 16.

Bibliography

Books, articles

Aborisade, Femi: *Globalization and the Nigerian Labour Movement*, Movement Against Privatization, Ibadan, 2002 (courtesy Drew Povey).

Acharya, Amitav and Buzan, Barry: *Non-Western International Relations Theory: Perspectives on and Beyond Asia*, Routledge, London, 2009.

Achebe, Chinua: *The Trouble with Nigeria*, Heinemann Educational Books, London, 1984.

Adeniran, Tunde: 'The Dynamics of Peasant Revolt: A Conceptual Analysis of the Agbekoya Parapo Uprising in the Western State of Nigeria'. *Journal of Black Studies*, June 1974.

Adichie, Chimamanda Ngozi: *We Should All Be Feminists*, Fourth Estate, London, 2014.

Akinyemi, A.B. (ed.): *Economic Cooperation between Nigeria and Eastern Europe*, Nigerian Institute of International Affairs, Lagos, 1984.

Ako-Nai, Ronke Iyabowale: *Gender and Power Relations in Nigeria*, Lexington Books, Plymouth, 2013.

Allen, Judith Van: 'Aba Riots or Igbo Women's War? Ideology, Stratification, and the Invisibility of Women'. In: Nancy J. Hafkin and Edna G. Bay (eds): *Women in Africa: Studies in Social and Economic Change*, Stanford University Press, Stanford, CA, 1976.

Amadiume, Ifi: *Male Daughters, Female Husbands: Gender and Sex in an African Society*, Zed Books, London, 1987.

Amadiume, Ifi: *African Matriarchal Foundations: The Case of Igbo Societies*, Karnak House, London, 1987.

Amadiume, Ifi: *Reinventing Africa: Matriarchy, Religion, and Culture*, Zed Books, London, 1997.

Amadiume, Ifi: *Daughters of the Goddess, Daughters of Imperialism: African Women, Culture, Power and Democracy*, Zed Books, London, 2000.

Amin, Samir: *Beyond US Hegemony? Assessing the Prospects for a Multipolar World*, Zed Books, London, 2006.

Ananaba, Wogu: *The Trade Union Movement in Nigeria*, Ethiope Publishing, London, 1969.

Arrighi, Giovanni: *Adam Smith in Beijing: Lineages of the 21st Century*, Verso Books, London, 2009.

Bahro, Rudolf: *The Alternative in Eastern Europe*, NLB, London, 1978.

Balogh, Andras and Salgo, Laszlo: *A gyarmati rendszer tortenete* (A History of the Colonial System), Kossuth, Budapest, 1980.

Bartha, Eszter: *Alienating Labour: Workers on the Road from Socialism to Capitalism in East Germany and Hungary*, Berghahn Books, New York, 2013.

Bayart, Jean-François, Ellis, Stephen and Hibou, Beatrice: 'From Kleptocracy to the Felonious State?' In: Bayart, Jean-François, Ellis, Stephen and Hibou, Beatrice (eds): *The Criminalization of the State in Africa*, The International African Institute, London, 1999.

Beckman, Bjorn et al: *Trade Unions and Party Politics: Labour Movements in Africa*, HSRC Press, Johannesburg, 2010.

Blackwell, William L.: *The Industrialization of Russia: A Historical Perspective*, Harlan Davidson, Arlington Heights, 1994.

Brezsnyev, Leonyid Iljics (Brezhnev): *Az SZKP es a szovjet allam kulpolitikaja* (The Foreign Policy of the CPSU and the Soviet State), Kossuth, Budapest, 1982.

Buber, Martin: *Der Glaube der Propheten*, Verlag Lambert Schneider, Heidelberg, 1984.

Campbell, John: *Nigeria Dancing on the Brink*, Bookcraft, Council on Foreign Relations, Ibadan, 2010.

Chabal, Patrick and Daloz, Jean-Pascal: *Africa Works: Disorder as Political Instrument*, The International African Institute, London, 1999.

Cohen, Robin: *Labour and Politics in Nigeria 1945–1971*, Heinemann, New York, 1974.

Chua, Amy and Rubenfeld, Jed: *The Triple Package: What Really Determines Success*, Bloomsbury Publishing, London, 2014.

Davidson, Basil: *Modern Africa: A Social and Political History*, Pearson, Edinburgh, 1994.

Davis, Mike: *Planet of Slums*, Verso, London, 2006.

Didi, Orike Ben (ed.): *Comrade Che at 80: Tributes*, Aklaka Heritage Books, Charleston, 2012.

Djilas, Milovan: *The New Class: An Analysis of the Communist System*, Harcourt Publishers, San Diego, 1983.

Dworkin, Andrea: *Pornography: Men Possessing Women*, The Women's Press, London, 1981.

Eke, Kenoye K.: *Nigeria's Foreign Policy under Two Military Governments, 1966–1979: An Analysis of the Gowon and Muhammed/Obasanjo Regimes*, The Edwin Mellen Press, Lampeter, Wales, 1990.

Elshtain, Jean Bethke: *Public Man, Private Woman*, Princeton University Press, Princeton, NJ, 1981.

Elwood, R.C.: *Inessa Armand: Revolutionary and Feminist*, Cambridge University Press, Cambridge, 1992.

Engels, Friedrich: *The Origin of the Family, Private Property, and the State*, Penguin Books, London, 2010 (last legal paperback edition in English).

Eze, Osita C. and Agbu, Osita (eds): *Nigeria–Russia Relations in a Multipolar World*, Nigerian Institute of International Affairs, Lagos, 2010.

Falola, Toyin and Heaton, Matthew M.: *A History of Nigeria*, Cambridge University Press, Cambridge, 2008.

Falola, Toyin and Ihonvbere, J.: *The Rise and Fall of Nigeria's Second Republic 1979–1984*, Zed Books, London, 1985.

Falola, Toyin and Goke-Pariola, A. (eds): *Politics and Economy in Contemporary Nigeria: Selected Works of Segun Osoba*, New Beacon, London, 1984.

Fanon, Frantz: *The Wretched of the Earth*, Grove Press, New York, 1963.

Feinstein, Alan: *African Revolutionary: The Life and Times of Nigeria's Aminu Kano*, Fourth Dimension Publishers, Enugu, 1987.

Ferreira, Abayomi: *Savagery in Politics: The Hindrance to National Development*, AuthorHouse, Bloomington, 2006.

Gaddis, John Lewis: *The United States and the End of the Cold War: Implications, Reconsiderations, Provocations*, Oxford University Press, Oxford, 1994.

Girard, Françoise: *My Father did not Think This Way: Nigerian Boys Contemplate Gender Equality*, The Population Council, New York, 2003.

Harvey, David: *The Enigma of Capital and the Crises of Capitalism*, Profile Books, London, 2010.

Iweriebor, Ehiedu E.G.: *Radical Politics in Nigeria, 1945–1950: The Significance of the Zikist Movement*, Ahmadu Bello University Press, Zaria, 1996.

Jeyifo, Biodun (ed.): *Oxford Encyclopaedia of African Thought*, Oxford University Press USA, New York, 2010.

Johnson-Odim, Cheryl and Mba, Nina Emma: *For Women and the Nation: Funmilayo Ransome-Kuti of Nigeria*, University of Illinois Press, Urbana, Chicago, 1997.

Kalmar, Gyorgy: *A Niger partjan*, Gondolat, Budapest, 1967.

Keller, Edmond J. and Rothchild, Donald (ed.): *Afro-Marxist Regimes: Ideology and Public Policy*, Lynne Rienner Publishers, Boulder, 1987.

Kew, Darren and Lewis, Peter: 'Nigeria'. In: Mark Kesselman, Joel Krieger and William A. Joseph (eds): *Introduction to Comparative Politics*, Wadsworth, Boston, MA, 2010.

Kolawole, Mary E. Modupe: *Womanism and African Consciousness*, Africa World Press, Trenton and Asmara, 1997.

Korbonski, Andrzej and Fukuyama, Francis: *The Soviet Union and the Third World, The Last Three Decades*, Cornell University Press, Ithaca, 1987.

Krugman, Paul: *End This Depression Now!*, W. W. Norton, New York, 2013.

Lasky, Victor: *The Ugly Russian*, New York, Trident Press, 1965.

Legvold, Robert: *Soviet Policy in West Africa*, Harvard University Press, Cambridge, MA, 1970.

Lenin, Vladimir Ilyich: *The Emancipation of Women: From the Writings of V. I. Lenin*, International Publishers, New York, 1934.

Levinas, Emmanuel: *Difficult Freedom: Essays on Judaism*, Johns Hopkins Jewish Studies, Johns Hopkins University Press, Baltimore, 1997.

Lopatov, Vladimir: *The Soviet Union and Africa*, Progress Publishers, Moscow, 1987.

Lukacs, Gyorgy (Georg): *Az esz tronfosztasa* (The Dethronement of Reason), Magveto, Budapest, 1954.

MacFarquhar, Roderick: 'China: The Superpower of Mr. Xi'. *New York Review of Books*, 62(13), 13 Aug.–23 Sept. 2015.

Madunagu, Bene (ed.): *Women in Nigeria Today*, Zed Books, London, 1985.

Madunagu, Bene and Madunagu, Edwin: 'Conceptual Framework and Methodology: Marxism and the Question of Women's Liberation'. In: *Women in Nigeria Today*, London, Zed Books.

Madunagu, Edwin: *Peter Ayodele Curtis Joseph*, CIINSTRID, Calabar, 2008.

Madunagu, Edwin: *Nigeria: The Economy and the People – The Political Economy of State Robbery and its Popular Democratic Negation*, New Beacon Books, London/Port of Spain, 1983.

Madunagu, Edwin: *In Lieu of Autobiography*, Clear Lines Publications, Calabar, 2010.

Madunagu, Edwin: *Understanding Nigeria and the New Imperialism: Essays 2002–2006*, Clear Lines Publications, Calabar, 2006.

Madunagu, Edwin: *The Tragedy of the Nigerian Socialist Movement*, Centaur Press, Calabar, 1980.

Madunagu, Edwin: *The Philosophy of Violence*, Progress Library, Ibadan, 1976.

Madunagu, Edwin: *For Our Departed Radical Patriots*, Clear Lines Publications, Calabar, 2010.

Madunagu, Edwin: 'Looking back: 25 Years Ago', *Guardian* (Nigeria), 7 Nov. 2002, p. 5.

Madunagu, Edwin: 'The Tragedy of 1989', *Guardian* (Nigeria), 3 April 2003, p. 5.

Madunagu, Eddie: *Problems of Socialism: The Nigerian Challenge*, Zed Books, London, 1982.

Mao Ce-tung (Mao, Zedong): *A nepen beluli ellentmondasok helyzes megoldasarol*, (Contradictions within the People; Hungarian edn), Kossuth, Budapest, 1957.

Mazov, Sergey: 'Soviet Policy in West Africa: An Episode of the Cold War, 1956–1964'. In: Matusevich, Maxim (ed.): *Africa in Russia, Russia in Africa: Three Centuries of Encounters*, Africa World Press, Trenton/Asmara, 2007.

Martin, Guy: *African Political Thought*, Palgrave Macmillan, London, 2012.

Maier, Karl: *This House Has Fallen: Nigeria in Crisis*, Penguin Books, London, 2000.

Matera, Marc, Bastian, Misty L. and Kent, Susan Kingsley: *The Women's War of 1929: Gender and Colonial Violence in Colonial Nigeria*, Palgrave Macmillan, London.

Matusevich, Maxim: *Africa in Russia, Russia in Africa: Three Centuries of Encounters*, Africa World Press, Trenton/Asmara, 2007.

Matusevich, Maxim: *No Easy Row for a Russian Hoe: Ideology and Pragmatism in Nigerian–Soviet Relations*, Africa World Press, Trenton/Asmara, 2003.

Meredith, Martin: *The State of Africa: A History of Fifty Years of Independence*, The Free Press, London, 2005.

McGregor, Richard: *The Party: The Secret World of China's Communist Rulers*, rev. edn, Penguin Books, Harmondsworth, 2012.

Mikell, Gwendolyn (ed.): *African Feminism: The Politics of Survival in Sub-Saharan Africa*, University of Pennsylvania Press, Philadelphia, 1997.

Miller-Young, Mireille: *A Taste for Brown Sugar: Black Women in Pornography*, Duke University Press, Durham, NC, 2014.

Mirsky, Jonathan: 'Fighting False Worlds and Worlds'. *New York Review of Books*, 4 June 2015, 62(10).

Montefiore, Simon Sebag: *Stalin: The Court of the Red Tsar*, First Vintage Books edn, New York, 2005.

Natufe, O. Igho: *Soviet Policy in Africa: From Lenin to Brezhnev*, iUniverse, Bloomington, 2011.

Nnoli, Okwudiba (ed.): *Dead-end to Nigerian Development: An Investigation on the Social, Economic and Political Crisis in Nigeria*, CODESRIA, Dakar, 1993.

Nolim, Charles E.: *Issues in African Literature*, Malthouse Press, Nigeria, 2013.

Nzimiro, Ikenna: *Nigerian Civil War: A Study in Class Conflict*, Frontline Publishing, Enugu, 1982.

Nzimiro, Ikenna: *Studies in Ibo Political Systems*, University of California Press, San Diego, 1972.

Nyikityin, Pjotr (Nikitin, Petr): *A politikai gazdasagtan rovid osszefoglalasa* (Political Economy: A Short Course), Kozgazdasagi es Jogi Konyvkiado, Budapest, 1962.

Offiong, Daniel A.: *Witchcraft, Sorcery, Magic and Social Order: Among the Ibibio of Nigeria*, Fourth Dimension Publishing, Enugu, 2001.

Okere, Theophilus: *Identity and Change, Nigerian Philosophical Studies I, Cultural Heritage and Contemporary Change, Series II, Africa*, vol. 3, Council for Research and Values in Philosophy, New York, 1996.

Okolo, M.S.C.: 'Re-establishing the Basis of Social Order in Africa: A Reflection on Achebe's Reformist Agenda and Ngugi's Marxist Aesthetics'. In: Beckman, Bjorn and Adeoti, Gbemisola (eds): *Intellectuals and African Development: Pretension and Resistance in African Politics*, CODESRIA, Dakar; Zed Books, London; UNISA Press, Pretoria, 2006, pp. 31–49.

Okoye, Mokwugo: *A Letter to Dr Nnamdi Azikiwe*, Fourth Dimension Publishing, Enugu, 1979.

Okoye, Mokwugo: *African Responses: A Revaluation of History and Culture*, Arthur H. Stockwell, Ilfracombe, 1964.

Okoye, Mokwugo: *Embattled Men: Profiles in Social Adjustment*, Fourth Dimension Publishers, Enugu, 1980.

Okoye, Mokwugo: *Points of Discord, Studies in Tension and Conflict*, Frederick Muller, London, 1973.

Okoye, Mokwugo: *The Beard of Prometheus*, Arthur H. Stockwell, Ilfracombe, n.d.

Olamosu, Abiodun: *Ola Oni: A Biography*, unpublished typescript, n.d., courtesy Drew Povey (July 2014).

Olukoshi, Adebayo O. (ed.): *The Politics of Structural Adjustment in Nigeria*, James Currey, London; Heinemann, Ibadan, 1993.

Olupona, Jacob K.: *African Religions: A Very Short Introduction*, Oxford University Press USA, New York, 2014.

Oni, Ola and Onimode, Bade: *Economic Development of Nigeria: The Socialist Alternative*, The Nigerian Academy of Arts, Sciences and Technology, 1975.

Onimode, Bade: *Imperialism and Underdevelopment in Nigeria: The Dialectics of Mass Poverty*, Zed Press, London, 1982.

Onimode, Bade: *Alternative Development Strategies for Africa*, vol. 1, Coalition for Change, IFFA, London, 1990.

Onimode, Bade: *A Future for Africa: Beyond the Politics of Adjustment*, Earthscan Publications, London, 1992.

Oniororo, Niyi: *Who are the Nigerian Comrades? The Story of the Opportunists, Revisionists, Reformists and Careerists in Nigeria*, Sketch, Ibadan, n.d.

Oniororo, Niyi: *Why the Nigerian Masses are Poor*, Oniororo Publications, Ibadan, 1993.

Oniororo, Niyi: *Nigeria's Future: Revolution Not Reformism*, Oniororo Publications, Ibadan, 1979.

Otegbeye, Tunji: *The Turbulent Decade*, VisionLink Nigeria, Lagos, 1999.

Ottaway, David and Ottaway, Marina: *Afrocommunism*, Africana Publishing Company, New York, 1981.

Ottenberg, Simon: 'Two Renowned Nigerian Scholars: Ikenna Nzimiro and Victor Chikesie Uchendu', *Dialectical Anthropology*, 31(1–3), 2007, Springer, pp. 11–43.

Oyeweso, S.: *The Political Thought of Mokwugo Okoye since 1950s*. PhD History thesis, Obafemi Awolowo University, Ile Ife, 1995, typescript.

Pankhurst, Sylvia: *Ethiopia: A Cultural History*, Lalibela House, Addis Abeba, 1955.

Peel, Michael: A *Swamp Full of Dollars: Pipelines and Paramilitaries at Nigeria's Oil Frontier*, Laurence Hill Books, Chicago, 2010.

Phillips, Layli (ed.): *The Womanist Reader: The First Quarter Century of Womanist Thought*, Routledge, New York, 2006.

Polonyi, Karoly: *An Architect-Planner on the Peripheries*, TERC, Budapest, 2000.

Pye, Lucian W.: *Asian Power and Politics: The Cultural Dimensions of Authority*, Harvard University Press, Cambridge, MA, 1990.

Rodney, Walter: *How Europe Underdeveloped Africa*, Pambazuka Press, Nairobi, 2012.

Rodney, Walter: *How Europe Underdeveloped Africa*, Bogle-L'Ouverture Publications, London and Dar-Es-Salaam, 1973.

Rossiyskaya assotsiatsiya mezhdunarodnih issledovaniy (Russian International Studies Association) and Torkunov, A.V. (eds): *Desyat let vneshney politiki Rossii* (Ten Years of Russia's Foreign Policy), ROSPEN, Moscow, 2003.

Rimi, Mohammed Abubakar: *Struggle for Redemption: Selected Speeches of Mohammed Abubakar Rimi*, Northern Nigerian Publishing Company, Zaria, 1981.

Robinson, Cedric J.: *Black Marxism: The Making of the Black Radical Tradition*, University of North Carolina Press, Chapel Hill, 1983.

Said, Edward: *Culture and Imperialism*, Vintage, New York, 1994.

Sassoon, Donald: *One Hundred Years of Socialism: The West European Left in the Twentieth Century*, I.B. Tauris, London, 2010.

Seidler, Victor J.: *Young Men and Masculinities: Global Cultures and Intimate Lives*, Zed Books, London, 2006, p. 174.

Service, Robert: *The Penguin History of Modern Russia*, Penguin, Harmondsworth, 2009.

Shawulu Kwewum, Rima: *The Gambo Sawaba Story*, 2nd edn, Echo Communications Ltd, Abuja, 2004.

Simor, Andras (ed.): *Neger kialtas – Fekete-Afrika* (Black Howl – Black Africa), Kozmosz, Budapest, 1972.

Sklar, Richard L.: *Nigerian Political Parties: Power in an Emergent African Nation*, Africa World Press, Trenton/Asmara, 2004.

Slovo, Joe: *Slovo: The Unfinished Autobiography*, Ocean Press, Melbourne, 1997.

Tar, Usman E.: *The Politics of Neoliberal Democracy in Africa: State and Civil Society in Nigeria*, Tauris Academic Studies, London, 2009.

Taylor, Ian: *The International Relations of Sub-Saharan Africa*, Bloomsbury Academic, London, 2010.

Tijani, Hakeem Ibikunle: *Britain, Leftist Nationalists and the Transfer of Power in Nigeria, 1945–1965*, Routledge, New York, 2006.

Timofeev, A.I.: *Nigeriya: Etapy razvitiya* (Nigeria: The Stages of its Development), Znanie, Moscow, 1978.

Tong, Rosemarie: *Feminist Thought: A Comprehensive Introduction*, Westview Press, Boulder, 1989.

Toyo, Eskor: *Marks i Keynes: Analiza porównawcza metodologii makroekonomicznej* (Marx and Keynes: An Analysis of Their Methodologies in Macroeconomics; in Polish), Tlumaczyl Bartlomiej Kaminski, Warsaw, 1977.

Toyo, Eskor: *Primary Accumulation and Development Strategy in a Neo-colonial Economy (A Critique of Dependence Theory and its Implications)*, unpublished typescript, Calabar, n.d.

Usman, Yusufu Bala: *For the Liberation of Nigeria*, New Beacon Books, London, 1979.

Usman, Yusufu Bala: *The Manipulation of Religion in Nigeria, 1977–1987*, Vanguard Printers and Publishers, Kaduna, 1987.

Uwazurike, P. Chudi: 'Ikenna Nzimiro – Anthropologist, Sociologist and Iconoclast: On the Intellectual Legacies of a Radical Nationalist', *Dialectical Anthropology*, 31(1–3), Springer, Netherlands, pp. 73–97.

Viinikka, Jussi: '"There Shall be No Property": Trade Unions, Class, and Politics in Nigeria'. In: Leo Zeilig (ed.): *Class Struggle and Resistance in Africa*, Haymarket Books, Chicago, 2002.

Zeilig, Leo (ed.): *Class Struggle and Resistance in Africa*, Haymarket Books, Chicago, 2009.

Zeilig, Leo: *Revolt and Protest: Student Politics and Activism in Sub-Saharan Africa*, I.B. Tauris, London, 2013.

Zirin, Mary, Livezeanu, Irina, Worobec, Christine D. and Farris, June Pachuta (eds): *Women and Gender in Central and Eastern Europe, Russia, and Eurasia: A Comprehensive Bibliography*, vols I–II, Routledge (For the Association of Women in Slavic Studies), London, 2015.

Zubok, Vladislav M.: *A Failed Empire: The Soviet Union in the Cold War from Stalin to Gorbachev*, University of North Carolina Press, Chapel Hill, 2007.

On-line sources

Abdul-Raheem, Tajudeen: 'Bye to all the B Stars of Global Pornography of Poverty: Blair, Brown, Bob and Bono', *Review of African Political Economy*, 33(107), March 2006, pp. 156–58, available at: www.roape.org/107/13.html (accessed 27 Feb. 2014).

Abdul-Raheem, Tajudeen and Olukoshi, Adebayo O.: 'The Left in Nigerian Politics and the Struggle for Socialism, 1945–1985'. *Review of African Political Economy*, 13(37), winter 1986, pp. 64–80, available at: www.roape.org/pdf/3709.pdf (accessed 27 Feb. 2014).

Adichie, Chimamanda Ngozi: 'We Remember Differently: Chinua Achebe at 82', *Premium Times Nigeria*, 23 Nov. 2012, available at: www.premiumtimesng.com/arts-entertainment/108378-chinua-achebe-at-82-we-remember-differently-by-chimamanda-ngozi-adichie.html (accessed 27 July 2015).

Barnard, John P.: 'The Story of Gambo Sawaba by Rima Shawulu', *Ufahamu: A Journal of African Studies*, 20 (1), Permalink: https://escholarship.org/uc/item/4j61p405 (accessed 27 July 2015).

BBC: *Nigeria, Gunmen Attack Kano Emir's Convoy*, BBC Africa, 19 Jan. 2013), available at www.bbc.co.uk/news/world-africa-21103322 (accessed 19 Nov. 2013).

Besenyo, Janos: 'Can the Arab Spring Present a Real Threat to Europe?' *Strategic Impact* (Romania), 1, 2014, pp. 32–44, available at: www.scribd.com/doc/241476196/Can-the-Arab-Spring-present-a-real-threat-to-Europe (accessed 24 July 2015).

Besenyo, Janos: 'Arab tavasz – politikai rendszervaltas az eszak-afrikai arab allamokban' – Kul-Vilag, a Nemzetkozi Kapcsolatok Folyoirata, VIII., 2011/4. – pp. 51–75, available at:. www.kul-vilag.hu/2011/04/besenyo.pdf (accessed 24 July 2015).

Besenyo, Janos: 'Harc az afrikai olajert, Kina gazdasagi ternyerese a fekete kontinensen' – Nemzetvedelmi Egyetemi Forum XI., 2007/4, pp. 36–37, available at: www.zmne.hu/Forum/07negyedik/afrika.htm (accessed 24 July 2015).

Besenyo, Janos: *Orszagismerteto: Kongoi Demokratikus Koztarsasag*, Sereg Szemle, Szekesfeharvar, 2010, available at: www.kalasnyikov.hu/dokumentumok/orszagismerteto_kongo.pdf (accessed 24 July 2015).

Besenyo, Janos: 'A francia Afrika-politika valtozasa' (with Ambrus Hetenyi Soma), *Sereg Szemle*, (MH OHP) IX/ 3–4, Oct./Dec. 2011, pp. 199–208, available at: www.scribd.com/doc/126276223/Sereg-Szemle-IX-evfolyam-3-4-szam-2011-oktober-december-199-207-oldal (accessed 24 July 2015).

Besenyo, Janos: 'Az orosz vedelmi ipar es Afrika' (with Zoltan Bokanyi), *Szakmai Szemle*, 2011/1, pp. 133–45, available at: www.kbh.gov.hu/publ/szakmai_szemle/2011_1_szam.pdf (accessed 24 July 2015).

Bloomberg: 'Mastercard Chases Africa's Poorest to Tap Continent's Growth'. *Bloomberg*, 21 Aug. 2013, available at: www.bloomberg.com/news/2013-08-21/mastercard-chases-africa-s-poorest-to-tap-continent-s-growth.html?cmpid=yhoo (accessed 23 Aug. 2013).

Democratic Socialist Movement (based in Lagos, Trotskyite political party; leader in 2014: Segun Sango). See: www.socialistnigeria.org/ (accessed 12 Jan. 2014).

Democratic Socialist Movement's Education Rights Campaign. See: http://educationrightscampaign.blogspot.hu/ (accessed 27 Jan. 2014).

Hirsch, Afua: 'African Hip-Hop Is Recreating America', *The Guardian* (UK), 3 Oct. 2012, available at: www.theguardian.com/world/2012/oct/03/african-hip-hop-america (accessed 16 Jan. 2016).

Hunwick, John: 'An African Case Study of Political Islam: Nigeria', *Annals of the American Academy of Political and Social Science*, 524, Nov. 1992, p. 151, JSTOR: www.jstor.org/stable/1046712 (accessed 19 Dec. 2012).

Hussain, N.A.A. and Akande, T.M.: 'Sexual Behavior and Condom Use Among Nigerian Soldiers in Ilorin, Kwara State, Nigeria', *African Journal and Clinical and Experimental Microbiology*, 10(2), May 2009, available at: www.ajol.info/index.php/ajcem/article/view/7514/29823 (accessed 15 Jan. 2016).

Immigration and Refugee Board of Canada, *Nigeria: Prevalence of Ritual Murder and Human Sacrifice; Police and State Response (2009–2012)*, 20 Nov. 2012, NGA104218.E, available at: www.refworld.org/docid/50c84a6d2.html (accessed 15 Jan. 2016).

International Labour Organization, www.ilo.org/public/english/iira/about/officers/otobo.htm.

Janis, Michael: 'Igbo and Fang: Feminism in West African Women's Fiction in the College Classroom'. Conference material, available at: www.hofstra.edu/pdf/community/culctr/culctr_guinea040209_viajanis.pdf (accessed 27 Dec. 2014).

Janneh, Fatou: *Marxist Historiography in West Africa*, typescript, available at: www.academia.edu/3551977/Marxist_Historiography_in_West_Africa (accessed 13 Nov. 2013).

Kimber, Charlie: 'Interview: Chimamanda Ngozi Adichie', *Socialist Review*, 310, Oct. 2006, available at: http://socialistreview.org.uk/310/interview-chimamanda-ngozi-adichie (accessed 27 July 2015).

Kenny O.P., Joseph: 'Sharia and Christianity in Nigeria: Islam and a "Secular" State', *Journal of Religion in Africa*, 26(4), p. 340, JSTOR: www.jstor.org/stable/1581837?seq=1 (accessed 19 Dec. 2012).

Kollontai, Alexandra: *Theses on Communist Morality in the Sphere of Marital Relations*, point 18, available at: www.marxists.org/archive/kollonta/1921/theses-morality.htm (accessed 26 July 2015).

Lukacs, Gyorgy (Georg): *Lenin: The Unity of His Thought*, ch. 3, 'The Vanguard Party of the Proletariat', available at: www.marxists.org/archive/lukacs/works/1924/lenin/ch03.htm (accessed 27 Jan. 2014).

Mahmud, Abdul: 'Where is the Left When Nigeria Needs It?', *Sahara Reporters*, 22 Oct. 2011, available at: http://saharareporters.com/article/where-left-when-nigeria-needs-it-abdul-mahmud (accessed 27 Feb. 2014).

Mama, Amina: 'The Challenges of Feminism: Gender, Ethics and Responsible Academic Freedom at African Universities', *JHEA/RESA* 9(1–2), 2011, pp. 1–23, available at: file:///C:/Documents%20and%20Settings/adam.mayer/My%20Documents/Downloads/1-Amina_JHEA_1_2_11%20(2).pdf (accessed 28 July 2015).

Marton, Kati and Germain, Adrienne: 'Bush in Africa: Saving Women from AIDS', *New York Times*, 9 July 2003, available at: www.nytimes.com/2003/07/09/opinion/09iht-edmarton_ed3_.html (accessed 4 Feb. 2014).

Musa, Abdulkadir Balarabe: *Yusufu Bala Usman: A Tribute*, available at www.dawodu.com/usman4.htm (accessed 4 Feb. 2014).

Nigeria Labour Congress Gender Equity Policy, available at: www.nlcng.org/search_details.php?id=11 (accessed 27 July 2015).

Nike (Dee Prodigal Daughter): 'Nigerians and their Foreign Accent Syndrome', NigeriaFilms.com, available at: www.nigeriafilms.com/news/18455/34/nigerians-and-their-foreign-accent-syndrome.html (accessed 16 Jan. 2016).

New York Times: 'Mokwugo Okoye, Nigerian Writer and Politician, 72', 26 Sept. 1998, available at: www.nytimes.com/1998/09/26/world/mokwugo-okoye-nigerian-writer-and-politician-72.html (accessed 1 Feb. 2014).

Osoba, Segun: 'The Deepening Crisis of the Nigerian National Bourgeoisie', *Review of African Political Economy*, 5(13), winter 1978, pp. 63–77, available at: www.roape.org/pdf/1306.pdf (accessed 27 Feb. 2014).

Osoba, Segun: 'Corruption in Nigeria: Historical Perspectives' *Review of African Political Economy*, 23(69), Sept. 1996, pp. 371–86, available at: www.roape.org/pdf/6903.pdf (accessed 27 Feb. 2014).

Ogundipe-Leslie, Molara (Omolara): '*Violence* by Festus Iyayi' (review), *Review of African Political Economy*, 8(22), winter 1981, pp. 108–15, available at: www.roape.org/022/17.html (accessed 12 Jan. 2014).

Sahara Reporters: 'Second Memorial Lecture for Mokwugo Okoye', 28 Feb. 2011, available at: saharareporters.com/news-page/second-memorial-lecture-mokwugo-okoye-march-2 (accessed 1 Feb. 2014).

Sango, Segun: *Nigeria on a Cliff Edge*, DSM Publication, Lagos, 2010, available at: www.socialistnigeria.org/page.php?article=1570 (accessed 27 Jan. 2014).

Schachtman, Noah: 'Inside the Brave New War', *Wired*, 16 May 2007, available at: www.wired.com/dangerroom/2007/05/q_tell_me_a_lit/ (accessed 27 Jan. 2014).

Shittu, Sola: 'Oniororo, Veteran Journalist and Human Rights Activist, Dies', Online Nigeria, 18 April 2005, available at: http://nm.onlinenigeria.com/templates/?a=1048&z=12 (accessed 4 Feb. 2014).

Socialistworld.net: '2015 General Elections and the Working Masses', socialistworld.net, 12 Sept. 2013, available at: www.socialistworld.net/doc/6466 (accessed 27 Jan. 2014).

Spivak, Gayatri Chakravorty: 'The Trajectory of the Subaltern in My Work', University of California Television, YouTube, available at: https://www.youtube.com/watch?v=2ZHH4ALRFHw, at mins 8:17 to 8:30 (accessed 27 July 2015).

Toyo, Eskor: 'An Open Letter to the Nigerian Left', *Review of African Political Economy*, available at: www.roape.org/pdf/3212.pdf (wrongly indicated in the author's list in the archive under 3211.pdf) (accessed 4 Feb. 2014), p. 85.

Valenti, Jessica: 'The Empowerment Elite Claims Feminism', *The Nation*, 12 Feb. 2014, available at: www.thenation.com/article/empowerment-elite-claims-feminism/ (accessed 27 July 2015).

Vanguard Nigeria: 'Sunmonu Revolutionized Labour with Workers' Charter of Demands', editorial, 14 Aug. 2012, available at: www.vanguardngr.com/2012/08/sunmonu-revolutionised-labour-with-workers-charter-of-demands/ (accessed 14 Aug. 2012).

Wedded Wonderland: 'Ten Nigerian Wedding Customs that Prove these Brides Know How to Party', 9 June 2015, available at: www.weddedwonderland.com/10-nigerian-wedding-customs-that-prove-these-brides-know-how-to-party/ (accessed 15 Jan. 2016).

Workers' Alternative: For the Unity of the Working Class, a Labour Party and Socialism (based in Lagos, not dated, no details given – perhaps due to semi-legal status), available at: www.workersalternative.com/ (accessed 12 Jan. 2014).

Workers' Alternative: 'Will Goodluck Jonathan's Emergency Succeed?' *Workers' Alternative*, 23 May 2013, available at: www.workersalternative.com/national-issues/171-as (accessed 27 Jan. 2014).

Films

Waterfalls, directed by Lancelot Oduwa Imasuen, produced by Nneka Onyekuru, approx. 2010.

Interviews

Edwin Madunagu, Calabar, Nigeria, 4–8 Jan. 2013.
Ashien Kingsley, multiple, Minami Uonuma-shi, Japan, 2006/2007.
Meetings with Usman A. Tar, Bill Hansen, Lucky Imade, Kimberly Sims.
Skype interviews with Drew Povey.

Index

Page numbers in *italic* denote the main reference.